Dark Star

by

Howard L. Enfiejian

ISBN: 1-4033-7603-4 (e-book)
ISBN: 1-4033-8977-2 (Paperback)
ISBN: 1-4033-7604-2 (RocketBook)

Library of Congress Control Number: 2002094584

This book is printed on acid free paper.

Printed in the United States of America
Bloomington, IN

1stBooks - rev. 12/12/02

To Morgaine and Corby:

May you live to see such times as these.

TABLE OF CONTENTS

INTIMATIONS

"...when you really want to know who you are or what the real significance of human life, human suffering, pleasure...is, very naturally you come back to silence. Even though you don't want to, you return to an area of no-sound. It cannot be explained, but in this silence you can realize, even if only dimly, what the real point is that you want to know. Whatever kind of question you ask or whatever you think, finally you have to return to silence. This silence is vast; you don't know what it is."

From: *"Returning to Silence"*,
1988
By: Rev. Dainin Katagiri

TIME OUT: January 1, 2034

For as long as the gods could remember, Oozum the Lord High Creator slept. Oozum slept, that he might know well the Dreams of Oozum, his Helpers and his Beloved. Oozum couched himself upon All That Is, and moved not, nor gave any sign of his awakening, so that the gods made their worlds but knew not where to put them, so lost were they during the Sleep of Oozum.

Silence reigned during the Sleep of Oozum, but the gods knew not Its wisdom or comfort, and they wandered through All That Is, clutching their worlds unto their hearts, weeping until their tears became blood.

So long was the Sleep of Oozum that it seemed as if the tears of the gods must drift forever in Space, which gave the tears their own sorrows such that they longed for the eyes who wept them. So terrible was the Sorrow of the Tears that they wept their own tears and so on until it seemed that the House of Oozum must fill with salt and blood.

Silence pitied the gods and their tears. So great was the Pity of Silence that it broke the Sleep of Oozum, scattering the Dreams thereof, which fled to the Edge of Things.

Oozum awoke and shared the Pity of Silence. He called for his servants Fate and Chance. "The gods of my House have made an infinity of worlds but know not their places and proper orbits. Go to the Center of Things and begin a Game. Rest and feast according to your needs, but never reveal to the other gods the Tally of the Game. It is to be a secret unto you and me. This will beguile the gods, and they will gather about you, and use such wisdom as is theirs to fathom the Tally of the Game. This I decree, that the gods may marvel at the mystery of my House and orbit with their worlds around the Game at the Center of Things, each in his proper sphere. The Game is not to end until I say it is to end. This is the Will of Oozum."

So it was that Fate and Chance began the Game at the Center of Things. The gods were delighted and all of them ordered their worlds within the House of Oozum. All, save Kishima the Hero Maker, for Kishima quickly grew weary of the Game and withdrew to the Edge of Things, where he wrought about himself a cave from pieces of the Forgotten Worlds. Silence ruled the cave, communing with the velvet whispers of Time, and comforting the Womb of Space, who longed for new creations. And so it

3

was that Kishima found himself a place that eased his mind into a sleep like unto the Sleep of Oozum. While Kishima slept, Silence walked along the Edge of Things, gathering about itself the lost Dreams of Oozum. "Be comforted, for I will lead you to the house of one who dares to dream the deep dreams."

The Dreams of Oozum were delighted, and followed Silence to the Cave of Kishima, where they gathered about his head and sang softly into his ears.

So passed the days of Kishima, until one day Time whispered into his ear that it was indeed time — time for the making of Heroes. Kishima awoke, looked upon the Game and its gods and turned his back on them, facing the Void beyond the Edge of Things. There, at the very edge, was a mountain of clay, which Silence had made during the Sleep of Kishima. "Go now and make Heroes and cast them into the Void, that they may learn that which is not yet known to Us and so expand the horizons of All That Is. Fear not for the ending of the clay, for I will bring you all that you need. This is the Secret Will of Oozum, who has spoken through me."

Kishima embraced Silence and turned to sit upon the Edge, his feet dangling into the Void. There his countless fingers fashioned the Heroes of his heart. Kishima was pleased with his work, sang praises to it, and sent his Heroes off to seek That which broods over the Void.

Kishima so loved the Heroes that arose from his clay that he sometimes stood at the Edge and wept into the Void. Sometimes, the Tears of Kishima rained upon the lesser gods in their orbits, and they marveled that a love so great could arise within the House of Oozum.

So great was the Love of Kishima that his Heroes carried it within their own hearts unto the end of their days.

-From Hymns for the Wayfarers Among Us by Shams Ibn Hassan, circa 2030 AD.

Hassan's book of hymns slipped out of Barbara Llandry's somnolent fingers and drifted inside of her cabin, quietly bumping into its Spartan surfaces. Were it not for its placement within a spacecraft, the cabin could have been mistaken for a monk's cell. After some minutes of free fall, the book glanced off Barbara's long, chiseled nose. She awoke slightly and pawed at her face. This sent the book careening into a porthole, where it bounced off and activated the on-switch of her reading lamp. Its halogen lights lanced her eyes, and jolted her awake.

From down the Argo's floatway came a man's phlegmatic voice, followed after a few seconds by the man himself.

"Trouble sleeping, my liege?"

"No...I'm all right. My book just bounced off the damned light switch."

"Getting into trouble with books are we? They could've digitized the Library of Congress for you. But NOOOOOOOO...you had to be little Miss Renaissance and bring along books."

"Eat my shorts Hal."

"You should be so lucky."

"In your dreams, maybe." She paused for effect and continued. "Good night, Hal." He closed the door to Barbara's cabin and kicked back up into the exercise module.

Barbara shifted slightly in her harness and stared out the porthole. Mars was visible at twelve o'clock. They were close enough now that it was clearly a planet and not just the red smudge of light that had seeded the loins of her childhood fancy. Barbara's mother, Laura, clearly carried the dream within her quickening womb and Barbara always figured that she and the deep dream had gestated together. What a marriage — both of flesh and ideas — her mother the engineer in charge of the Argo's construction; her father, Gordon, the astrophysicist who integrated telescopes of one sort or another into the hulls.

They would be pleased if they could see the Argo hurtling toward their dreams.

Barbara let her gaze drift among the stars and thought, as she often did, about two loving faces superimposed on a vertiginous Midwestern sky cleft in two on clear nights by the Milky Way. She remembered being a toddler reaching up to strong arms that would toss her into the air. She would stare into the faces for as long as she could and then throw her head back, face toward the sky, and imagine that she was flying to the stars. She never fell. Her father always caught her and tossed her to her mother, who wrestled her to the ground and tickled her all over and told her how much she loved her.

Barbara nodded off again, and after awhile dreamed about being tossed into the air. Only this time she did not come down. She hovered among an infinity of opalescent starpoints. As she floated among them, they turned into legions of sad eyes that looked upon her and wept into the deeps of space. When the tears touched her, they were a warm, dark rain that made her feel safe within the Womb of the World. Within the Womb, a woman's voice said, "I love you Barbara. I love you so much it hurts..." over and over again.

It was not long before the eyes winked shut and faded away. Barbara slipped gently into a darkness blacker than the space around her. She drifted out of her unzipped sleeping pod and was held within her cabin only by the tether fastened to the wall. Her legs slowly curled up until her knees touched her cheeks.

Like most complicated machines, the Argo had its share of gremlins. One of them was forever popping open the door to Barbara's cabin despite all attempts to secure the latch. Well into the night, the door bounced open and banged against the wall of the floatway. This awakened Hal Major. He pulled himself down the floatway and grabbed the handgrips opposite Barbara's cabin.

He paused a moment to contemplate her face and the fine white scars that covered it like a web spun by a deranged spider. She insisted that they were hideous, but Hal saw them differently. To him they were the serendipitous flaws of a fine raku vase bringing to perfection the beauty of its form. He tucked her back into her sleeping pod.

Smiling shyly at her, Hal exited Barbara's cabin and shut the door behind him.

WINDOWS AND DOORS: January 2034

Commander's in-flight personal log:

Time. I finally have some time. You could say that I have all the time in the world. I mean, it isn't as if I can leave this titanium rat can, which is good. I'm feeling the weight of memory and the need to let it settle and ferment. You might say that I need to write my memoirs. The outer events of my life are well known and I have no desire to elaborate them here. My real interest is in the innermost life, specifically to those moments of silence and stillness that are pregnant with oft-overlooked meaning. It's a daunting task, but I have help from the stars. When I look through the portholes, I can see that they are not much brighter than during a clear night on Earth. However, they are far steadier than on Earth. And steadying.

During this first leg of the mission, the constancy of the stars reminds me that memory dwells in the quiet places of the world. Stillness is its natural home, where it grows by accretion until its innate currents meld time, space, and being into a subtle, aureate essence. This alchemy is easily overlooked by those whose impatience binds them to noise, busyness, and haste. Others, who have that fey sight peculiar to old souls know that memory is sentient, that it lives in simple, timeworn things — trees, furniture, barns, letters, jewelry, gardens, old people, unmolested houses. The list never ends, and is so long and so ancient that it never really began, such is the paradox of time and infinity; but within this paradox resides an inherent simplicity. It arises from a resonance between remembrance and rememberer that makes of us vessels of knowing. On a deep enough level we all know where we have been and where we're going, because we live at the crossroads of time and infinity. The present moment and everything in it is the field in which we are called to labor. It is our allotment of eternity.

My own labors began in the middle of nowhere, in an old house that dominated Milton, a town in Iowa whose existence was justified by a rail line and four grain silos. On clear days, I could stand on the tracks facing west and see the town of Windsor on the horizon. When the sun set behind it, Windsor's silhouette beckoned to me like some misplaced Emerald City. But I knew that if I walked the ten miles to it, I would be in another town with four grain silos and a rail line running through it. As the years passed, Windsor taught me that our most distant longings are actually mirrors reflecting our innermost selves, and that our starting points and ending points are the same.

Milton and Windsor were but two stops in a series of rural Iowa towns that channeled the grain output of the American Midwest to an unstable and ravenous world. They were not even listed on most road maps, being considered too inconsequential, I suppose, to interest outsiders.

This suited my paternal grandfather perfectly.

Dr. Richard Xavier Llandry was an art dealer, and an expert in detecting fakes. His magisterial doctoral dissertation was for years a benchmark in its field, so much so that his services to that end were in constant demand. This posed a dilemma for a man who enjoyed solitude and a simple life, so he moved back to his ancestral house in Milton and did much of his work by telecomputer. When it was necessary that he examine an object, he would either travel to see it or have the piece shipped to the house. In this way, Richard Llandry made many powerful friends and eventually found himself the steward of a terrible secret and the artifact that went with it. Both came to him through Natasha, an intimate and unforgettable friend.

Natasha.

You hover over these pages much as you have over my life — distant, indistinct, inscrutable, and yet in the end the arbiter of what I have decided to do for you and Grandpa. In the crucible of my heart, you and Grandpa have melded, each into the other, forging in the heat of your union a Philosopher's Stone that is transforming the baser elements of my loneliness into gold. The miracle is unfolding both within and without. I feel it.

I never knew you by anything other than your first name. Over time, I learned that you were a Russian Jew, of legendary beauty, who settled in Manhattan after World War II to become one of its leading art dealers, especially among that breed of collector whose habits are secretive, for whom public attention to their collections is anathema. Evidently, you were a shadow in more lives than mine.

But I also knew of you as Grandpa's mentor and friend, the latter despite the fact that you were so many years his senior. He spoke often and adoringly of you, so much so that I fancy he would have married you had you been closer in age. All of this, however, I surmised indirectly from my nest in the cornfields of Iowa.

We never met, and for that I will be forever sorry. For a time, I was also sorry about the sadness that Grandpa brought back with him after one of his last trips to visit you in New York, a sadness bound to a tightly sealed crate of which he refused to speak, that disappeared into the basement vaults as if it had never been.

Strange things those vaults, in a house such as ours. In 1864, when it was built, the basement was simply that: an empty, dirt-floored hole in the ground bounded by fieldstone. From then on, though, sundry forward-looking Llandries were inspired to make any number of abortive attempts to convert the basement's rooms into busy places — workrooms, storerooms, pantries.

But most of these endeavors foundered or failed outright, as if under a curse, and they were either abandoned or consigned to outbuildings where they mysteriously fared much better. It was as if the basement's original tenant was jealous of its occupancy and hostile to intruders.

An unlikely tenant it was in America of the 1860s, a time of industrial revolution and mechanized warfare. The masons who laid the foundations and the carpenters who set the joists overhead unwittingly sealed a piece of the vast Midwestern sky into the earth, for the breath that the men drew during their labors and panted into the rock walls was of a piece with the air overhead, blown in from Canada, the Rockies, the Gulf, each according to its season, and all of it part of the sky. When the work was done, the sky's breath settled into the foundation. And what is stilled breath but silence? Silence took up residence in the basement and brooded upon the secrets it had gathered during its former lives as wind and sky, rain and snow. Over time, the house became so steeped in stillness that its occupants fancied they could hear spiders spinning their webs. Sometimes, in the deep of night, the Llandries -- always a fanciful lot -- imagined that they could hear voices long ago subdued by death and reduced to dusty whispers by the passing years.

But I digress. On a more prosaic level, Grandpa needed the basement vaults for his work. It often happened that he received objects that were either too precious or too delicate to be left lying around the house, and so into the vaults they went until he was done with them. Avatars though they were, the vaults never betrayed the spirit of the house, despite their elaborate technology. If anything, the vaults deepened the stillness with their imperturbable, sepulchral immobility and interior blackness. Nothing less could have contained Natasha's crate and its attendant melancholy.

Natasha died shortly after the crate disappeared into the vaults, and with her passing Grandpa's sadness deepened for a long time. Sometimes, mostly at night when he was alone in his study, I could hear him choking on sobs that left him breathless. At the time, I didn't know what to do but decided to leave him alone. I've learned since that men like to crawl into their caves to lick their wounds. They come out when they're ready. Given Grandpa's penchant for privacy, I think I did the right thing.

But it's all right now. The thing of which Grandpa refused to speak until his death is now secure within a metal casing strapped into the Argo's hold, along with Grandpa's last letter to me, articulating his dying wish that I find a final resting place on Mars for the thing that caused so much sorrow on Earth.

Consider it done.

HAVENS: January 2034

Commander's in-flight personal log:

As the days drift by, I find myself falling into a persistent dream about a caravan making its way through Central Asia along the silk routes to China. My thoughts always settle on twilight, specifically on that crack in time when a crystalline mystic blue suffuses cloudless skies whose whispering stars intimate that they are the seats of gods too distant, and perhaps too reluctant, to have revealed themselves to us yet.

Everything in this faraway place is rock, and mountains flank the horizons. I stand on a hard dry plain, always about a thousand feet from the travelers -- far enough away to muffle all sound and yet not so far off that I cannot see the flow of the journey, imperceptible though it may have seemed to someone in the mountains. Here, I am patient, and patience is the touch of a lover's hand against my face after too long an absence, a touch that rivets me into the moment with its erotic mysticism. My vision in this place is clear, and soon my mind becomes clear in equal measure. Thoughts fall away. I am a lake reflecting the heavens and find within them depths of solace that I have rarely known.

The blue without and the blue within deepen. A few stars quietly appear in the velvet sky. They are known to me and, I suspect, are known also by the travelers. Our modern understanding of these stars would have meant nothing to these people, but they did have names for them. Beautiful names. Aldebaran. Vega. Deneb. Alderamin. Alphirk. Shedir. Caph. Ruchbah. Mirphak. Capella. Menkelinan. Castor. Pollux. I too know these names, but most of them mean nothing to me; nevertheless, their lush beauty as they flow past my lips form kisses that beckon me into times far earlier than my own, into places I could not possibly have visited, into places where half-remembered faces dimly seen pass in the night, and eyes rendered black by the deepening skies gaze into me, through me, into places where whispers just beyond the range of my hearing beckon me like a long-lost lover. He draws me into a moist and mystical darkness that thrills me -- all of me -- as he quickens my womb with the seed of a million stars.

As I said, most of these names mean nothing to me, but not all of them. Castor and Pollux are two such. Castor and Pollux -- the Dioscuri of ancient Greek myth -- hatched together from a

17

single swan's egg along with their sister, Helen, who would eventually be the cause of so much mischief between the Greeks and Trojans. Castor the Fates declared to be mortal, Pollux immortal. The brothers' love for each other was so great, however, that they cheated the Fates and contrived a common destiny as they rose to the heavens to become the Gemini. Such a difference in the way we see things! To us, Castor is a class A1V star with an absolute magnitude of 1.20. It is neither variable nor binary. Its twin, Pollux is a class K0 III star with an absolute magnitude of 0.20. It is non-variable binary star.

We moderns cull such useful information from our study of the heavens. So too did the ancient Greeks, but for them the sky also held their mythos. Thus did the heavens become an Olympian place of timeless, mythic moments. Imagine mortality and immortality forever juxtaposed in a place of legend where time necessarily falls away in the face of the paradox immanent between the love of a being that never dies for a being whose days are numbered. Here, mortality meets immortality, time meets eternity, and at their crossing lives love.

The day ends in blackness and the caravan comes to rest.

This is a contemplative moment seen, as I just said, through a crack in time, and I am not oblivious to the dangers everywhere facing the travelers. Hunger, thirst, theft, disease, war. All of these ancient dangers form such an odd contrast to the journey we are making. China must have seemed as far away to those people as Mars does to us and yet, if nothing goes wrong, we have little to do except eat, sleep, exercise, talk, and think. If anything serious does go wrong, we'll freeze, fry, bake, or explode.

These pleasantries notwithstanding, the Argo is a peaceful place. Linda Maddock and Hal Major spend a lot of time in narcostasis. I suspect that Linda is homesick at the thought of leaving her husband and son for so long. Hal just likes to sleep. He usually wakes up to eat, pee, and exercise, kind of like the guys I went to school with. I like Hal. I like him a lot. He reminds me of someone that I once knew long ago — very long ago — but I don't know whom. I feel as if I should remember, but I don't.

I enjoy my own company enough to prefer being awake. The silence of space flight is exquisite and I want to imbibe it through my every pore. Already it's happening, and the Argo has become for me a place of dreams and musings. It's not lethargy or torpor that I'm feeling. Rather, the experience is that of a centered and calm lucidness. When I'm in that place, I can observe my own inner workings from a distance. The odd thing is that as my inner detachment increases so too does my sense of intimacy with myself. Life becomes vivid, I feel involved, and I gain a knowledge of my own contrary currents. I now understand that obsession with any one current creates turbulence, confusion and error, whereas detachment creates perspective, perspective creates acceptance, and acceptance honors time and memory.

This knowing has a shape. The shape is a matrix of circles and centers. My center is to my periphery as I am to the Argo. It's my detachment as pilot, engineer, and commander that keeps her running, especially the astronomical arrays. The Argo is a flying eyeball fixed on the heavens. She too is a center observing her surround. Could it be that the universe is a lattice in which one being's center is another's surround ad infinitum, from Alpha to Omega? No one being in its essence is more or less important than any other, since each of us has been created to channel the energy of the whole.

This is liberating.

The Argo isn't just a quiet place. It's also a memorial to my parents. Their spirits are suffused, some of their friends might say entombed, in everything. They designed it. They persuaded our apathetic government to fund it. They died finishing it. But their tomb is my womb. I feel myself gestating something on this long, quiet journey. A very long time ago, I knew what that something was. But somehow I forgot and now I haven't a clue as to what it is. Nothing is clear yet, save for a faint voice encouraging me to go to Mars. That's all I can hear. What really creeps me out sometimes is that this ostensibly inner voice feels as if it's coming from someplace, and someone, very far away.

Havens blend into havens. The Argo as a haven necessarily morphs into my parents as my most cherished of havens. They often told me how I started talking when I was nine months old, rapidly became fluent, and turned into a sponge so quickly that they found themselves home schooling me. They took me everywhere with them. Laboratories, space centers, and any number of universities were my first classrooms. I found the proficiency tests that the state required for home-schooled children so trivial that I never so much as set foot in a public school. It is often said that knowledge is power. But knowledge as power doesn't go far enough. My parents taught me that knowledge is also love. Affection, respect, and enthusiasm were the vessels they used to slake my inborn thirst for understanding.

And then they were no more.

As nature abhors a vacuum, so did I, and it was natural that my grandfather took me in. As Mother and Dad made increasingly frequent trips to the space station where the Argo was nearing completion, I found myself spending more and more time with Grandpa and his Magic Kingdom of a house. Richard Llandry was a natural teacher, who led me to worlds of wonder beyond imagining.

And therein hangs my life.

STARBURST: May 2002

"Ten, nine, eight, seven, six, five, four, three, two, one..."

Flames seared the late-afternoon air. Steam shrouded the launch pad. The ground shuddered in sympathy with shock waves from the engines.

"...lift off. We have lift-off."

With gyroscopically guided thrust from their liquid-fueled partners, the solid-fueled engines generated the requisite 7.7 million pounds of thrust, heaving the shuttle Daedalus off her launch pad at Cape Canaveral. She assumed a standard trajectory and within minutes achieved her escape velocity of 17,450 miles per hour and injected herself into a fixed orbit inclined at 28.5 degrees to the equator, thus balancing her kinetic energy against the pull of the Earth.

An observer following the Daedalus as she ascended into orbit would have experienced an acoustic oddity. As the altitude of the shuttle increased, the sound of the engines decreased, and this despite their implacable fury. A moment's reflection would have revealed, however, that the sound diminished because there was less air available to conduct it. In fact, sound itself would soon be left behind altogether as the Daedalus approached mach 3, thus enveloping the ship in a cocoon of silence.

Not so for the crew. They carried their atmosphere intact and endured the bellowing of Titans trapped within an underworld of tanks, pipes, turbopumps, preburners, combustion chambers, and nozzles. It is a credit to human endurance that this ordeal, and the crushing gravity that ensued from it, perturbed neither the Daedalus's pilots nor her passengers.

It was an impeccable performance, right out of the book.

Which is how so many disasters begin.

#

"Eeeeeyahhhh! We have liftoff! Yes! Yes! Yes!"

Her arms outstretched, Barbara leapt from her accustomed spot on the rug in front of Richard Llandry's television, galloped through the parlor and the kitchen, bounded onto the back porch and sailed over the railing onto the grass below, all the while imagining the combined thrills and terrors of rocket-powered flight. Despite the fact that nobody seemed to give much of a damn about the space program in general and the Mars mission in particular, hungry news services could generally be counted on to broadcast shuttle launches that involved any aspect of the seemingly interminable construction of the Argo. Every time one of them took off, so did Barbara.

On that day, Richard had the foresight to open the doors between the parlor and the porch before the Daedalus's launch, and so the sailing was clear all the way to the lawn. During the previous launch, he had neglected to open the porch door, with the result that Barbara flew right into it and snagged herself on the screens like a bug in a spider's web. After his initial fright, Barbara thought the old man would never stop laughing. However, Barbara and Richard now understood each other and she spent the rest of the afternoon unscathed, daydreaming about what the astronauts who would fly the Argo would find when they reached Mars. She returned to Earth at dusk when the smell of steak sandwiches enticed her back to the kitchen.

The screen door shut and a pair of little eyes appeared over the edge of the stove top just as the last of the pink in the steaks fried away.

"Hey Grandpa."

"Hey Pookie."

"That stuff has a lot of grease in it, right?"

"I suppose so."

"I hear doctors say that kind of stuff can kill you."

"Yep."

25

"So why are we eating it?"

"Because it tastes good and I like it. So do you, if I'm not mistaken."

"But aren't you being kind of stupid?"

Richard looked at Barbara, and as always became pleasantly distracted as he looked into her unnervingly intelligent eyes. Coming from most children, such questions would simply have been rude. But Barbara was never rude. The worst one could say in these instances was that she was inclined to be blunt.

"No, Pookie, it's not stupid. You can't go through life being afraid to die. You get more years out of relaxing and having fun."

"Sounds good to me. Are they ready?"

"Yep."

Despite the fact that she had only seen him a few times in her brief life, Barbara noticed that Richard and her father were as different as a father and son could be. Gordon was always talking about something and he always seemed to be moving, even when he was supposed to be sitting still, such as during dinner. Her mother was much the same, and so family life always struck Barbara as a contest over who could say the most in the shortest possible time. Meals were, the most frenetic. Barbara typically sat between her parents watching the conversation bounce back and forth like a tennis ball. This probably accounted for what would become Barbara's lifelong tendency to be quiet most of the time and blunt when she did speak — it was the only way she could get a word in when her parents were excited about something, which was most of the time.

And then there was Grandpa. Everything about him was quiet. He walked like a cat. His clothes did not rustle. He never seemed to move his eyes quickly; in fact, he never seemed to do anything quickly at all. He seldom spoke spontaneously, and when he did, his words sounded like crushed-velvet curtains fluttering in a breeze. He spent so much time reading and thinking that Barbara thought at first he was in another world most of the time, except that he also seemed uncannily aware of everything around him. He was also mysterious. For a man who seemed, in the eyes of a child, to be on death's door, Richard Llandry rode the biggest, meanest looking Harley Davidson motorcycle that Barbara had ever seen, and he rode with a lot of rough men and women who treated him like the father they never had.

Considering all of this, Barbara decided that her grandfather was an OK guy. They ate slowly and quietly while the sun set behind the corn tassels in the garden next to the cob house. As often as she thought polite, Barbara studied her grandfather's face. She hardly knew him, but yet she felt so safe when he was around. After awhile, she ventured a question.

27

"Grandpa, Daddy tells me you sell old stuff for a living."

"You might put it that way."

"Do you make a lot of money doing it?"

"That's rather an odd question for a little girl."

"Oh...just wondering, that's all."

"Your mother tells me you never 'just wonder' about anything."

"Well, okay, but even so things don't add up. If you spend all your time around old stuff, then why do you care so much about space and things in the future? You know what? Mommy told me that you paid for her to finish engineering college when she was only Daddy's girlfriend. Then she started crying and I asked her if she was sad and she said no, she just couldn't believe how nice you were to her."

"Oh...it wasn't that hard. Her parents never had much money, and then they were both killed when she was only half way through engineering school. Besides, your Mommy and Daddy liked each other so much back then that I was sure they'd get married anyway — sort of keep the money in the family."

"Well, okay, but what I mean is if you've got it made doing whatever it is you do then why do you care about all that other stuff?"

Richard looked at Barbara for a long time and then took out a pipe, filled it with tobacco, and stared at it for a long time before lighting up.   Finally, he looked at Barbara.

"Oh hell, I don't know.   Why to we do any of the things we do?"

Another long pause.

"Maybe this will explain things.   I notice that Gordon and Laura read to you a lot."

"Oh yea!   I love books!"

"That's good.   Did they ever read to you about the last ice age?"

"Uh-huh.   It was during the Pleis-to-cene gla-cial ep-och.   Did I say that right?"

"Uh, yea...I think so."

Richard was starting to wonder if he were out of his league with this child.

"Anyway, I was going to say that the ice ages were times of horrible cold and crazy weather.   For thousands of years the ice came and went.   It covered whole continents, almost.   The only way people could survive was to always be looking for new places to live, new animals to hunt, new plants to eat, new ways to make tools.   They always had to know how to change.   It was simple, really. Change or die.   Move or die.   Learn or die. Learn or rot."

The pipe had gone out.   Richard relit it and continued.

"What I'm saying is that the world is a lot like it was back in the ice ages, sort of.   It's shrinking and we need to learn a lot of new things so that we can take care of what we have and grow beyond it.   Or we'll die.   It's that simple. We learn to move into space or die. I can't believe I'm having this conversation with a six-year-old."

"Don't worry, Grandpa. You'll get used to it."

"I hope so. I like having you around."

"Thanks, Grandpa. I like being here. It feels good."

"Do you want anything else?"

"No, thank you. I think I'll go upstairs and listen to the radio. Maybe they'll have some news about the Daedalus."

"Okay Pookie, see you later."

To himself, however, Richard was thinking, "I wouldn't count on it, sweetie; nobody gives a rat's ass."

\#

The trouble began as the Daedalus approached the Argo. Strictly speaking, it was not really trouble. It was simply an intermittent burst of chaos within the ship's unprecedentedly complex onboard computers. It was not chaos as simple disorder, however, or the accumulating consequences of small engineering errors. Rather, it was chaos as the alter-ego of highly ordered systems, a tendency for small perturbations in complex systems to grow radically and in unpredictable ways. The Daedalus was such an ordered system.

"We interrupt this program to bring you this breaking news." The announcement roused Barbara from a doze just as the phone rang downstairs. By the time Richard hung up the phone, Barbara was at the bottom of the stairs, pale, sweating, breathing hard. Richard got down on his knees so he could talk to her face to face.

"Did you hear it on the radio?"

"Yea..."

"Listen, Barbara. That was Mission Control on the phone. Nobody knows why the shuttle's thrusters are going crazy and no one can stop them. As I recall, something like this once happened on one of the Gemini flights. The ground people figure the Daedalus is going to hit the upper atmosphere in a few minutes and crash somewhere near Washington, Iowa, which isn't so bad because that's mostly farmland, like around here. It so happens there's a military turbocopter at the Iowa City airport, and the pilots said they'd fly us out there. Do you want to go? We'll do what you want."

"Uh...okay Grandpa. Let's go." Barbara's breathing decayed further into a series of wrenching gasps. "Washington...that's on...the west side...of the house..." She staggered onto the back porch, lurched over the railing and ran onto the west lawn. Richard started to follow her but then thought the better of it. He called the airport to confirm the flight.

The night was clear and the sky awash with stars. Barbara tried to breathe slowly and scanned the western sky for anything moving. She was old enough to

31

understand that the Daedalus would be moving very fast and would literally pass in the twinkling of an eye.

Richard had barely hung up the phone when it happened. A large white star appeared high in the western sky, arced briefly, plummeted, and disappeared behind Milton's rooftops, trailing specks of exploding light behind it. The falling star was as silent as it was swift.

Nobody noticed. No one came out. Television screens flickered inside the neighboring houses. The occasional car drifted by, going nowhere in particular. Somewhere, a dog was barking. It was a night like any other, in the midst of which a star-filled chasm opened up in a little girl's heart.

For the first time in Barbara's life, the sky seemed too big. She wanted desperately to grow and fill it so that she could embrace both the stars and what was now only a memory of two people who had brought them down to earth for her delight. Instead, all she managed to do was clutch the air and scream.

"MOMMMMYYYYYYY!!!! DADDDDYYYYYYYY!!!! I LOVE YOUUUUUUUU!!!!"

#

The nature of complex problems is such that simple solutions are not often realized until it is too late. This was the fate of the Daedalus and her crew. It was not until the ship was tumbling into a re-entry interface at 400,000 feet that the pilot thought to simply shut down the computers and restart them. She did so and was, in fact, able to abort their misfiring of the thrusters. Unfortunately, restarting the computers, engines, and attitude controls in the few remaining seconds before the Daedalus was committed to re-entry was another matter altogether.

Skeins of superheated air seared the hull before incinerating into a three-thousand degree plasma that shattered the nose cone and slammed the pilot's face through the back of her head before she had time to scream. An instant later, two passengers — a man and a woman — unlatched their harnesses and clutched one another desperately, each absorbing the agony of the other. They barely had time to say, "I love you," before their superheated bodies exploded.

And then came the radio blackout that bedevils all spacecraft during re-entry. The ground crews had no choice but to sit still and hope that the Daedalus would begin communicating after she passed through the re-entry interface.

It never happened. The window re-opened but nothing flowed through it but a terrible static whose implicit horror enveloped Mission Control, as well as all of its remote tracking stations. The silence was broken only by reports that impact had occurred in an Iowa cornfield.

#

Barbara was never able to remember much of what happened between the fall of the Daedalus and her arrival at the crash site. For the rest of her life, she would hold within her mind nothing but vague images of being gently buckled into the front seat of Richard's Corvette; of being led with equal gentleness to the turbocopter; of flying through stagnant air; of landing on a field blacker than night.

Then her mind cleared.

She stood at the edge of the crash site next to Richard, who was talking intently to a group of nervous officials who Barbara vaguely recognized. Local rescue squads had been marshaled hastily to delineate the perimeter of the crash site and construct a grid to facilitate removal of the debris. They were well into their work when Richard and Barbara arrived. No one noticed her and therefore nobody told her that the crash site itself was off limits, so she quietly slipped away from Richard and walked in.

Barbara found herself wandering on scorched earth blacker than the richest topsoil, through air that stung her eyes, nose, and throat, and stank of things that were never meant to burn. To look at it, one would never have known that the rubble strewn about had once been an immense and graceful spacecraft. The last thing that any of the rescue workers expected to see within the crash site was a small child.

34

She walked unseen among the wreckage. She spent long moments staring into rubble so utterly burned that it could have been anything -- plastic, steel, thermal tile, fabric — and so it struck Barbara as being very strange that she should suddenly be smelling fried chicken.

Or so it seemed. She realized that she had not eaten for hours and assumed that she was just imagining things. But the odor persisted, so much so that she decided to track it down. She picked her way through the rubble, sniffing the air like a skittish rabbit, gradually adjusting her path until she came upon a pile of rubble as horrifically nondescript as everything else around her. It seemed to be the source of whatever it was that she was smelling. Barbara sifted through the rubble until she found what she was looking for. Like everything else at the crash site, it was black and still warm from the inferno of re-entry. With the precociousness that infused everything she did, Barbara recognized...

...two shoulders, two arms, two forearms, and two hands clasping each other so tightly that the fingers were seared into a tangle of bones. She bent closer. Under the brilliant starlight, something on the fingers glinted. She bent even closer and saw two gold rings melted into each other. Barbara went stiff with realization. A banshee's wail rent the night and startled the investigators, who looked up from their work to see a small girl running frantically from something deep within the crash site.

No matter how often she stumbled and fell, Barbara sought out Richard with the sureness of a homing pigeon. The sheen of his white hair under the starlight was a beacon signaling the way home and she focused on it to the exclusion of all else. She did not stop when she reached him but scrambled up his body until she reached the lapels of his jacket. She pulled them apart and tried to crawl inside, as if she could hide inside his chest. But the fright was too much. Barbara collapsed onto Richard's shoulders, stinging his ears with screams that were broken by wrenching gasps for air. It took awhile, but she eventually quieted down.

"Barbara, honey, there's a doctor here who can give you something to calm you down and make you sleep."

"I don't wanna calm down! I don't wanna sleep! I just...wanna be...sad."

Richard did not press the issue as once again Barbara's mind faded to gray and she was aware only vaguely of being carried back to the turbocopter, then after awhile to the Corvette, and finally to bed, where she fell asleep without sedatives.

#

She left her body someplace and seemed to be floating in a warm, golden light, minutely aware of countless energies surging around and through her. She was awash in currents of love, kindness, and caring. The light before her condensed into glittering golden motes that condensed still further into a lavender book. Barbara read The Book of Life emblazoned on its cover.

A strong, ancient hand also materialized from the golden light and opened the book. It was filled with the names of people admitted to eternal life. The hand turned the pages until it came to Barbara's name, written in Gothic script with indigo ink. The hand left Barbara's field of view and returned with a quill pen.

The hand struck her name from The Book of Life.

Barbara fell from the golden light, which soon shrank to a pinpoint, back into her body. Rough hands tossed her into a black abyss. That was when the ululations started, punctuated at intervals by a deep, self-satisfied, sadistic laugh. Taloned hands with obscenely long fingers reached up from the abyss and flailed at Barbara's clothes until their claws sank into her skin, holding fast her arms and legs. Tears of blood slid off her wounds and disappeared into the void below.

The laughter continued to rise from the depths until something like a human bat descended upon her. Everything became silent except for the sound of claws and fangs sinking into her chest with wet, ripping sounds. It was not until the bat-thing started tearing her chest apart that Barbara realized it was trying to eat her heart out. Shards of skin, muscle, and bone fell into the black ink below, from which the sounds of demonic feasting arose and shoved aside the silence. Gordon and Laura were calling for her but they were in the golden light and could not reach down far enough into the darkness to save her. mind.

Screams filled the house, bouncing off windows, walls, tapestries, paintings, rugs, and statues, as Barbara arched her back and tore at her blanket. Down the hall a door slammed and slippered feet ran towards her room. Richard disentangled her from the bed clothes and held her gently but firmly until she woke up and stopped struggling. He rocked her back and forth and side to side for a long time.

"Shh, shh...Don't be afraid, sweetie; everything's going to be all right. You're not alone. You're Grandpa's little girl and I love you. Don't ever forget that."

Richard held Barbara and rocked her quietly in the darkness. All the while, tears that were not entirely her's pattered onto the carpet beside her bed.

CRICKETS: June 2002

Ching Ho broke through,
looked deeply into
the Reclining Buddha of Wat Po.

And then his head exploded.

Bone shards lanced the sky
and became stars.
Brain-grease splattered the ground,
tripping up alike
the pious and the worldling.

Ching Ho remained still,
until the blood cloaking his shoulders
dried to dust and wafted
along the city streets,
leaving no trace.

No one noticed.
Dogs barked.
Parrots screeched.
Cabbies played chess.
Hucksters peddled mangoes
and lichi nuts.

No one noticed
save an old monk, sitting
at the Buddha's mother-of-pearl feet,

Howard L. Enfiejian

**who saw the Infinities
through Ching Ho's eyes,
smiled and bowed.**

**Anonymous, ca. 2014 A.D.
Written on a scrap of paper
found in a gutter somewhere in Bangkok**

For weeks after the accident,
Barbara's earth and sky were filled with
sorrow, and her dreams still
occasionally rent by howls from the Pit.
During the rainstorms that blew in from
the prairies and the Great Lakes,
Barbara could often be seen sitting by
herself on the porch swing at the side
of the house, hugging one leg and
rocking the swing with the other in a
silent arc punctuated by the creaking of
150-year-old chains. She stared a lot,
mostly into empty space, but every so
often her gaze drifted randomly over the
cob house, the garden and compost heap,
the yard, the tidy houses along the
street. Her eyes bore into these things
with a fixity, an intentness of purpose
that hinted at the desolation of exiled
longings looking for a new home. During
these storms, she often dreamed that the
sky was crying onto an earth so parched
by grief that it would soak up forever
the sorrows of the heavens.

Evening storms were especially hard.
Barbara imagined the Argo, abandoned and
orbiting through the ink of a night that
would never end. This endlessness
constricted each passing moment into a

straitjacket whose suffocating grip often choked tears out of her. The swinging would stop as she huddled into a trembling life-sized netsuke that was all arms and legs.

None of this was lost on Richard. He knew that Barbara was inclined toward privacy and so he often left her alone. But just as often he knew that no child, however private, should be left alone to nurse so much grief. This certitude drove his catlike appearances onto the porch, where he drew Barbara into his arms and, silently, they shared the pattering of the rain and the vastness of the night. Things went on thus for almost two years. But it was not all desolation. Milton was doing its work of healing, albeit so indirectly that Barbara hardly noticed the changes.

It was the farmers who started it all.

The ineluctable warming of the skies and greening of the fields fostered other energies conducive to calming Barbara's mind. For one thing, Richard's home schooling made it possible for the diurnal rhythms of the local farmers to regulate Barbara's habits, although none of them could have possibly known it. Their work in this respect was much like that of a bee who, intending only to harvest nectar for her hive, succeeds nevertheless in fertilizing the plants that in turn support the survival and evolution of all higher life on the planet.

In the same way, the grumbling of farm equipment on the horizon, beneath the cerulean skies of countless clear dawns, awakened Barbara with the gentleness of a bell ringing in a far off mountain temple. The farmers' measured comings and goings, both in the fields and in town, stamped the unfolding hours with Nature's blessing, imbuing Barbara with an expansive sense of time inclusive of anything the hours saw fit to hold. Nothing in and around Milton was ever hurried, and yet so much was done on any given day that the farmers welcomed the lavender twilights and the rest that went with them.

On these clement evenings, the twilight dimness that suffused the house brought with it Richard's measured footsteps through the kitchen, the clatter of a screen door, and the creak of a porch swing bearing up under its wonted load. Curiosity sometimes impelled Barbara to follow Richard at what she fancied to be a discreet distance in the hope of discovering what was so beguiling about the porch at that time of day.

At first, she could not figure it out. Hiding on the far side of a hutch that had sat next to the porch door for 150 years, she never saw much of anything. After sitting down, Richard draped his arms and legs over anything that presented itself, and that was about it for a half hour, until the deepening night nudged him indoors. At that, Barbara would pretend to be busy doing something other than spying.

After about a week, however, she noticed other things. Within moments, Richard's bearing would change from his usual demeanor to something else. His gaze, normally focussed to the point of being unnerving, softened such that he seemed to be looking at nothing and everything at the same time. His broadened vision was accompanied by commensurate changes in his hearing, or so Barbara surmised as she scrutinized Richard's every feature in the soft light. He inclined his head slightly, as if listening to sounds that no one else could hear. His stillness made him invisible. Passersby who invariably waved whenever they saw Richard pottering about the yard went on their way, oblivious to his presence. He was transparent to children cutting through the lawn within feet of the porch. Birds occasionally landed on his shoulders and preened his hair before flitting on. All the while, the chirping of the crickets that abounded during these evenings assumed an immediacy impossible to ignore, as if it were encrypted with secret messages.

And then, at the behest of an unseen impulse, Richard would rise and go about the business of the evening. His was an intense quiet that Barbara was unable to ignore, so great was the fascination that mounted within her after a few weeks of watching.

"Hey, Pookie."

"Hi, Grandpa. How'd you know I was here?"

"You've been hiding behind the hutch for the last three weeks."

"Yeah, okay, but how'd you know."

"I just sense things."

"But how? I've been as quiet as a mouse and you haven't looked at me. Not once. You're not even looking at me now."

"I don't need to."

"All right all ready! But how?

A hint of petulance, at which Richard smiled.

"Come on out and I'll show you."

The sun had just nestled into the western horizon and was shining through the tassels of the corn that Richard had planted in the garden beside the cob house. The light, crenated by its passage through the plants, split into fine beams that tumbled among the garden's greenery like so much iridescent golden hair. Errant breezes wafted the foliage and with it the light, as if it were airborne, giving the impression that supernal beings, for the moment earthbound, were cavorting among the leaves. Barbara stepped onto the porch and sat next to Richard, her face quietly expectant. He shifted to accommodate her but remained otherwise still.

"There's not much to it, actually. The first thing is to get comfortable.

There's no point in doing anything unless you can breathe easily."

Barbara slumped into the swing and propped her feet on the porch rail. Her belly, relieved of its accustomed weight, undulated easily with her breath.

"What do I do now?"

"As I said, not much. Just look around and let go of your thinking. Let your thoughts flow without directing them. That's when things start happening."

"What things?"

"It's hard to tell. Let's just say that you'll start communing with the spirits."

With that, Barbara sat up and looked around with heightened interest, first into the house, then around the grounds, and finally at the fading light in the garden.

"Grandpa, I never knew the house was haunted! Why didn't you tell me? That's so cool!"

"Shh, shh, shh, sweetie. That's not quite what I meant. It's just that...if you let go of your thinking for long enough, you'll realize that things, all kinds of things, everything actually, is whispering all the time. You just have to be quiet enough for long enough to hear it. It takes practice, although some people come by it naturally."

"But Grandpa, you can't stop thinking. I think all the time."

"That's not quite what I meant either. I guess I'm not explaining this very well. You never stop thoughts. They're like stomach juices -- they're always flowing. What I'm saying is to ignore the story teller in your head. That's what takes practice. It's not something you can really do; you just have to let it happen. The trick is that if you sit still and just breathe, then the story teller gets bored and takes a nap. Your thoughts start flowing their own ways. They won't bother you. That's when you'll hear the whispers."

Barbara relaxed back into the swing. Richard rocked it gently. But the story teller would not go away. It kept tugging at her awareness, tempting her to be everywhere except where she was, impulsively conjuring plans and as impulsively dashing them to bits, fabricating furtive itches and pains, and after a while tugging at her limbs in a subversive campaign to move just for the sake of moving. When it was just short of being unbearable, Barbara's mounting unrest was aborted by the softest of touches on her left hand. She thought it was a moth and was about to shoo it away when she noticed a warmth that only Richard's hands could impart. It banished her unrest and revealed a still center that invited attention. The story teller hobbled away to an obscure corner and sulked.

That was when Barbara noticed the
light, or rather the lack of it. The
day was far enough advanced, the sun
deep enough within the corn, to ease its
burdens on the eye, yet not so far gone
as to obscure subtleties of shape,
texture and contour in a twilight whose
lavender tints shimmered off the white
clapboards and millwork that bracketed
the porch. Softness suffused
everything. With a quiet thrill,
Barbara saw things with a clarity she
would never have believed possible in
such obtuse light. With this clarity
came an inbreath that reached deep
inside her belly and dissolved all of
the tension left over from the day. The
more she looked, the more she saw.
Thoughts of past and future persisted
but became irrelevant in the face of a
Now that was complete and sufficient
unto itself. Without realizing it,
Barbara had become as transparent to the
world as Richard.

Sounds came next. They arose with an
immediacy that was odd because almost
nothing was making any sound. Save for
the clattering of iced mugs in the root
beer stand across the street, the rare
passing of a car, and scraps of
conversation floating on the breeze, the
only things making noise were the
crickets that lived in and around the
porch.

Even they were mellow, as crickets
go. Their chirping set up a cadence
that soon became a mantra opening a path

within Barbara's mind to places that she never knew were there. It lulled the gatekeeper in Barbara's ears and soon she was hearing with the same purity as she was seeing.

The dun haze of twilight had just overcome the dimming day when fireflies began to rise from the lawn, their evanescent glitter making of the air over the grass a starfield in miniature. Suns winked in and out of existence within seconds, to be replaced by other suns that glowed ever brighter as the darkness deepened. Each passing lightpoint hinted at worlds, at dust-mote planets, whose lives were shorter even than those of their parent suns, so much so that they left no trace upon the darkness to mark their passing. Aeons boundless beyond reckoning passed before Barbara's eyes in the time it took for the sun to yield its hegemony over the western sky to the lesser lights of lamps, cigarettes, televisions, and the occasional candle.

Still, the crickets and fireflies persisted in marking time with sound and light unnoticed by those whose attention was caught only by the more obvious signs of life around them. To Barbara, these obscure creatures were gods in miniature, architects of a universe spread before her feet, filling the darkness with their private pursuits.

As her eyes and ears took in the immensity, real and imagined, around her, an interior immensity opened from somewhere within, although Barbara would not understand its import until years later. All she sensed at the time was that the space inside her belly grew in proportion to her awareness of the small and subtle things around her. The feelings that arose in resonance with this experience she could only liken to those of infancy. Gordon and Laura had once told Barbara that she started talking when she was only nine months old, but she could remember much further back than that. She recalled clearly a time when she could not talk, a time when her mind was devoid of words, and, by implication, of thoughts as they are commonly understood. Hers was a life of unmitigated immediacy, untrammeled by filters and judgements. She could be unblinkingly riveted by the lambent reflections from an ordinary kitchen plate, until someone moved her and she became rapt in the immediacy of something else.

Barbara's mind was filled, cluttered almost, with these snippets of memory. But as she sat with Richard, she realized how intensely they had constellated themselves around his house. Why, she would never know, save that, for the rest of her days, the house would be an icon of being through which she could make sense of things. It had already done a laudable job of kindling her primal memories into a comet's tail of itinerant glory.

It all began in the kitchen, with visions of things that could not have been there but nevertheless were. Laura must have been cradling Barbara in her arms such that she could only see the ceiling. After some moments, its uniform olive-green firmness dissolved, became a window through which she saw clouds billowing into a cerulean infinity whose silence had been absolute and inviolate since the beginning of time. The window itself dissolved and Barbara found herself soaring among the clouds, flinging herself off cotton-ball cliffs into the yielding whiteness below, bouncing up again through the limpid blue to ever greater heights.

After a time, Barbara noticed a mote drifting among the clouds. The very act of noticing drew her towards the mote and into it. She found herself in a cozy, albeit somewhat Baroque, parlor whose walls — all ivory and gold — shut out the sky but preserved its light. A window that occupied most of one wall afforded a view of the clouds. Barbara willed herself toward the window, and in so doing noticed a man and a woman lounging upon a settee. They were unfathomably old and unfathomably young, and they looked at her with a love she could not plumb.

Then she dropped.

Like a meteor.

But it was a controlled fall, much as a meteor's incendiary frenzy is consistent with the laws of celestial mechanics. Within moments, Barbara leveled out. She was flying down Main Street, several hundred feet above the tops of its oldest trees. She reached the center of town and the slate mansard roof of Richard's house. Without hesitating, she descended slowly through the house and back into Laura's arms.

Laura must not have noticed anything amiss, because Barbara sensed that she was being carried, slowly and somewhat aimlessly, from the kitchen, briefly through the living room and into the dining room. She looked up at the ceiling, and it too dissolved, revealing a night-bound pastoral scene. A large, full moon shed just enough vague and grainy light to reveal a stone balustrade enclosing a flagstone patio. A man, in what Barbara would later recognize as Victorian garb, stepped up to the balustrade, laid his right hand upon it, and looked up at the moon.

This scene gave way to another -- to a group of people, also in Victorian dress, lolling amidst the black trees of an ancient grove, in the deepest hours of the night. The scene was well, if diffusely, lit from an invisible source, there being no moon, fire, torches or. lamps in sight. Just as Barbara was settling into the scene, she was ripped away from it, probably by Laura strolling back to the kitchen, because the next thing that Barbara peered into was a glass-paneled bookcase next to the kitchen door. It dissolved into a stark and abstract white space bounded only a seamless white floor. Endless lines intersected the space and the floor at various angles. To the extent that Barbara's infant brain could interpret ordinary space, the orientation of many of the lines made sense. But there were others that came from impossible directions, did impossible things within the white space, and disappeared into equally impossible directions.

Barbara was not alone in this place. People, dressed in loose clothing much like togas, wandered among the lines. They paid her no heed, but instead followed one line or another with a meditative intensity that precluded distraction. The wanderers' movements were slow and peaceful, and yet oddly indecisive, as if they were venturing into spaces alien to their sensibilities. The scene faded, and Barbara was sensible once again of being cradled, kissed, hugged, and held up to admiring eyes. One pair of eyes, powder blue, stared into hers with an intensity that rivaled her visions from moments before. They held her with as much warmth as her mother's arms. At the time, she was too young to understand that the eyes belonged to her grandfather.

As the evening deepened, these and other thoughts arose in Barbara's mind as effortlessly as a bubble's ascent through water. These visions were among her first memories of life and they had persisted, unaltered. She had not a clue as to what they signified but, sitting in the warm darkness with Richard, she wondered whether entire worlds somehow crossed paths deep within the house. Or maybe the worlds held their concourse within her, within the vastness that she had found in her belly.

Barbara inhaled deeply and fidgeted. This broke the spell and drew Richard's attention. His eyes met her's and he smiled.

"How about some root beer, Pookie. I'll race you."

As if on cue, Richard and Barbara bounded over the porch rail and dashed across the street into the halogen brightness of Frank's root beer stand.

#

Frank's iced mugs stuck to a customer's fingers and lips just long enough to break the torpor of hot summer nights. The root beer, which Frank brewed himself, had the same effect. Barbara looked back and forth between her drink and the porch swing, now motionless against the darkness of the unlit house.

"Grandpa, that was fun. Can we commune with the spirits every night? I won't bother you. I promise."

"Sure, Pookie, whatever floats your boat. You might get a little bored, though. Listening to the spirits is kind of an old-man thing. You don't want to shrivel up before your time, do you?"

"Don't worry, Grandpa. I won't. Besides, the crickets are pretty cool when you really listen to them."

"Well, Pookie, here's how I figure it. I don't know how long crickets have been around, but people of one sort or another have been around for three, maybe four, million years. That's a long time to be listening to night-time sounds. I'll bet the farm that it's good for us. It recharges the batteries."

Barbara gave Richard a precociously appraising look. Then, tentatively, she ventured to say something that had been on her mind for a long time.

"Thanks, Grandpa."

Richard looked up from his root beer.

"For what?"

"For not talking to me like a little kid all the time. I hate it when grownups do that. I've got a brain, you know."

She paused.

"And Grandpa?"

"Hmmm?"

"Guess what? I don't want to be sad all the time anymore. I'm tired of it. And when I'm with you I almost feel okay. You're like a mommy and daddy all rolled up into one."

Richard's eyes moistened for a few moments, then cleared.

"Thanks, sweetie. I'm doing my best."

After that, they sat quietly amidst Frank's busyness and listened to the crickets serenade the evening into night.

PREMONITIONS: January 2034

Commander's in-flight personal log:

My earliest memory of Grandpa's house, or of anything else for that matter, is of looking down on it from an unearthly height. I was surrounded by a vast, warm light, and had no sense of a body. I was a happy ball of sentient light surrounded by other happy balls of sentient light. An omnipresent voice was talking to me, laying out a task that I was to undertake during my upcoming life. I don't remember what was said, but I agreed to it. The nature of the task, and my memory of it, has subsequently faded, but its aura and its sense of mission has never left me, despite the fog that tends to settle over us with time and age.

At this point, I absolutely must digress and mull over this preincarnational dream.

I remember when I was little, maybe eight or so. It was a lazy, Gothic sort of Saturday in late Autumn when black storm clouds boiled in from the Prairies and brooded over the house. There was nothing to do but build a fire in the parlor and snuggle, which we did, Grandpa with a snifter of Armagnac, I with a Coke. We got to talking about mother and dad and why they died when I was only six. My world caved in then and I thought I would never get the pieces back right.

Talking must have put me in a bad way, because before long Grandpa silenced me with a look and disappeared upstairs into the library. I heard him rooting around for a while, and then things got quiet again. He returned, his thumb jammed into a volume of Plato's dialogues, and sat down again, cradling me in his arms and opening the book in my lap. The chattering of the fire within the hearth punctuated the soothing intervals of quietness that calmed me down and suffused the parlor, as if the house itself were straining to hear what Grandpa had in mind. When we were settled, I found myself staring at the closing pages of The Republic.

Grandpa began reading me a myth about a warrior named Er, who bought the farm after an especially nasty battle, and was given the task by the gods of chronicling the sojourn of the soul through the afterlife, between death and rebirth. Plato says that Er completed his task within twelve mortal days, but I got the impression that at least a thousand years passed in Hades before Er returned to his undecayed body. It was as if he had experienced a sort of relativistic time dilation. I guess death and its attendant mysteries stretch time out before us at least as much as our futile attempts to match the speed of light.

Souls recently arrived in the afterlife received judgements that could hurl them into Tartarus or fling them into heaven, depending on the relative merits of their lives. This part of the journey alone could span thousands of years. But it didn't last forever. Eventually the souls either exhausted their merits or expiated their sins, after which they encamped in a meadow for seven days to talk about their experiences in their respective worlds. On the seventh day, the souls began a four-day journey that brought them to the Spindle of Necessity, a World Axis around which revolved the heavens. Within the spindle lived the Daughters of Necessity -- Lachesis, Clotho, and Atropos — who are more commonly known as the Fates. They were a musical bunch. Lachesis sang of the past, Clotho of the present, and Atropos of the future. The souls came first to Lachesis, who scattered lots among them. They chose their own lots, without interference from the gods, at which point a prophet came to the souls and scattered life patterns among them, also to be chosen freely. The life patterns specified everything but the quality of a soul's life. This was the responsibility of each soul individually and rendered imperative its duty to cultivate the Good.

After freely making their choices, the souls were led back to Lachesis, who assigned each of them a genius — a Daimon -- to be the guardian of that soul's choice and the agent of it's destiny. The Daimons in turn led the souls to Clotho, who ratified their destinies, and thence to Atropos, who rendered irreversible the web of destiny and choice. Their decisions made and sealed, the souls passed beneath the Throne of Necessity. And then something fascinating happened. After all that fuss and bother, everybody forgot everything. It happened when the souls passed from the Throne of Necessity to the Plain of Oblivion and camped by Lethe, the River of Forgetfulness, where they drank a measure of water which Plato claimed "no vessel can contain." That evening, in the midst of utmost blackness, an earthquake flung the benighted souls into the sky to their rebirth.

It was a short but immense story, much like my earliest memory of awaiting my birth among all those other souls and the unfolding of my destiny in Grandpa's house. It had a strange effect on me. As I thought about mother and dad, the words of the myth flowed through me. Necessity. Fate. Freedom. Things that were. Things that are. Things that will be. Choice. Destiny. The Good.

The Genius.   The Daimon.   Oblivion.
Forgetfulness. Rebirth.

And memory.

At the deepest level, the most profound level, always there is memory. Grandpa made sure I understood that the Daimon never forgot anything even if we did, that it was our partner in life, that if we let it, the Daimon will lead us to our Destiny. Our future holds the pay dirt, not the past.   Without realizing it, I had entered Plato's mythic sensibility, and learned that on some level my parents already knew and accepted what they were doing when they climbed into the Daedalus for the last time.   Plato's gods also taught me that in their realm on the far side of the universe, death, which seems to be the end of all our striving here on Earth, is in truth the beginning, and birth the unfolding of memory from death to destiny.   Considering my parents' fiery ends, I found it ironic that Er returned to life while lying on his funeral pyre, just moments before being immolated.

After that I felt a lot better.

But back to my story.   When next I have any memory of Grandpa's house, I am four years old and still young enough to perceive things with that freshness of which only children and sages are capable.   We were driving down to Milton from the University of Chicago and it was late.   Main Street was deserted and lit only by the stars.   Nothing moved except the occasional meteors that blinked in and out of existence overhead.

The house finally came into view on our right. Marked by four huge, hoary maple trees at the corners of the grounds, it was as dark and still as everything else in town, but with a difference, at least for me. When we parked and I got out of the car, I was seized by a moment of recognition that I couldn't understand, save for the certainty that I belonged here, in this place. The house was uncannily familiar. When I stepped onto the dew-sprinkled lawn, I sensed that Grandpa's house wasn't just a building. It was alive with a brooding presence that was as deeply rooted as the oak trees from which its timbers had been hewn. The starlight gave hints of ironwork that framed a slate mansard roof. The house's many chimneys thrust their bulk into the sky and I fancied that the stars were embers that had escaped the chimneys to gambol in the heavens. The white siding was barely visible, making the house seem as if it would fade into vapors with the coming dawn.

The front porch light came on suddenly and broke my reverie. The light framed Grandpa with an aura that matched that of the house. He seemed to me to be as ancient as the trees around him, and just as strong. Noiselessly, he descended the porch steps and gave us all soft, warm hugs. As he bent down to hug me, his head passed for a moment into the darkness and I thought that I could see stars dusting his soft gray hair and closely cropped beard. The illusion faded, but not the impression that it made upon me. As the years passed, I came to realize that Richard Llandry was indeed a man who carried entire worlds within himself.

I was the last to enter the house. Grandpa had turned on a couple of soft lights that only deepened the mysteries around me. I vaguely saw walls hung with paintings, family pictures, and Oriental carpets that ascended to meet a ceiling framed by intricate plaster cornices. A chandelier cut from quartz crystals hung from the center of the ceiling to illuminate a large, red marble fireplace. The furniture was old, comfortable, and well used.

But before all of this, what struck me first, what inscribed itself upon my brain with indelible ink, was the scent of the house. What most adults would have dismissed as the faint odor of mold and dust that permeates old houses was a marvel to me, accustomed as I was to the forced freshness of laboratories, classrooms, and modern houses. To me, the scent of the house was an incense that spoke of old trees, autumn leaves, and the persistence of memory. As a child of four years, I was of course unable to articulate my impressions in this way. But what I lacked in expressiveness was more than compensated by the untrammeled purity of my senses.

For me, Grandpa's house was the vessel of a life that held all things within itself, and so began a series of trips that ended with Grandpa's house becoming a home whose memory I will carry with me, beyond my grave, to the End of Days.

#

Grandpa had a library. Situated on the second story of our house, it was a cheery white room, awash with books on everything. Daylight found its way everywhere. The room had ample east-facing bay windows which opened onto the upper branches of maple trees planted during the Civil War, just after the house was built. This always made me feel as if the library were a tree house, especially in the morning when the sun filled the room with dancing swatches of green, and squirrels played at jumping from the branches to the windowsills and back again.

I always felt clear in that room, as if I were Emerson's transparent eyeball. Light flowed through me, thought flowed through me, feelings flowed through me. I was all flux, and yet centered. It was during those moments that I reveled in losing myself among the arabesques of Grandpa's Kashan carpet. Woven in Iran in 1955, it had a ruby-red field in whose center was a medallion broken into smaller, intricately nested curves that tricked the eye into seeing seemingly endless progressions of pattern and color. From this center shot, at intervals, a series of interlaced vines which twirled among themselves such that you could pick any spot -- a leaf, a flower -- and return to that same spot by any one of a number of routes, all of them different. Infinity nestled within the finite. The finite gave hints of infinity. Change dwelt within changelessness. And all of this happened within a space of ten feet by fifteen. This inclines one to be thoughtful, which happened bigtime one day when I was about ten, and studying relativity theory for the first time.

I must have started daydreaming. Watching those arabesques endlessly curving in upon themselves created a whirlwind inside of me. My spine was its axis and my brain its dizzy funnel. But deep within the funnel there was a quiet spot. There, I was calm.

In that state, I wrestled with my questions as Jacob did with the Angel. What if the world of three dimensions was just a perceptual quirk? What if our brains just happened to be wired to see things that way? What if there were no survival advantages to seeing things in four or more dimensions, so we just stopped seeing them? Maybe the ability, if we ever had it, just fell into disuse. What if the nearest star, or Mars for that matter, were just a stone's throw away, only we long-ago forgot which way to throw the stone. Reaching the stars may only require us to shift our consciousness and our perceptions. Maybe certain mystics and philosophers have always understood this.

Stars.

Those of us in the northern hemisphere get our bearings in the sky from Polaris, the Pole Star, called Alracubba by the Medieval Arabs. We know it now as a binary Halo Cepheid variable with a period of 3.960 days, 687 light years away, and displaced slightly from true north, around which it traces a circle along with everything else in the heavens. It is visible to us at a right ascension of 2 hr 49 min and a declination of 89° 14′. Alracubba's closest approach to true north will not be until 2102 A.D. Its absolute magnitude is unknown to us.

"Unknown" is the operative term here. How many of us would have the slightest idea of what I just said? Take this further. How many of us could tear ourselves away from the virtual world of television, walk outside into the real world on a clear night with our children, and so much as point out Polaris to them, to say nothing of yielding to the foreplay of "Alracubba" on the lips?

The ancient races of Central Asia grounded themselves on bedrock far deeper than the sand dunes over which we moderns stumble in our craving for certainty. To king and slave alike, the tiny circle traced in the night sky by the Pole Star was a door opening into Paradise. An axis -- the World Axis --

plunged through this Sky Door and anchored itself on the Earth. Around this axis the universe revolved and everyone found his way home. It was a grounding in myth that explains why many ancient temples were covered by domes with holes, or something equivalent. It's a way we had of centering ourselves by being rooted in both Heaven and Earth.

It also explains rugs like Grandpa's. The craft of weaving such rugs disappears into the preliterate history of the human race, probably in or near Central Asia. The borders of a rug are a Sky Door, the central medallion, if it has one, the World Axis, and the designs in the field visions of Paradise.

Paradise.

It's where you find it.

That morning paradise for me was being pulled back from my reveries to the morning sun filling that white library and a voice from downstairs.

"Hey Pookie, it's time for breakfast!"

I'd trade my place on this mission for just one more breakfast alone with that man. But you're dead, Grandpa, which slams that Sky Door.

Forever.

TIME PASSAGES: January 2034

Commander's in-flight personal log:

...but at least we dream, and dreams open other Sky Doors. Such as the door of memory. And of time. If you ask most people, they'll say that time moves from past to present to future. Obvious, right? I'm not so sure. Years ago, when I looked deeply into how I experienced time, what I sensed was that a future moment passed into the present and disappeared into the past. So for me time passes from future to present to past. The past for me is a repository. It has no power over us, and too many people spend too much time trying to deal with the issues of a murky past. There's nothing to be dealt with. The future is what causes things to happen. It calls us into life and action, like the call of Mars for me, Hal, and Linda.

But with the passing years, I've sensed that these musings don't go far enough. I may only be seeing half the picture.

When Einstein's theories were making their first impact on the world, the mathematician Hermann Minkowski remarked that, "Henceforth, space by itself, and time by itself, are doomed to fade away into mere shadows, and only a kind of union of the two will preserve an independent reality." It is as if the universe were a hypercube of four or more dimensions. If we learn to move among all of the spatial dimensions, might we not also learn to move someday along the temporal dimensions as well, as H.G. Wells predicted in The Time Machine? Can we do this by bending spacetime with our minds? I wonder. I really have to wonder.

On the first day of winter in the year 1240 AD, a Japanese Zen Master named Eihei Dogen delivered a sermon to his disciples at the Kosho Horin Monastery that later generations have come to know as "The Time-Being". It was another morsel that I culled from Grandpa's library. It's cryptic, and I've read it often enough to have memorized it without, unfortunately, having much real understanding of it.

I like to imagine storm clouds gathering around Kosho Horin to hear Dogen speak, much as they often did around Milton at certain times of the year. If the gods of Thunder and Lightning could have silenced themselves for a while, they would have learned from the Master that, "...yesterday and today are both in the moment when you directly enter the mountains and see thousands and myriads of peaks.

Yesterday's time and today's time do not go away...Do not think that time merely flies away. Do not see flying away as the only function of time. If time merely flies away, you would be separated from time. The reason you do not clearly understand the time-being is that you think of time only as passing...The time-being has the quality of flowing. So-called today flows into tomorrow, today flows into yesterday, yesterday flows into today. And today flows into today, tomorrow flows into tomorrow...Just actualize all time as all being; there is nothing extra...Mind is the moment of actualizing the fundamental point; words are the moment of going beyond, unlocking the barrier." This and more the Gods would have learned before the winds blew them to other lands.

What this says to me is that a shift in consciousness is all we need to transform our perception of space and time in a way that reveals the true dimensionality of the Universe.

#

Words. So many wonderful words lived in Grandpa's library, and all of them were collected carefully by his discerning hand -- a hand that was hooked up to a brain that was endearingly cracked at times. I mention this because my thoughts are turning to the Milton Methodist Church and the matter of its Ladies' Auxiliary.

I suppose they meant well, but the ladies simply didn't understand with whom they were dealing when they invited us to Sunday services one day when I was six. It wasn't long after mother and dad died that the ladies made it their business to be worried that a man of Grandpa's vintage would be ill-equipped to rear a child alone. Some people in Milton were like that. Evidently, they were born without Grandpa's capacity for imaginative solitude, and so it was partly out of having nothing else to do on one broiling Saturday afternoon in August that the ladies showed up on our front porch and made a racket with the verdigris-bronze doorbell.

Grandpa wasn't religious in any conventional sense and so his exchange with the ladies was terse, despite their determination to get inside the house and gawk at its legendary contents. They left, however, with the consolation prize of having cajoled him into bringing me to Sunday services the next morning. They would even come and escort us, their unwashed Pagan captives, to church themselves.

Silly ladies, who had just made...

...a bad mistake, as I realized when I saw the look in Grandpa's eyes after he politely but emphatically shut the door against further annoyances. He paused a moment, smiled, turned to me and said, "Pookie, would you like to help Grandpa play a little trick on those church ladies tomorrow?"

"Sure!"

"That's my girl!"

With that, he plopped onto one of a pair of Stickley rockers nested among the bay windows that matched those in the library directly overhead, and began browsing a Bible whose pages were thoughtfully worn, considering that its owner never went to church.

The next morning, I was primed. At the anointed hour, the ladies came calling and Grandpa greeted them in tones silky enough to have charmed the serpents of Eden. Their leader, one Louise Higgenbotham, was a local gad-about whose cadaverous body never quite caught up with her necrotic face as she bustled about town in pursuit of one marginally useless errand after another. Louise's evident disregard for her impending corporeal ruin, seen against Grandpa's own taut figure — he was her senior by at least ten years — told me who respected whose body as God's Temple.

But what I remember most about Mrs. Higgenbotham that day was her outfit. Despite the heat that was baking the prairies, the pavements, and the road, everything about her that could be buttoned, zipped, tied, or otherwise bound, was. Just looking at her made me sweat, despite the silk chiffon dress I was wearing, which was as light and diaphanous as decency, or at least Christian decency in Grandpa's estimation, would allow of little girls in church.

He was wearing a midnight-blue Saville Row suit with such aplomb and disregard for the heat that one would suspect he had an air conditioner in his breast pocket, which was good, because he was planning to crank up the theological furnace a bit.

Mrs. Higgenbotham and her entourage began chiseling away at our pitiable ignorance with their most practiced holier-than-thou-poor-Pagan condescension, which Grandpa countered with a smile that had charmed women the world over. While so doing, he ushered me onto the porch and locked the door with a finality suggesting that further intrusions would once more be most unwelcome.

Matters became noticeably strained the moment Mrs. Higgenbotham noticed Grandpa's tie. Descending from a perfect Windsor knot, and ending decidedly at crotch level, was an embroidered belly dancer whose charms grabbed susceptible onlookers and wouldn't let go. With an expression, and voice, carved from wood, Mrs. Higgenbotham suggested that Grandpa's taste in ties wasn't quite...Christian. Perhaps she could help him select another?

Grandpa was ready for that one.

With the air of a passably intelligent yokel who had never been anywhere or done anything before in his life, he became thoughtfully confused and said, "But Mrs. Higgenbotham, it occurred to me while I was dressing this morning that this was quintessentially Christian, and in fact very much in keeping with Scripture. Don't you agree, Barbara?"

That was my cue.

"Certainly, Grandfather! Why just the other day you were reading to me from the Old Testament about how King David unified the Kingdom of Israel. After all the wars were over, the first thing he did was take off most of his clothes and dance in front of the Tabernacle. I guess it was too sexy or something, because one of his wives got really mad and never talked to him again. Why would she do that, Grandfather?"

"We can discuss that another day, Barbara, because Scripture–especially the Songs of Songs–teaches us that the poor woman was misguided, and wasted her life by being so...so buttoned up."

With that, he eyed Mrs. Higgenbotham's plethora of buttons, ties, zippers, and straps, and proffered his arm so as to brook no refusal. And so it was that the entourage began it's way down Main Street, Grandpa arm-in-arm with the local Gorgon.

He wasn't done with her yet. Not by a long shot.

He started chiseling away at her with stream-of-consciousness ramblings that only a drunk or a lunatic would have understood. I learned then that my grandfather had a gift for bullshitting people with endless gushers of pseudointellectual drivel -- and for doing it in one breath. He drew such a breath and began.

"I realize it's a little late, what with services starting in just a few moments, but would you, as a senior member of the congregation, share any insights -- garnered no doubt from a lifetime of study -- that you might have on the ways in which a Christian might distinguish between prefigurements versus Preincarnational manifestations of Christ in the Old Testament?"

"The question, I feel, is not only of theological interest, but one of great practical import to Christians everywhere and for all time (all remaining time, anyway), serving as it would to not only deepen our appreciation of the Incarnation and Presence of our Lord, but also to serve as a kind of cipher against which the appearance of not only the Antichrist but also of his much prophesied false teachers might be recognized soon enough for pious souls to save themselves from the Lake of Fire."

"I certainly meant no disrespect for those Old Testament patriarchs who could be construed as Prefigurements, but I feel -- and have felt for years -- that such precious insights would enable us to recognize those pretensions to holiness and divinity (which no doubt the Antichrist and his minions would foster) that were simply of the flesh."

"But by 'the flesh' I <u>am</u> <u>not</u> referring to our discussion on the porch. At that, he paused to stroke the tie along the dancer's breasts and thighs, as I recall, as if lost in the most pious reflection. After some moments, during which the silent thunder of our soles grinding along the pavement was rendering the group insensate, he resumed.

"No, that is not the flesh to which I'm referring. I am thinking mostly of that dross which will be blasted to the Pit after the scales fall from our eyes during the End Times, and speaking of End Times, it has always struck me as extraordinary that the Bible would speak so clearly about both the beginning of time and the end of time, and maybe if we paid particular attention to this aspect of scripture, then we would be able to discern the truth among otherwise untestable theories of cosmology. Such a Sacrament for the mind! And speaking of sacraments, didn't Christians understand them to be the outer manifestations of an inner and spiritual grace...?

It was thus that Grandpa filled the entire half-mile walk with the most exquisite babbling. My part in the mischief was over, so I turned my mind elsewhere, mostly to the slowly approaching church.

I had passed it many times, although usually pretty fast, while in Grandpa's Corvette or on the back of his Harley. As such, the church was always a blur on the periphery. My first slow approach that day was the beginning of my respect for honest architecture wedded to the prairies. The church was rust-red, its bricks having been baked to a fierce hardness by six generations of incineration under the Midwestern sun. During those six generations, not one gray-slate shingle on the roof or eighty-foot steeple had split. The cross atop the steeple always caught the sun and sparkled with it's gold, although I never remember anyone's ever polishing it.

My ruminations were over by the time we reached the church, which was just as well because I had to take Mrs. Higgenbotham's free arm and help her up the front steps of the church. She had the punch-drunk look of a boxer who has received one too many blows to the head. I could tell by the way she immediately listed to the right on entering the church that she was desperate to sit in the back, but Grandpa would have none of it. With the most urbane protestations to the contrary, he led us squarely down the middle aisle and up to the right front pew, where people generally didn't sit for fear of being conspicuous -- it was squarely in front of the pulpit. He stood facing the largely assembled congregation until we were all seated, which didn't take long because most of the ill-fated sisters had managed before then to blend into the crowd. Grandpa sat down and reverently arranged his tie on his lap, at which point he assumed the expression of a pilgrim in a faraway land, wrapped in the pious expectation of gifts from heaven.

Up to then, I couldn't see the minister. He was seated in a plush wing-backed chair by the choir. He rose and mounted the pulpit, at which point the congregation fell silent. To my pleasant surprise, it was Reverend Murphy, a sweetly self-effacing man who often tipped a few glasses with Grandpa in Jake's Mule Barn. That was where I had heard some of the words he had just impaled Mrs. Higgenbotham with, only in Reverend Murphy's presence they made sense.

Jake's Mule Barn! Be still, oh my heart! If anyone ever reads this stuff, please excuse yet another digression. The routine of the mission has left me with almost too much time to think.

Winters in the Iowa fields were silent, white, and hard. Winds blowing in from the lakes made obligatory fortresses of the humblest homes, and many a glass was tipped at Jake's Mule Barn by refugees from the cold. Grandpa was often among them, with me in tow, and thus many of my early memories were bound up with lounging among tipsy men in bib overalls — men quick to laugh and argue, men with eyes as shrewd as the fields were hard.

Built originally as an apothecary shop around 1870, the building subsequently housed a succession of languishing dry goods stores whose owners never removed the original furnishings, partly because they were so bulky, and partly because they were too versatile to give up. Shelves and glass cabinets that originally held reagents, drugs, and lab equipment, in later generations stored dry goods, sick-room products, and candy. The building's latest incarnation as a bar brought the building back to its roots, the difference between the effects of laudanum on the one hand and booze on the other being academic at best.

Every owner in unbroken succession, including Jake, kept the apothecary's lab untouched. Arrayed in plain view across the back of the building, moldering instruments with no obvious purpose to the unpracticed eye drew the curious and idle, which was never bad for business. Something else that wasn't bad for business arose from another aspect of the building's benign neglect. The owners seldom threw out advertising displays, with the result that people entering the bar stumbled into a time tunnel littered with reminders of the past. This jumble of memorabilia wasn't just the cutesy appeal to nostalgia that so many businesses affect, but an archeologic treasure trove of enticements for sick-room products long ago rendered obsolete, for candy that hadn't drained any child's piggy bank within living memory, for bras and panties tailored in the hopes of arousing post-Victorian lusts, and also for more familiar things: Coke, Pepsi, Dr. Pepper, shoe inserts, corncob pipes.

For me, Jake's was a catacomb for history and reliable memory. In our interior mindscapes, these things are never static, but evolve as personal mythologies every bit as malleable as the epic poetry sung by the ancient bards. By life's end, our earliest memories bear about as much resemblance to the events which formed them as a dinosaur does to a dog. But at Jake's, these faded displays were the relics of daily life as once we lived it, every bit as rare in their own way as Old Master paintings.

In Jake's Mule Barn I could cut loose and drift in time. From the nowness of my life, I could go to a place where the dusty gossip of lives gone by still resonated in the cobwebs that no one ever bothered to sweep away. If I sat very still, and was just a little drunk, I could still hear it. And so, I suspect, could everyone else. For hours, Jake's drew people whose eyes lingered over the reminders of who we once were and, within the hubbub of bar life, regulars could always be seen -- especially the elderly ones -- sitting very still, as if listening for something just beyond the range of hearing.

Over this same span of years, however, the leftover reagents in the lab came to pose their own set of problems. The old druggist, one Walter Henry, died without leaving instructions as to their disposal, and so scores of ground-glass bottles with illegible labels sat undisturbed under generations of dust on wooden shelves black with age. As the years passed, each owner in turn showed a tendency, to put it mildly, to be disinclined to spend money on the building, so that by the time Jake won it in a poker game, it was a House of Usher on an otherwise immaculate street.

Jake, who understandably loathed building inspectors and paid them off well, never called in the EPA to dispose of the bottles for fear of what else they would find in the place. It actually wasn't a bad arrangement. Jake's waitresses and bartenders learned to sidestep the shelves with their loads of drinks and pizzas in exchange for the continued quiescence of whatever was in the bottles. To my knowledge, no one ever got hurt or gave birth to a two-headed baby.

None of this bothered the clientele, an assortment of bikers, farmers, pensioners, and people with government checks of various sorts who were drawn together by a shared, if unvoiced, need for darkness. This is good and, to my way of thinking, much better than church. We all carry shadows within us. We need to catch them. Own them. Give them form. Like the gargoyles on a Medieval cathedral. Otherwise the shadows will catch us. Own us. Give us their forms. Turn us into caricatures of ourselves.

This need drew people into Jake's Mule Barn and kept them there, so much so that some of the customers seemed unaware of the existence of natural light. It was the sort of place where people fleeing their spouses could enter by the front, slip out the back, disappear, and rest assured that no confidences would ever be broken. Pretty women could have a quiet drink in a corner for as long as they wanted without being bothered. The list of tacit courtesies went on and on.

And through all this coming, going, hiding, and evading, the bottles in back kept their secrets. One day, years after the Sunday morning in question, I was rooting among those bottles during a slow, and therefore safe, time of day. After cautiously wiping away decades of grime, I found that many of the bottles contained arsenic, mercury, nitric acid, fuming sulfuric acid, and other things that made me wonder whether Mr. Henry was occasionally asked to undertake discrete assassinations or, as was more likely, mercy killings. Given the state of pharmacy back then, it wouldn't have surprised me to find a stash of cocaine somewhere on the premises. Considering what could have been unleashed from those bottles, it's proof of God's goodness that Jake's Mule Barn never caught fire.

It was here that I developed a taste for hot scotch at a tender age.

And it was all because of Jake's screen door.

I knew that winter had come to stay when Jake took the front screen door off its hinges. It was one of those doors that was forever out of square, never fit its frame, and was pulled tenuously shut by a spring that had worn out sometime during the Great Depression. The whole contrivance worked only during the gentlest of weather, and even then not very well. The subarctic winds that blew in from Canada set the door careening like the shredded sails of a ship floundering in a gale every time customers came or went. When this became sufficiently annoying, two hastily jacketed waiters would be seen practically ripping the door off its hinges in their frenzy to escape the cold. But Jake was too cheap to replace it with a storm door, and therein began my love of hot scotch.

No matter where Grandpa and I sat, I always seemed to be in the way of icy drafts that tore through the bar every time someone opened the door. Since there was nothing much to do in Milton during the winter other than drink or go to church, this happened a lot, and so it was a deliverance of sorts one night during a mounting blizzard when I first smelled a mug of steaming brown liquid that was topped off with brown sugar and steeping around a cinnamon stick. It was being nursed by Somebody-Or-Other Braunschweiger, a farmer well-known to Grandpa, whom he was regaling about the evils of corporate agribusiness. I paid no attention to what they were saying, so absorbed was I by the hot sweetness tickling my nose.

A string of imploring stares enabled me, after a while, to establish furtive eye contact with the farmer. With an equally furtive smile, he pushed the mug toward me. Not knowing the sting of alcohol, I took what I fancied to be a manly swallow. The subsequent fire in my mouth seared my brain and blistered my toes, suffusing everything in between with a warmth that transported me to warmer climes. While my brain simmered, Grandpa and the farmer winked at each other, at which a discreet grandfatherly hand slid the scotch away from me and signaled the waiter for some hot chocolate topped with marshmallow fluff. Thus began a clandestine winter ritual that Grandpa accepted as a harmless initiation into the pleasures of dissipation. God bless him.

Mug in hand, I often picked my way — some would say staggered and lurched — to a pot-bellied stove that was vented, against the dictates of common sense and building codes the world over, directly through the middle of the bar's uninsulated ceiling. The whole contrivance had been in place for so long that it was sinking at a glacial pace through the floor. None of this bothered me in the least when I found that I could dodge the worst of the drafts by sitting close to the stove and propping my feet on its fender. This lent a certain charm to the endless winter storms.

For as long as anyone could remember, and there were people in the bar pushing a hundred, a huge blue stoneware basin sat on the stove untouched save by the occasional waiter who would fill it brimful with water. This was Jake's idea of a humidifier, inheriting said concept as he had from his predecessors. None of these worthies had ever once cleaned the basin, with the result that it was caked by an inner shell of mineral deposits at least an inch thick.

This fascinated me.

I knew, from Grandpa's somewhat neglected plumbing fixtures, that mineral deposits from evaporating water accumulate imperceptibly, so I knew that decades of perfect stillness must have elapsed for the equivalent of geologic strata to have laid themselves down within the basin's interior.

I often looked around and sensed something perfect about the arrangement. In the center of the bar was an easily overlooked time capsule within whose rim the years had accreted themselves grain by grain. And then, on a larger scale and in felicitous duplication of this microcosm, there was the bar. Its senescent hulk, undisturbed for at least as long as the basin, had acquired a patina formed by the dings and dents made by both the regulars and the itinerant customers who had passed through Milton on their way to someplace else. It was a place where time went nowhere in particular, settled in quiet corners, and otherwise drifted with the dust devils that were forever blowing in from the street. Looking deeply into the basin and then up at the shadows around me, I could lose myself in a river of half-formed memories. These memories, and the barely audible words they somehow evoked, reminded me trenchantly of those long-forgotten words I heard before I was born. They were inside of me somewhere. Such altered states were an almost daily wintertime ritual that would be interrupted softly by a well-worn voice calling me back to the snow and the ice and the frigid walk back home.

But back to my story.

As Reverend Murphy approached the pulpit, he cast a mildly curious eye at the front pew. At first, I could see him register the incongruity of Mrs. Higgenbotham sharing a pew with my grandfather. Then he saw the tie. He stifled his surprise and mounted the pulpit with an incandescent smile.

People further back probably sensed nothing in him beyond an unwonted joy. From ten feet away, however, I could see a man trying desperately not to pee in his pants. I knew that he knew that if he gave way, all would be lost. It was only through an impressive display of clerical discipline that Reverend Murphy confined his hysterics to an indefatigable grin that persisted through everything he said and did for the next hour.

After the service, Grandpa left Mrs. Higgenbotham to the ministrations of Mr. Higgenbotham, a forbearing man who seemed to have caved in on himself over the years, much like a barn whose owner sees no further use for it. It wasn't long after rescuing his wife that Mr. Higgenbotham entered Jake's Mule Barn by the front door late one night and exited through the back door forever.

I hear he looks much better now.

#

Maybe someday, eons from now, we'll understand the essence of time, memory, and being. Maybe we'll learn to see time and space as they are. Maybe we'll find it easy to bend space and time with our minds. Maybe Grandpa and I will be able to meet and have a quiet drink somewhere, somehow, somewhen.

I'd like that.

QUIESCENCE: Gods' Eye View

The universe at-large is a noisy, violent place, much like a rock concert gone berserk. Supernovae, gamma-ray bursts, quasars, black holes, protostars all conspire to fill space with the primal cacophony of creation. Such a universe is far more hospitable to guitar riffs than it is to toccatas and fugues. It is cause for wonder, therefore, that anything could be still, quiet and at peace amidst such seething. But it's there. It is the interval of no-sound between the notes that gives music it's meaning; it is the dark, subtle, contrapuntal yin to the effusive yang that we see so readily around us.

The Argo's enhanced VASIMR propulsion system reduced the outbound limb of the Mars mission to a mere four months, while its systems generally maintained themselves within normal limits. The crew thus found themselves often in narcostasis at the same time, each member's breathing a nidus around which stillness gathered itself — a buffer against the cosmic tumult around them and fortification against the things to come.

That these advantages should accrue to people blazing heroic trails is good, because there are threads within the tapestry of spacetime that only the Fates can see. This gives them an arguably unfair advantage over those of us who have been consigned to lesser links on the Great Chain of Being. Where the Fates have clarity, we fly blind through the mists and must rely upon the promptings of our angels and daimons. Such reliance demands that we leap into the Void, trusting that they will follow and show us our destinies.

It is said that cohorts of souls exist whose task it is to travel together toward a dimly discerned end. As these journeys unfold, a few souls will depart, while others return. These detours are neither distractions nor follies; on the contrary, these wayward souls enrich the wisdom of the group with their unique experiences. Such was the case with the Argo and its crew. From a god's eye view, Linda Maddox's and Barbara Llandry's destiny lines had been entwined longer than either of them could have ever known. Over forgotten aeons and lives beyond reckoning they had, together, fought with flint knives, borne children, labored as peasants, died as queens, and so on in a vast journey that neither of them could have imagined in its entirety. Also on this soul's journey was something in the

Argo's hold that should have been alive, that should have breathing but wasn't. It swayed slightly in its cradle whenever the Argo made course corrections to assure its tryst with Mars. That Barbara's and Linda's trajectories would soon diverge was something that no one could possibly have foreseen.

REUNIONS I: early summer, 2006

"So you're the smart one."

Barbara Llandry looked up, startled, from her reading on the porch swing to see a small, blond girl in a black leather jacket leaning against a motorcycle on the side lawn. Her eyes were green, shrewd, and appraising, and they looked piercingly at Barbara. When the girl's eyes met Barbara's each of them felt a thrill of recognition, as if each saw in the other a multitude of well-known faces from other places, in other times.

"I don't have to go to school, if that's what you mean," said Barbara.

"Yeah, that's it. You're Doctor Llandry's granddaughter. I hear your mom and dad got blown up or something a few years ago," said the girl.

"Uh, yeah, you might put it that way," said Barbara, averting her gaze to the grass.

"Oh, sorry," said the girl, "that was rude." At that, the girl proffered her right hand. Barbara jumped over the porch rail. Landing lightly on the grass, she strode over to the girl and shook her hand.

Again that mutual thrill of recognition.

"I'm Linda Maddock," said the girl.

"I'm Barbara Lla...but I guess you knew that already. You're new here," said Barbara.

"Yep, me and my mom moved here last week. My dad, Herb, has been here for a few months setting up a business. Your Gramps and Herb are going to be business partners," announced Linda.

"Your Dad's in the art business?" asked Barbara.

"Nope, Herb's in the motorcycle business. It's much cooler than all that art stuff," said Linda. At that, she stepped away from the motorcycle. It's ruby red paint vied with its chrome and immaculate V-twin engine for Barbara's attention, each trying to grab more light than the other.

"Herb built it for my birthday. I just got it!" Linda could barely restrain her pleasure and pride in her father's skill. You wanna go for a ride?"

"Sure! But aren't we too young to go by ourselves?" asked Barbara.

"Nope," said Linda with a Cheshire-cat grin, "let's just say that Sheriff Norton and me have a little agreement. He looks the other way and I don't tell his Goody-Two-Shoes wife that he plays poker at Jake's Mule Barn."

"Isn't that a little underhanded?" ventured Barbara.

"You bet! It's the only way to get things done. Just ask your gramps," advised Linda. At that, she mounted the motorcycle and nodded at Barbara to get on the back seat.

When she was settled, Barbara asked Linda, "Why do you call your own father Herb?"

Linda shrugged her shoulders dismissively, saying, "It's his name."

At that, Linda started the engine, coaxing the motorcycle across the soft, lush grass. As they pulled out onto Main Street, Richard Llandry stepped onto the porch. He smiled contentedly as the sound of the motorcycle's engine faded in the distance. When all was quiet again, Richard closed Barbara's book and quietly disappeared with it back into the house.

#

The stable at the edge of town had been falling into ruin ever since the automobile displaced the horse as the preferred mode of transportation. The building was tired, and listing like a drunk about to collapse when Herb Maddock bought it for a dollar as part of a municipal reclamation project. Within days a gang of men with pierced bodies and tattooed arms descended on Milton like Huns. More than a few of them were known to Richard and Barbara as denizens of Jake's mule barn.

The men converged upon the barn. Foundations were repaired, and crooked timbers set straight. Siding was restored and painted red. Stalls were converted to service bays. An immaculate mobile home was towed in and installed on one side of the stable. Then came the tools -- implements for everything germane to the restoration of old motorcycles. After that came consignments of bikes in every conceivable stage of abuse and neglect.

Finally a sign arrived. It read, "Herb's Ineffable Motorcycle Rehabilitation: Consultants To the Discerning Road Rat." It had just been hung above the main bay doors when Linda and Barbara pulled up. Barbara's first impression upon dismounting the bike was one of pleasure at seeing a ruin being given a new life. Then she noticed a man standing off to the left of the shop, in distracted contemplation of the sign. The man turned around as Linda cut the engine.

"Hey pumpkin," said the man in greeting.

"Hey Herb," replied Linda as she trotted up the grass to hug her father. Herb looked up and smiled as Barbara approached and stopped at a polite distance.

"You must be Richard's granddaughter. You're a dead ringer for him, except for the beard of course," said Herb.

Barbara smiled shyly at Herb and walked closer to him, extending her right hand in greeting.

"We don't do handshakes around here," said Herb, "just hugs. You like hugs?"

"Sure do," said Barbara, with a look of simple pleasure.

Barbara found herself in a strong yet gentle embrace that was so much like her dead father's that her eyes started leaking long-repressed tears. But as her eyes moistened, the emptiness within her did not feel quite so burdensome. Herb saw the look in Barbara's eyes, understood what it meant, and discretely changed the subject.

"Hey pumpkin! Your going to have to do some serious growing to catch up to your friend here," said Herb. Linda straightened up defiantly saying, "No problem, old man! I can do anything I want! I could make myself grow if I wanted!" At that, Herb grabbed Linda's thick blond hair and started pulling it upwards, saying, "Well then, grow, girl, grow!"

"I will not and you can't make me!" With both hands, Linda tried to pull her hair down, all the while kicking, or trying to kick, Herb in the shins.

As Herb and Linda continued their horseplay, Barbara stepped back and watched. Herb had the strangest face she had ever seen. She was used to being around men and women with pierced faces and tattoos, but Herb was unique. The left side of his forehead was dented. Whatever had caused the dent had also displaced his left eye slightly down and sideways, with a result that Herb looked as if he could see in two different directions at once, like a lizard. He also had an assortment of scars in various places that could only have been acquired by someone who lived at the brink of either death or insanity.

Herb and Linda had wrestled each other to the ground and were trying to rub each other's faces in the grass when a woman appeared from around one corner of the stable. She stopped, placed her hands on her hips, and assumed a stance of practiced forbearance. Herb was losing the contest, and perforce eating dirt, when the woman sauntered forward and kicked Herb's backside.

"Hey butt head, what are you doing to your daughter!"

"What am I doing? Ask her! She's the one rubbing my face in the dirt!"

At that, the pair released their death locks on each other and sat back on the grass, looking a little cowed.

"Linda, go into the trailer and cleanup. And you! Pick the dirt out of your teeth and give me a hand with something!"

Herb's wife would have been described as "a real looker" by the elderly regulars at Jake's Mule Barn. Her body — perfect by any standards — could have been a subject for any number of stunning statues, photographs, and paintings. As it turned out, her body was itself the canvas for an assortment of small tattoos depicting mythological animals, all flatteringly placed and rendered with consummate skill. The effect was completed by tight cut-off blue jeans and a makeshift midriff blouse that did little to conceal her ample breasts. She was one of those women who are proud of their bodies and yet sweetly self-effacing about it. After she had thoroughly chastised Linda and Herb, the woman looked at Barbara and smiled.

"Hi, I'm Sarah Maddock. You must be Barbara."

"Yes, ma'am." Once again, Barbara held out her right hand in greeting, but Sarah ignored it, enfolding her instead in a mother's embrace that Barbara had not known for years. She melted into it.

"Welcome to our home, Barbara. Don't mind Herb and Linda. Those two lose track of their brains when they start messing with each other. You want to stay for a cookout?"

"Sure," said Barbara, "but I better call my grandpa first."

"Don't bother," said Sarah, "he'll be by any minute now."

"Would you like some help?" asked Barbara.

"Okay," said Sarah, "follow me."

Sarah put an arm around Barbara's shoulders and together they walked to the north side of the stable. Arrayed in front of the trailer was a panoply of ribs and other assorted meats cooking slowly, circumfusing the trailer with the odors of home.

"That's a lot of food," said Barbara. "Who's it for?"

"The guys who worked on the stable for Herb. You've got to keep the help happy or they won't come back," said Sarah.

The guests started cruising in as Sarah and Barbara busied themselves with arranging drinks, salads, and bread. The guests had about them a rough-hewn eclat rendered all the more memorable by their motorcycles, which were more works of art than means of transportation. The women were much like Sarah -- naturally and unaffectedly sensuous. Their collective presence was raw and rough, soft and yielding.

The combined odors of well-oiled leather, perfume, and hot meat clarified feelings that Barbara had been having for some time, but did not understand until now. An incense had been ignited within her whose smoldering would soon make of her body a censer for the erotic fires of puberty. Barbara's reverie was broken by a tap on her shoulder. It was Linda, nodding toward a tall man in the distance walking toward the stable and asking, "Isn't that your gramps?"

"Uh...yeah, yes it is," said Barbara, somewhat distractedly.

"Herb's right. You look just like him, and I bet you're gonna be as tall as him too someday," said Linda.

Richard Llandry approached, wearing chinos and an open-necked denim shirt. He smiled and waved to the two girls before disappearing among the guests, who greeted him warmly and made room for him among the makeshift tables that Herb had set up for their comfort.

"Come on with me and I'll show you Herb's shop," said Linda.

The two girls strolled to the front of the stable. Along the way, the odors of new wooden siding and fresh paint hinted at the new life that would soon rise from the stable's long and dreamless sleep. As Barbara and Linda entered the main service bay, the smells of cooking gave way to the smells of restoration. Paint, oil, gas, grease and solvent fumes competed with each other to dominate the air around well-organized piles of decrepit motorcycles. Their gas tanks carried names little known to most people: Vincent, Ace, Crocker, Indian, Norton, Henderson, and Emblem, as well as better known names such as Harley-Davidson and Buell.

In the main work area rose two motorcycles nearing completion. Barbara walked slowly around the machines, marveling at these Phoenixes rising from the wreckage around them. She asked Linda what they were. Linda brightened and explained. "They're Herb's masterpieces. This one is a 1928 Harley

Davidson two-cam twin. It's the fastest street-legal bike that Harley's ever produced. The other one is just too cool for words. It's a Crocker. Only 64 were ever produced and each one was made by hand. People used to call them the Dusenbergs of American motorcycles."

"What kind of people can afford these things," asked Barbara.

"Rich ones, mostly. You wouldn't know it to look at him, but Herb can call all kinds of famous people on the phone and get through every time. That's what makes Herb and your Gramps natural business partners. Each of them can drum up business for the other."

"Speaking of Herb," asked Barbara, "what's the deal with his face? It's really messed up."

Linda explained through a smirk that she could not control. "Let's just say that Herb had a little disagreement with a concrete wall at Pocono Raceway. He was in the lead, and the second-place guy wouldn't stop bird-dogging him. Herb finally got clear of him when the front tire exploded, and that's all she wrote. The wall smashed right through a thousand-dollar Kevlar helmet and didn't stop until it was part-way into his skull. He was in the hospital for about a month. The doctors put him back together, mostly. But they didn't want to mess with his skull. When Herb woke up, he was his usual self again, so the Docs decided not to fix him since he wasn't broke. Mom says it's because

Herb never uses that part of his brain anyway. His sponsors were really sorry. They gave us a pile of money and Herb used some of it to set up his own shop. He was doing high-class restorations for other shop owners, and was itching to have his own place."

"So here you are," said Barbara.

"Yep, here we are and I think we're gonna like it," said Linda.

"What are you doing now that school's out," asked Barbara.

"I'll work for Herb. I know how to use all these tools and I can fix anything," boasted Linda, "and soon, Herb's gonna show me how to use an airbrush. I can't wait!"

"I guess you'll be a first-rate motorcycle mechanic when you grow up," said Barbara.

"Nope. I wanna fly — for the Air Force or maybe even the Marines. That's why I want to be around tools and machines. That plus it's fun," said Linda. "What are you gonna do when you grow up?"

"I'm going to Mars," said Barbara nonchalantly.

Linda looked closely at Barbara.

"You really mean it, don't you?" said Linda.

"Yep," said Barbara.

The girls fell silent for a few moments as Barbara surveyed Herb's exotic tools. Her eyes fell upon a new staircase that led to a loft. A fresh sign was affixed to the rail. In a lush, feminine script it read "S and M Tattoos." Both the initial and final Ss were formed into fanciful whips. Beneath this was a smaller sign whose plain, bold lettering shouted, "If you are drunk, stoned, under age, or just plain stupid, THEN GET OUT OF HERE!"

Barbara chuckled at the sign. "Who's S and M?"

Linda replied, "Sarah and Marguerite— my Mom and my aunt. They're tattoo artists. Pretty good ones too. Their appointment book is filled for the next six months. My aunt has a place in Iowa City. I've been bugging my Mom for a tattoo, but she just tells me to read the sign and figure out which kind of low-life I am. Herb says maybe for my 16th birthday."

Linda paused as a Cheshire-cat grin formed itself on her lips.

"Guess what?" She said.

"What?" said Barbara.

"Mom says your gramps has an awesome tattoo on his back. It's a great big dragon flying out of a cloud," taunted Linda.

"No!" Barbara was stunned. "How does your mom know?"

"She did it a long time ago and she says it's one of her best pieces ever," said Linda.

Barbara mused, "Every time I think I understand Grandpa, something turns up that knocks me back to square one."

"Yeah," added Linda, "your gramps is one of those nerdy guys who's really cool when you get to know him."

Just then, Sarah's stentorian voice boomed, "Linda! Barbara! Dinner!"

The girls trotted back to the trailer, where someone had lit a bonfire against the coming night. The smell of meat was now palpable, and blended with the musky odors of leather, smoke, and hot metal in a way that aroused everyone's bacchanalian instincts to that of a high revelry whose energy pulsed with the rock-and-roll music thundering out of the trailer.

Linda excused herself and went off to harass Herb about something. Barbara on the other hand was driven into the crowd by a sudden craving for fleshy closeness and meat. She passed up trays of salad, bread, and soda and went straight to the rack of ribs that Sarah had just laid out. She loaded a plate with ribs and hot sauce and sat down in front of the fire. She was lost in the Stone Age pleasures of the meal when she felt a light kick to her backside.

"Hey Barb! Doesn't your gramps ever feed you?" It was Linda. "Look at you! You're a mess!"

"Linda, these ribs are unbelievable! How does your mom do it," said Barbara.

Linda replied, "We don't know and it's not for lack of spying. Mom likes to cook alone. She throws stuff at us if we even peek around the corner when she's making something special. Now let me clean you up. Jesus, girl! I can't take you anywhere! Come on."

Linda steered a slightly flustered Barbara into the trailer. When they emerged, the fire had burnt low, and the adults had formed small, intimate groups. The girls laid back on a soft grassy incline close to the fire. For a long time, neither of them spoke. They lay quietly on their backs and watched the embers escape the fire and rise into the warm evening sky where they twinkled briefly like newborn stars and then faded into the blackness.

Linda spoke first. "I guess your parents' spaceship is still out there. Is anybody working on it?"

"A little," answered Barbara, "but mostly a bunch of people in Washington are screaming that the whole thing is too expensive, too dangerous. The usual crap."

"No guts," said Linda. "You and I may just have to go to Washington and kick some butts — fly the sucker to Mars ourselves if we have to."

"I'd like that," said Barbara. "I think we'd make a good team."

"Damn straight, ma cherie," said Linda.

The girls fell silent again.

The fire had burnt to a bed of coals when Linda sensed someone approaching quietly like a cat looking for a mouse in the darkness. The figure paused in front of the fire and sat down beside them. Linda rose first.

"Oh... hi Dr. Llandry."

"Don't get up, Linda; I'm just here to collect Barbara."

Barbara had nodded off and Linda poked her sharply in the ribs. "Wake up! Your gramps is here to take you home! The girls both rose.

"Thanks for inviting me to your party, Linda. I really enjoyed it," said Barbara.

"Good. Come back anytime. I'll show you Herb in action. He's smarter than he looks," said Linda.

"Okay. Count on it," said Barbara. "Goodnight."

"Same here. Goodnight Dr. Llandry," said Linda.

As if by tacit agreement, Richard and Barbara walked home in silence, each of them alone with their thoughts — Richard secretly hoping that Barbara had found a surrogate family in the Maddocks, Barbara knowing that she had, and neither of them voicing their convictions to the other.

Midnight found them sitting quietly on the porch swing, watching for the occasional meteor to cross the sky. Barbara broke the silence with a chuckle.

"Grandpa, Linda told me you have a tatoo."

"Rats! I swore her to silence. The child must be destroyed."

Richard spoke so nonchalantly that it took Barbara a moment to realize that he was kidding. She smiled. "Put her bike in a trash compactor. She'll die on the spot."

Richard's eyes twinkled in the dark. "Count on it."

They went back to watching the sky.

REUNIONS II: late summer 2006

"Hey, girl!"

It had become a familiar and welcome routine. First, the faint but gravelly sound of a V-twin motorcycle engine in the distance that became louder as it approached Richard Llandry's property; then, the soft sound of tires rolling on lush grass; and finally, Linda Maddox's clear and forever friendly voice. Barbara looked up from her reading on the porch swing.

"Don't you ever stop working?", said Linda.

"It's not really work, so I don't mind doing it," said Barbara.

"You're so weird," said Linda.

At that, Linda dismounted the bike and removed a brown paper bag from one of the hard saddlebags. Along with the bag came the stench of a dead something-or-other that had been sitting in the sun for too long.

"Look at this!" demanded Linda.

"I don't need to. I can smell it," said Barbara.

"It's just a dead raven," said Linda, "don't be such a wuss!"

Barbara jumped over the porch rail and landed a few inches from her friend. The stench of the carcass grew in proportion and Barbara wretched a few times before acclimating to it.

"Oh God, Linda," said Barbara, "what are you doing with that thing?"

"I have an idea," replied Linda, "and you gave it to me."

"Huh?" Barbara looked questioningly at Linda.

"Remember last week when you showed me that picture of Leonardo da Vinci's airplane? You said he copied it from birds and it would have worked, except that Leonardo didn't have enough power to make it fly. Well, think of it the other way around. If we build the same thing from ultra light materials, then we won't need as much power to launch it. I could make profiles of the wings so we know what kind of airfoil works for a bird." Linda's excitement at the thought of building Leonardo's aircraft was infectious. Barbara examined the raven with renewed interest.

"Then," said Linda, "when we know the shape of the thing, we'll singe off the feathers and look at what holds the wings together. That's where you come in."

By this time, Barbara had taken the bird from Linda and was flexing its wings as well as her imagination. The possibilities unfolded in her mind, while a soft voice from faraway told her that Linda's idea would work.

"Okay Linda, I'm in," said Barbara, "what do I do?"

"Here's the deal," said Linda, "Herb tells me that you're a stinkin' genius with numbers. I can make all the measurements of the wing and I can build it. What I can't do is scale the measurements up to where one of us can fly the thing. I don't know how to figure out the lift either. I can be the draftsman and the builder, but I can't crunch the numbers. Can you?"

Barbara did not answer right away. She thought the project through. At each step, she knew what she could to and, more importantly for such a hazardous project, what she could not do. She could learn the new material.

"I can do it," said Barbara with calm assurance, "but what do we do about power?"

"Got it covered," countered Linda. "We'll attach a tow line from the wings to one of Herb's ATVs. The pilot has roller blades on. The rider starts towing the wings in a straight line, like on a runway, until the pilot takes off. And then, if she's got the cajones, she can release the tow line and see where the wind takes her."

"Which hopefully isn't straight down," said Barbara.

"That's where I'm counting on you for all the right numbers," countered Linda, "those plus controls — probably just a few wires to shift the pilot's weight and warp the wings. You still in?"

"Sure. But school's starting in a few weeks," said Barbara; "won't that cramp your free time?"

"Nope," said Linda, "I see something once or do something once and I've got it forever. After school I go straight to the library. It never takes me more than an hour to do my homework, and then I'm free. And you know what? I always get As and Bs. Never a C in my whole life! And that's without even breaking a sweat."

Linda had a way of being modest and boastful at the same time that most people, including Barbara, found endearing. When Linda spoke of her strengths, it was as if she were talking about someone else or reading excitedly from a book.

"Let's start now," said Barbara.

"Uh...sure. Yes!" said Linda.

"Let me just tell Grandpa where I'm going," said Barbara. She opened the screen door that separated the porch from the kitchen and shouted, "Hey Grandpa, I'm going over to Linda's to start a project!" From deep within the house came a voice. "Okay ˙Pookie."

If Richard only knew what he had just unleashed.

#

It was not long after she had met the Maddox's that Barbara had shown a penchant for motorcycling. At the end of her first and only day of instruction, Barbara was popping wheelies, jumping small hurdles, and negotiating tight high-speed turns. Later that night, she slipped into the Jake's Mule Barn and struck a deal with Sheriff Norton; and so began another of Milton's subtle diurnal rhythms as the sounds of two V-twin engines making their way up and down Main Street joined those of the tractors and harvesters that crawled everywhere along the horizon.

It was also not long after Barbara had met the Maddoxes that the locals started referring to Herb's shop as Jake's Other Mule Barn, given the propensity of both enterprises for sharing customers. These were of two types. The first consisted of men and women who worked part-time for Herb as artists and machinists. As a group, they could recreate every part and every finish ever applied to any brand of motorcycle ever produced. Their services were in demand all over the country.

In contrast to these people were the hangers-on and wannabes, people who enjoyed being seen with the creative, convention-flouting fringe but who were too spiritless to get involved with it. One got the feeling that this was how they approached everything.

It was into this melange of people that Barbara and Linda rode on the day they decided to improve upon Leonardo da Vinci's airplane. The loiterers parted to make way for the girls like a listless Red Sea. The girls, always careful not to disturb any of the workers, parked their bikes by the trailer, well away from the shop.

"Let's go upstairs," said Linda, grabbing the raven and heading for S and M Tattoos. Barbara followed and noticed that Linda was leaving in her wake a stench that distracted even the most intent of the artists. Oblivious to the disturbance that she was creating, Linda nonchalantly entered the shop. She ascended the stairs and came upon her mother and a customer.

"Geez, Linda! What's that smell?" demanded Sarah.

"It's just a dead bird, Mom," said Linda with a carefully rehearsed coolness, "Barbara and I are starting a project."

"Well you're not starting it here! Who knows how much filth and corruption's on that thing! Out!" As Sarah resumed her work — a greywork dragon on the shoulder of a young, muscular, flame-haired woman — Linda descended the stairs and gestured to Barbara that she stay quiet and go outside.

Once they were outdoors, Barbara suggested that they did not need the whole bird, just it's wings. They sat on a picnic table where Linda produced a pen knife and began to feel along the raven's dark sides. She moved her fingers tentatively but deftly in the manner of a craftsman.

"All we need are the wings, Linda'" Barbara reminded Linda, "you can leave the shoulders alone. Wings are just modified arms."

"You're the science geek," murmured Linda as her probing fingers moved more purposefully along the bird's flanks. When she felt where the wings should be cut, Linda picked up her knife and began using it like a finger. The blade pierced the raven's skin and slid through its flesh, seeking the joints that she had felt on the bird's lean surface. With only a few barely perceptible cuts, the wings fell softly to the ground. Linda lifted up the wings with a satisfied smile and flexed them against the sky.

"Are you sure these are hands? They don't look like hands to me," said Linda.

"Don't worry," replied Barbara. They're hands all right. Body plans in nature are highly conserved among different species."

"You don't say," said Linda with a facetious grin.

"I do say," countered Barbara. She was about to say something else but paused to sniff the air. Then she sniffed herself. Finally, she stepped toward Linda and smelled a lock of her hair.

"Hey girl," said Barbara, "we stink as much as this bird! If we don't wash up, no one's going to let us anywhere near them."

Linda slid off the table and sniffed herself. "Oh yuck! You're right. I smell like death!"

She picked up the bird's carcass and hurled it into the air for one last flight. It formed a blot in the sky before it fell and disappeared into the canopy of a small wood that adjoined the Maddox's backyard. Linda trotted over to one of the service bays and soon returned to the picnic table with a jar of alcohol. She immersed the wings within the jar, sealed it tightly, and placed it in the shade next to the stable. The girls entered the trailer. Minutes later, puzzled passers by saw a jumble of denim pants and leather vests flying out of the Maddox's kitchen window, followed by the sounds of giggles and running water.

#

The next morning, Linda woke up early and checked the wings. Their overnight soak in the alcohol had rendered them soft, and pliable and odorless enough to handle without disgusting anyone, especially Sarah, by whose graces Linda had been allowed to convert a corner of the tattoo parlor into a small workshop with good natural light. Not being one to let the proverbial grass grow under her feet, Linda had arrayed a set of drafting tools within easy reach of a table flanked by two adjustable office chairs. She was set up and ready to work when Barbara rode up and parked her Harley next to the stable. She removed a laptop computer from the motorcycle's tail bag and entered the main service bay.

"Morning, Herb. Hi guys," she said in greeting.

"Hey, Barb," replied an assortment of male and female voices.

"Where's Linda?"

Without speaking or looking up, Herb nodded toward the tattoo parlor.

Barbara knocked politely on the railing and ascended the stairs. She came upon Sarah, who was tattooing an image of a man pushing a lawnmower just above the pubic hair line of a woman who Barbara recognized as one of Herb's airbrush artists. Doing her best not to stare at the woman's crotch, Barbara nevertheless broke into a laughing jag when she saw the humor behind the tattoo. Both of the women smiled slyly at Barbara's increasingly ribald sense of humor.

"Hey, girl," came a voice from the parlor's far end, "people are trying to work here!"

Barbara choked back her laughter long enough to locate Linda, who was seated at her drafting table. She stuck out her tongue at Barbara as she crossed the parlor and sat on one of the office chairs. Linda had pinned the raven's wings meticulously to a sheet of white foam-core on whose surface was inscribed a series of parallel lines spaced one-centimeter apart. The wings were beautiful in death, and as Barbara contemplated them she felt sad over this small death and the irony of a powerful bird, stripped of its wings and rotting in an obscure wood behind an old stable in the middle of nowhere. Images of her parents shattered remains and final death embrace played slowly through her mind like the frames of an old silent movie fraught with scenes of desolation. Linda looked up from her drafting table. She changed her tone.

"Barb? You all right?"

This roused Barbara from her reverie. Taking a slow, deep breath, she looked up.

"I'm fine. Just thinking, is all."

"You want to start later?" asked Linda.

"No. Let's do it," said Barbara as she regained her composure.

The girls went back to studying the wings. To Barbara, they were reminiscent of the delta-winged designs that were integral to the design of stealth military aircraft. She got up and stood behind Linda, gesturing over the drafting board.

"Simplify the rear contours of the wings by drawing straight lines here, here, and here," said Barbara.

Linda complied with a deftness far beyond her years. Herb and Sarah must have long ago recognized their daughter's talent and taught her well. In less than two minutes, the outline on the foam core became a hybrid between a delta and a W. The shape took on a stark beauty.

"I guess the parallel lines are markers for making cross-sections," said Barbara.

"Yep," replied Linda. Placing a flexible straight-edge over the wing, she aligned it over one of the guide lines. Holding the straight edge precisely along one of the guide lines, Linda picked up a beard trimmer and carefully cut a channel through the feathers. Clearing away the debris and down feathers, Linda formed a precise channel down to the skin. She picked up a red indelible marker and drew a guideline on the wing. Pleased with the results, she settled down to work.

The honey-bee white noise formed by the clippers was soothing and conducive to concentration. Barbara turned on the computer. She had devised a two-part plan for designing a pair of wings that would be likely to fly. The first part required that she design virtual wings in the computer and the second that she test them in a virtual wind tunnel.

Barbara had a clear view of the one intact wing. She opened a three-dimensional graphics program and configured it to accept the data that Linda would soon be generating. As she was bigger in general than Linda, Barbara formed a prototype fuselage using her own weight and height. She had finished a simple prototype when Linda looked up.

"I'm finished with this wing," she said, "and I'm guessing that you won't need numbers for the other one."

"Right," said Barbara as she typed a few final commands into the program, "We'd just be making extra work for ourselves. When we finish the one wing, I'll just create a mirror image."

Barbara got up and scrutinized what Linda had done. It was perfect. And beautiful. The combination of the blood-red lines and the remaining black feathers, which intersected them at varying angles conspired to make the wing look like an element from an abstract mobile. It belonged in the air. Linda looked hopefully and somewhat shyly at Barbara.

"You like it?"

"It's beautiful. Linda, you're an artist."

Linda beamed with a simple pleasure that filled the room. She was too proud to admit it, but Linda was beginning to see Barbara as both a friend and mentor. What she did not know was that Barbara saw her in the same way. Each of them felt good about herself when in the company of the other. Linda was the first to break the moment.

"So how do you want me to feed you the numbers?"

Barbara appraised the wing briefly and said, "start at the wrist and make your way to the wing's tip. For every line that you make, give me measurements every centimeter."

"Okay."

Linda picked up a pair of calipers that, of their own seeming volition, became extensions of her fingers. She quickly established a routine as she measured the wing sections and called out the numbers to Barbara in a brisk efficient voice. Each number was answered by a staccato of keyboard taps. The bursts of sound quickly formed a quiet tide whose ebbs and flows moved in a soothing rhythm made all the more pleasant by the muted voices coming from Sarah and her customer at the other end of the room. Barbara loved quiet moments. She would lose all sense of time and fall into a dynamic stillness replete with creative possibilities. It was as if she were being rewarded for understanding that the best way to use time is to forget all about it.

"I guess that's it for now," said Linda. "You want some lunch?"

"Sure," said Barbara. "Just let me set the program to work while we're gone." As she did this, Barbara had a thought. "Say, Linda; you've never been inside my Grandpa's house, have you? Let's eat there."

"No, I haven't. But I know a lot of busybodies who'd love to get in there," said Linda.

"Okay then, let's go." At that, Barbara tapped the 'Enter' command on the laptop's keyboard and stood up.

As the girls rode away, the computer quietly calculated a piece of their shared destiny.

#

Linda had never spent much time around Richard, and so it was with considerable curiosity that she opened the screen door on the front porch and entered the main parlor. Barbara followed upon Linda's heels and let the door swing shut with a distinctive 'creeeeaak-and-clunk' that had announced visitors for four generations.

Rumors about the house, its contents, and its enigmatic but convivial owner had long ago become part of Milton's folklore. As is typical with rumors, however, they were easily undermined by the reality that they purportedly depicted. Linda saw this immediately when she paused to admire the room. Life with Sarah and Herb had nurtured within Linda a connoisseur's instinct for sensing the level of honesty and integrity in any object, regardless of the medium in which it was made. The parlor itself, the Isfahan rugs, the furniture, the prints on the walls, the exotically bound books, bespoke these virtues with a friendly understatement that lent a coziness, a nuzzling comfort, to these rare beauties. The room was an enchantment rendered real. Linda suspected that the rest of the house was the same.

Linda's reverie was broken by a soft voice at her back. She turned and saw

119

Richard entering the parlor from the kitchen, followed by an invisible swell of kitchen odors in which the smells of grilled cheese with bacon predominated.

"Hello, Linda. Hey, Pookie."

Richard proffered his hand in greeting. As Linda shook it and looked up, she felt as if she were standing in front of an old, grey tree that had just lowered a branch as an invitation to climb and enjoy the upper limbs.

"Your mother just called to let me know you were coming. She also hinted that grilled cheese and bacon would make your day," said the tree as it reassumed its human form.

The girls followed Richard into the kitchen and sat at the places set for them on a table made from an immense plank of walnut that struck Linda has being the oldest thing on Earth. She fancied that it was a great and dark god of a river whose black, brown, and red currents swirled into eddies that existed for a few moments before breaking up and rejoining other currents whose pace had been set in a land before time, and whose destiny it was to float inexorably to a place where time, after a seeming eternity, would itself vanish as if it had simply been a dream.

Linda surprised herself. She was not prone to reveries like this, and she suspected that the house had something to do with it. This was in itself a strange thought for her to be having, so she directed her attention elsewhere.

Richard had by this time served lunch — grilled cheese and bacon with a tray of dill pickles and potato chips on the side — and sat opposite Linda. He immediately got up again, muttering something to himself, and returned with a pitcher of iced lemonade. As he filled three tall glasses, she discreetly took a long look at him.

She was struck by how much Barbara resembled her grandfather. There could be no doubting her friend's ancestry. Both of them had the same long faces, with angular features whose severity was tempered by slight curves. What remained of Richard's original hair color was the same relentless black that framed Barbara's face so dramatically. But where Richard's eyes were an endearing robin's egg blue, Barbara's were the sapphire-blue of two dark stars. They were eyes that looked upon other worlds, and many adults were profoundly unnerved when they looked at Barbara squarely in the face. Linda smiled when she realized that her parents and their friends were not among them. She looked up at the sound of a polite voice.

"I hope these sandwiches are to your liking?"

"Uh, yes Dr. Llandry. Thanks. They're better than what my mom makes, but don't tell her. It might hurt her feelings."

Richard smiled. "Consider it lost in the vaults."

He and Linda then started talking shop. She quickly relaxed in the presence of this man, to whom mystery clung like a second skin, and who thus became the subject of so much speculation. Conversation floated on its own caprice, shifting easily as it unfolded to include welding, metal lathing, lacquer finishing, airbrush work, and other things that impassioned people devoted to their art and craftsmanship.

Barbara was quiet during much of the meal. Linda's knowledge of tools and techniques never ceased to amaze her. The girl was a prodigy, and her parents knew it. They also had the rare ability to nurture Linda's talents without applying any pressure or letting their own egos thwart her growth. It was also interesting to watch her grandfather as he talked to Linda. Barbara was starting to appreciate Richard's knack for relating to intelligent children without patronizing them. He was genuinely interested in what Linda was saying and treated her as a miniature adult. It was a blessing for her to be living with a man like that. Child prodigies too often grew up in a limbo, not really being adults or children. They had abilities that exceeded those of most adults, and yet coexisted with a child's emotional needs. Richard Llandry knew how to balance the two as if they were one.

The girls eventually found themselves staring at empty plates.

"Are you two still hungry?"

"No, Dr. Llandry. That was good. Thanks. Barbara and me...uh, I...have to get back to work," said Linda.

"Yes, I suppose you do," said Richard. "Herb tells me that you two are working on a special project. Very hush-hush and all that."

Linda smiled puckishly at Richard and said nothing as she followed Barbara outside. He stood at the window, watching and listening to the pair of motorcycles as they disappeared down Main Street.

He smiled and cleared the table.

\#

Barbara and Linda sat in front of the laptop's screen staring at the ghost it had conjured during lunch. The prototype looked about as flight worthy as a dodo bird, and not much prettier. Linda tilted her head to one side like a perplexed but intelligent dog.

"You think that thing will fly?"

"Probably not," said Barbara.

"So we've gone belly up?" asked Linda.

"No, we're still okay," said Barbara, "I decided not to trust myself with the final design because I don't understand all the math yet; so I called around and talked to some people that my mom and dad used to work with. I finally found a guy at Lockheed who e-mailed me a simple wind tunnel program with a really cool twist to it. The software takes the results of a given test, tags its flaws, and feeds them into another test. It does that over and over again until it finds a shape that'll fly. The wings evolve in a virtual world. There's just one catch."

"Herb says there always is," quipped Linda.

"We need to know the thing's weight," said Barbara.

Linda looked at the screen again. "You're sure about the wing span?"

"Yep; the computer scaled up the dimensions with the ratios it got from your numbers and my body weight," said Barbara.

"So if you die, it's my fault," said Linda.

"No big deal. I'll just haunt you for the rest of your life," said Barbara.

"It's not your ghost that I'm worried about," said Linda. Without elaborating any further, she pulled a few catalogs from a shelf next to the drafting table and started poring over them. Fifteen minutes later, Linda closed the catalogs, added a column of numbers, and looked at Barbara, who had busied herself with configuring the wind tunnel software.

"Okay, ma cherie, here's the deal;" said Linda, "forget the fuselage and replace it with a harness like a hang glider, which is what this thing amounts to. Add a pound or two for cables and controls, and this bird weighs in at 10 pounds."

"You're kidding!" said Barbara.

"Too heavy?" Countered Linda.

"No, it's great!" said Barbara as she entered the number and started the program. "Okay, now we've got some feathers to singe."

By this time, there was a marked funk in the air. It was not a stench exactly, but it was weird enough to repel anyone who did not know what was going on and so, anxious not to be evicted, Linda immersed the marked-up wing in the alcohol bath while Barbara removed the intact wing and took it outside. She sat on the cool, lush grass in the shade of the trailer while Linda went into the shop to talk to Herb.

The afternoon was quiet, cool, and conducive to reflection. Barbara laid the wings on the grass in front of her and just looked at them. The black nestled low in the green and opened into a bottomless hole out of which flowed a stream of impressions that drained into a corresponding space deep within her. The Earth was opening up to her and whispering its secrets. The more it whispered, the bigger Barbara felt inside until she fancied herself to be coextensive with the Earth. She shuddered with the fecundity of a girl becoming a woman.

A pair of steel tongs landed in her lap.

Barbara looked up to see Linda standing over her with a blowtorch. "Hey girl, you're not going goofy on me again, are you? You really creep me out when you do that."

"Try it sometime; it's refreshing," said Barbara.

Linda grunted, "uh-huh," and fired up the blowtorch. "It'll be easier if I do this myself. Hand me the tongs." As Linda singed the feathers, Barbara saw Sarah looking out the kitchen window at the two of them, not knowing what to make of the sight of Linda standing in the middle of the yard in the middle of the afternoon singeing the feathers off a dead bird with a blowtorch.

"Oh, man...this is one hell of a stink!" Linda grimaced as she finished singeing the feathers. In one movement, she snuffed the blowtorch and tossed the wing to Barbara.

"Here, you take over! I'm gonna puke if I don't get away from that thing."

Barbara felt her own gorge rising as she caught the wing gingerly with her fingertips.

"Calm down and don't go all mental on me," she said.

Barbara ran into the stable and returned with fresh alcohol, a scrub brush, and a battered pan. Sitting at the picnic table, she poured some of the alcohol into the pan, dropped in the wing, and cleaned off the remaining stubble within a few minutes. Linda had recovered sufficiently by then to pick up the wing. Holding it against the sun, she repeatedly flexed and extended it, all the while squinting speculatively through the skin at the bones. "Hey Barb, do you have that picture of Leonardo's plane handy?"

"Yep. It's in the computer. Why?"

"If I remember it right, then the Maestro did a good job with the struts and controls so we don't need to reinvent them," said Linda.

"That would be great. I'll go upstairs and print a copy," said Barbara. Several minutes later, the girls were standing side-by-side comparing Leonardo's plan with the backlit wing.

"You know, Barbara, I think the old geezer's got it licked. If you can come up with the best wing shape, I can adapt his control structure. Was he always this smart?" asked Linda.

"Pretty much," replied Barbara, "Grandpa has a facsimile of his notebooks in his library. He'd be happy to show it to you. Come on over tonight after dinner."

"Cool," said Linda, "you wanna close up for today?"

"Okay, but keep the wings until tomorrow, in case we screw up," said Barbara.

\#

Sunset found Linda in Richard's parlor, sitting cross-legged in a rocking chair, with an oversized vellum book nestled in her lap. The visions of a man born 500 years too early floated off the pages of his notebooks and rose to form an ensorcelling cloud around her head.   Leonardo would have adored the sight.

Barbara passed the time by communing with the house. She listened to it with all of her senses, unable to shake the conviction that it was alive.   From the day she first came to live with her grandfather, Barbara could hear the house whispering to her at odd moments when nothing else was going on.   But to describe her impressions in terms of hearing alone did not do justice to the experience.   It actually began with her sense of smell.   The patient odors of age mingled with the incense of ongoing life.   They stirred memories within her that spanned abysses of time and space too vast to have been laid down within her own short life.   Had she known that smell was the oldest of the senses, that it connected intimately with ancient centers of the brain responsible for preserving memory, she would have suspected that she was tapping the collective memories of mankind.

She imposed no thoughts of order on the experience.   Smell, touch, sound, and light interlaced themselves each among the others to weave a net that formed itself around her contours and made of her body an organ of subtle knowing.   Barbara knew, and yet did not know, what the house was trying to tell her. And that was all right. The house was patient.

Barbara's reverie was cut short by a stabbing "rrriiiiinnngg!" from a telephone across the room. Rising from his rocker, Richard parked his meerschaum pipe in an ashtray and sauntered across the room to answer the phone. It was a curious pipe that often made Barbara smile. More a statue than a pipe, it's soft white mass had been sculpted into an impish face whose bacchanalian smirk, forever frozen in time by the carver's blade, made light of all that it surveyed. The effect became surreal whenever Richard lit a wad of fresh tobacco in the pipe's deep bowl. The clouds of sweet smelling smoke that escaped the little man's head made it look as if his brain was on fire.

"Linda, your mother's on the phone," called Richard from across the room.

No answer.

"Linda. Your mom wants to talk to you," said Richard more forcefully.

No response.

And then, with the forbearance of a veteran parent, he shouted good-naturedly, "HEY LINDA!"

Startled, Linda levitated about three inches from the rocker cushion and landed on her backside with a muffled thump. Looking a little disoriented she said,"Yes, Dr. Landry?"

"Your mom's calling to check on you and I said you might as well stay for the night. How about it?" said Richard.

"What time as it?"

Pulling up his right shirt sleeve, Richard squinted at his watch through the dim light. "It's 11:30."

Where did the time go, she wondered.

"I'd love to stay, if you guys don't mind."

Richard cordially bade Sarah good-night and hung up the phone. Back in his rocker, he looked at Linda. "Good book?"

"Yea," replied Linda, "I can't believe that one guy had the time to invent all this stuff."

"They say that Leonardo only slept three hours a night, which is more than you two will get if you don't go upstairs. Before I forget, Linda, you can take the book home with you tomorrow, if you like," said Richard.

"Thanks, Dr. Landry!"

Midnight snacks, goodnight hugs, and the dubious intimacy of a shared toothbrush left Linda staring at Barbara's bed.

"This thing's a bed?"

"Yes, you fool, what you think it is?" said Barbara as she slid under the covers.

"It's bigger than my whole goddamned bedroom! And it's got curtains! I don't even have curtains in my own freakin' windows!"

Linda was working herself into a lather.

"Oh you poor child. Just shut up and get into bed!"

"Yes, my queen," said Linda.

Once under the covers, she continued to stare at the curtains.

"So what's the deal with the drapes?"

"The bed's about 300-years old. Houses weren't heated back then. You want to complain about anything else?"

"I'll think of something," said Linda.

The girls lay quietly for some minutes. Linda sensed that Barbara was listening to something. She couldn't imagine what it could be, so she broke the silence.

"What are you listening to? I don't hear anything," said Linda.

"The crickets," replied Barbara.

"You're listening to crickets? Why?"

"That's how God talks to me," said Barbara as if it were in the most obvious thing in the world.

"God talks to you through fish bait?" said Linda.

"Sure; it makes me feel good," said Barbara.

"Whenever floats your boat," yawned Linda. She rolled over and fell asleep. Barbara stayed awake, smiling into the darkness as the crickets lulled her to sleep.

#

The trajectory of the dead raven's last flight landed it noiselessly on the detritus blanketing the floor of the woods. After bouncing and rolling a few times, the bird came to rest upon its back. Flightless, stripped of it's wings, and forever still, the bird faced the sky. Its clouded eyes stared into the blue empyrean overhead and, with the passing seasons, sank into their sockets and shriveled to dust. The winds that sometimes wandered among the trees picked up the dust gradually and wafted it to faraway places with the wistful longing of a lover blowing a kiss to his beloved where, over time, it once again would be enfleshed within new life.

REUNIONS III: early Autumn 2006

The computer had done its job. Several thousand evolutionary iterations simulating different wind conditions had produced a work of art that was begging to fly. Viewing the ghostly prototype from different angles, Barbara and Linda became convinced that a form so beautiful must perforce fly. The wings reminded Barbara of something that Richard had recently taught her about Japanese aesthetics — that beauty in one facet of an object is intimately and invariably associated with other facets of its beauty, hence the observation, easily made in Buddhist temples, that a visually stunning bell will produce a stunning sound in equal measure. Linda was thinking more viscerally. A ball of enthusiasm had formed deep within her, throbbing with the impending joy of a craftsman contemplating the plans for her masterwork. She felt everything that Herb had ever taught her dancing in thoughtful circles around an aerial form awaiting its birth. For different reasons, but at about the same time,

133

each girl felt a tingling spider of joy tickle its way up their spines, from their tail bones to the base of their skulls and burst with the knowledge that the Fates had favored them with a glimpse at their destiny.

With that they set to work.

It did not take long for Barbara and Linda to form, as if in resonance with the rest of Milton, a work routine that was governed by the diurnal disciplines of farming. Linda's days ebbed and flowed like tides, and comprised school, homework, a nap, and work on the wings until dinner, which Herb preferred to eat at 7 PM. She went to sleep early and awakened early so that she could start the day in the shop, with her commercial work — the extra jobs for Herb's customers that always ended with a satisfying handful of money. School was, for her, an annoyance wedged between the two halves of otherwise agreeable days.

Barbara took a broader approach to the project. Its design phase revealed her so-called deficiencies in mathematics, although by all other standards Barbara was a prodigy just as she was. But she craved understanding and could not tolerate gaps in her knowledge of the things that were important to her. So she turned the wing design into an ongoing homework project, using the wind tunnel software as a study guide. When she came across an unfamiliar aspect of the design principles and mathematics used by the software, she paused and studied them. The software became a gold-standard. She tested her proficiency by trying to duplicate the wing design at a given phase in its evolution by using a pencil, a pad of paper, a calculator, and her own mind. Only when her results matched those of her computer did she move on.

Barbara had by now exceeded Richard's knowledge of mathematics and science. She was flying on her own power and seemed to know, at some level, where she was going. All Richard could do was to provide whatever Barbara needed. Beyond that, he could only marvel at what was unfolding under his own roof.

He was not the only one.

One month passed.

Barbara and Linda stood at the gate to the Schultz farm. Early autumn was settling into the trees, which responded by donning shrouds resplendent with jewel toned greens, reds, yellows, and purples. The fertile soil answered the bite of the air by stiffening under the girls' shoes as they trudged uncertainly toward the Schultz's house. It was the season for the many small deaths whose frigid decay would compost into new life.

The Schultz family had worked the land for five generations, each of which had prospered and added new holdings to those of their predecessors, and George Schultz was no exception. His acquisitions, plus those of his ancestors, had made him the largest and wealthiest farmer within a 100-mile radius of his house. He also had several very long, very straight dirt roads connecting his holdings. For these, the girls had a use.

George Schultz was not exactly known for his friendliness, and so Linda and Barbara climbed the front steps timidly, breathing heavily through a fog of free-floating dread as each step they climbed squeaked a warning that they go no further. They inhaled deeply and knocked on the door. No answer. Secretly relieved, they had turned to go when they heard footsteps clumping toward the door. It opened. The girls looked up.

They would have screamed and run away, had their voices not dried up in dusty spasms and their feet not stuck to the steps. Their first impression was that they were about to be crushed by an immense denim-covered boulder. And then, having regained their composure at roughly the same time, the girls realized that they were looking straight up at a very big, very tall, denim-clad man who had an equally proportionate potbelly. He wore bib overalls that were partly unbuttoned on each side to accommodate his cetacean girth. A captive toothpick chattered back and forth along his front teeth, quavering, as if seeing its own fate reflected in the girls' eyes, Linda was the first to coax her voice from its hiding place.

"Mm...mm...Mr. Schultz?"

"Yep."

Barbara, thinking to rescue Linda, attempted to follow-up.

"Hi...uh...hello, Mr. Schultz...I'm Bar..."

"I know who you are. You're Richard Landry's granddaughter," he said flatly.

George Schultz turned his dead-looking but shrewd eyes on Linda.

"And your Herb Maddox's girl. Damn good mechanic."

Another unnerving pause, during which no one spoke.

"What do you want?"

"Barbara and I are building a hang glider and we'd like to test it a little on one of your dirt roads."

The farmer looked at the girls for some moments, as if he were sizing up a couple of skittish heifers. Then, he nodded.

"Go on. But I'm not liable if you get yourselves killed."

So saying, he turned and closed the door, the receding sound of his plodding steps voicing his only farewell. With the ogre gone, the spell that had glued their feet to the steps dissolved and they trotted back to the main gate, where they had parked an ATV on which the wings, having been separated for the purpose, were carefully loaded. Within minutes, they located one terminus of the longest road on the property. The corn in the adjacent fields, having been set aside as seed corn, had not yet been harvested. It's dirty-blond immensity was reminiscent of a giant's scalp whose stubble had been neatly parted in the middle by a gargantuan comb.

Dismounting the ATV, Linda and Barbara assessed the terrain. Small tributary roads connected randomly placed barn-red outbuildings, each of which had been constructed as needed to meet the mounting demands of the Schultz's ever-expanding holdings. The contrast of bright red against dirty blond was innervating, and rendered all the more so by the crisp air and gray storm clouds mounting on horizon. It was a gathering of spirits, come to see two of their enfleshed sisters give flight to their mortal clay.

The girls assembled the wings and harness with the efficiency of two hands laboring at the behest of one brain. Having secured a tow-line between the wings and the ATV, they paused to assess their most likely flight path. Unless they hit an outbuilding, their airspace was unobstructed; the road was wide and mostly level.

Only one detail remained, and Barbara was the first to address it.

"Which one of us goes first?"

"I don't know," said Linda. "Maybe we should toss a coin."

Barbara replied, "No...that's not fair. I did the math and I designed the

airfoil.   If I screwed up, there's no
reason you should take the hit."

"But I'm lighter than you and I've
been building things longer then you,"
countered Linda.   "If she does take off
and there's a problem.   I'll know what
it is and I'll know how to fix it after
I land."

"Or crash..." said Barbara.

"Think positive and think big, ma'
cherie," said Linda.   "She'll fly and I
won't ditch her.   It's like they say.
Failure is not an option."

"Okay...let's do it," said Barbara
reluctantly.

Linda put on a pair of roller blades
and a helmet fitted with an intercom.
Checking the wings one last time, she
climbed into the harness.   Barbara put
on the mate to Linda's helmet and
mounted the ATV.

"Can you hear me?" asked Linda.

"Like a bell," said Barbara.

Starting the ATV and throttling the
engine, Barbara shouted, "can you hear
me over the noise?"

"Like a bell," answered Linda.   "And
you don't have to shout.   Let's go."

Barbara put the ATV in gear and
slowly engaged the clutch.   Linda would
need a minute or two to gain her
balance, so Barbara throttled the engine
just enough to get the ATV moving.
About a minute into the test, Barbara
heard Linda over the intercom.

"I'm good.   Speed up a little."

Barbara responded by smoothly accelerating to the upper limit of first gear. A few more seconds, and she shifted into second year. Linda spoke next.

"I'm getting lighter! Everything is okay. Open her up! I'm okay to go!"

Barbara throttled through the upper range of second year.

"I'm okay to go!"

Shifting into the low end of third.

"I'm okay to go!"

The upper range of third.

"I'm okay to go!"

The lower end of fourth.

"Oh Mama! I'm okay to go!"

Linda's exhilaration mounted in proportion to Barbara's anxiety. The thought of hurting her friend was almost incapacitating, but she persisted and throttled through her anxiety into the midrange of fourth gear. Suddenly the rear end of the ATV lifted slightly, and fell back onto the road.

"YEEEEEHAAAAA! I'm up!"

The ATV lurched violently to one side as Barbara recovered from the shock of having two acoustic ice picks hammered into her ears. Back on the road again, Barbara looked up at Linda. She had risen about twenty feet into the bracing air and was maintaining a course dead center over the road behind the ATV.

For the first time ever Linda Maddock was struck dumb, rendered mute by the epiphany of flight. For as far back as she could remember, something, maybe even someone, had been urging her to fly. Now that she was doing it, she wanted to keep doing it. She wanted to leave the earth and fly until she reached the far side of Forever. Barbara increased her speed toward the upper end of fourth gear. Linda rose another 10 feet.

And then something happened.

Her ecstasy shattered into pixie dust at the sound of struts groaning and whimpering as they approached the limits of their strength. Their increasing speed had forced the wings into a flying V. Linda dropped 10 feet in less than a second.

"Oh shit! Slow down Barbara!"

An adrenaline fury surged through Linda's arms with a power far beyond her years as she gripped the control cables and forced the wings back into alignment. At the same instant, Barbara backed off on the throttle and Linda regained control of the wings. The ordeal was terrifying yet oddly thrilling.

"I'm setting you down, Linda."

"Okay."

Barbara slowed the ATV, judging as best she could Linda's rate of descent against the approaching end of the road. She landed like a clumsy and confused duck. But she maintained her footing and came to a stop without falling or grazing the wings. She was still soaring in spirit as Barbara dismounted the ATV and ran toward her, shouting.

"Oh, Jesus! Linda, are you all right?"

"Never better, ma cherie! But I think your airfoils are too good. They create too much lift. The structure can't keep up with it. But I can fix that. Leave it to you to be an overachiever."

"Linda!"

"What?"

"I can't wait until you fix the struts. I have to try it. Now!" insisted Barbara.

"Okay, but don't break anything," said Linda. "Compared to me you're a freakin' Amazon, so expect the wings to fold sooner than they did with me."

"I promise not to hurt your baby!" said Barbara.

It only took a few minutes for the girls to ready themselves for another test. They started much as they did before, except this time they secured the tow line to the front of the ATV. That way, it would not lose traction as the wings gained altitude. It took Barbara a little longer to take off than it did for Linda, and the wings started deforming sooner. Being forewarned, Barbara compensated immediately. As she gained altitude, she felt the stresses on the wings mount. But compensating was well within her strength, and afforded pleasures of its own. She was in control, having no sense of struggling with the wings; the effort diminished her sense of having fleshy boundaries, such that she did not know where her arms ended and the wings began. She was a bird flying under the power of a dream bravely pursued. She was strong, and pregnant with possibilities.

Linda broke in, announcing her descent,

Barbara landed well and released the harness as Linda dismounted the ATV. For a few quiet moments, they just stood where they were, looking at each other. Each had something she wanted to say to the other but could not find the words. Then, as if of one mind, they ran toward each other and embraced. The need for words dissolved until Linda stood back and said, "Woman, we're going to Mars! We're going to get on your mom's and pop's spaceship and find us some Martians."

Barbara laughed. At that moment, in that place, it did not seem so far-fetched.

"There's just one problem," she said.

"What's that?" asked Linda.

"We have to go to flight school first," replied Barbara.

"Oh, yeah...I forgot about that," said Linda.

\#

Walter Brown looked up from his work when he heard the sound of an ATV in the distance. For the last 30 years, Walter had worked as one of George Schultz's tenant farmers, and in all that time, he had never known his boss to allow kids to play on his land this early in the year. The harvest had to be in and the ground thoroughly frozen before George grudgingly let any children — along with their ATVs, dirt bikes, and cross-country skis — onto his land. It was not out of meanness that he did what he did. He just did not want anybody tearing up the soil.

It was with this in mind that Walter squinted into the horizon from which the sounds were coming. He vaguely made out the forms of two young girls, one of them tall and the other one short, fooling with a funny-looking hang glider. As he watched the girls, Walter felt a tingling something-or-other deep inside his gut. It felt happy and sad all at once, and set him to thinking, however briefly.

Being a tenant farmer was not the most exciting job in the world, but for once farming was a secure profession. With all the strange weather and famines going on around the world, a man could find a market for thistles, if thistles were all he could grow. All in all, it was not a bad life. He had friends. The work was steady but not hard. Walter's wife could stay home which, to his way of thinking, was where a woman ought to be. It was a comfortable life and he was satisfied with it, so he went back to work and let the sensation fade whence it had come.

#

George Schultz put the girls out of his mind the instant he closed the door. He finished his lunch and had settled down in an oak rocking chair as old as the farm when the sound of the ATV caught his attention. Suddenly unable to concentrate, and wondering what a smart rich kid could possibly have in common with the daughter of a banged-up grease-monkey, he rose, opened the kitchen window, and located the ATV. Watching the girls fly their contraption, he started wondering how his life would have turned out had he left the farm, but he soon banished the thought. His eldest brother by many years had left the farm to join the army and got himself killed on Omaha Beach. His dog tags were the only things anybody could identify. His body fell apart when they came to bag him. No one ever found his head. It must have been washed away with the tides.

And that's what you got for leaving behind a sure thing.

#

The girls' duly trumpeted their success. Neither Richard nor Linda's parents really expected the thing to fly, or at least not much. A cookout was improvised, complete with ribs that Jake allowed Herb to mooch from the bar. When the meal was over, and as twilight descended on Milton, Linda and Barbara became quiet, and seemed content to just sit and stare into the embers. Richard looked at them carefully, first at one and then at the other, back and forth, several times.

And then he spoke.

"So girls, what do you want to name your bird?"

Linda raised her head and looked at Richard.

"Oh, man! I didn't even think about it. Let me see..."

A few seconds later, Barbara looked up quickly, as if surprised by an unexpected thought.

"Let's call her the Phoenix."

Linda parted her lips to say something, but stopped and whispered "Phoenix" to herself several times. It felt good as it formed on her mouth and jumped off her tongue. It was a name that flew. "Let's go with it," she said. The girls went back to contemplating the embers. Herb and Laura, who had spent the evening being quietly pleased with their daughter, smiled but said nothing. Richard looked at Barbara. His eyes glinted with a smile that was barely visible beneath his beard.

HARVEST TIME: Autumn 2006

Five weeks passed.

As the fields lapsed into their annual, frigid torpor, and as plants everywhere withered into the ground, the Phoenix grew and ripened. Struts were reinforced and tested; control cables were refined and tested; the contours of the airfoil were tweaked and tested.

And people were starting to notice.

The Phoenix had become as airworthy as Barbara and Linda knew how to make her. And so, after perusing and squabbling over scores of paint chips, the girls finally agreed on a simple finishing scheme. Deep-blue metal-flake paint would cover the Phoenix's dorsal surfaces and a corresponding blood-red her ventral surfaces. Being inveterate Trekkies, they stenciled the sigil of the Klingon Empire in reverse colors to the Phoenix's top and bottom — blood red on the top and deep blue on the bottom. They finished early on a warm, clear night in which the incandescent dust of the Milky Way, tossed by a careless god into a glittering arch, watched over the darkness. If nothing else, the girls' precocious hands and minds had created a work of art. Fully assembled, set up in Herb's main service bay, and lit by the encircling suns of overhead work lights, the Phoenix glowed in the center of an aura that soothed even as it inspired.

"This is just too cool!"

Linda pranced like a neurotic dervish around the Phoenix, admiring her from every possible angle. Barbara was quieter. She stood still, her eyes softly unfocussed, savoring a pride that cupped her brain within a golden bowl. Linda stopped admiring the Phoenix long enough to tap Barbara on the shoulder and said, "We only have to do one more thing."

Barbara started a little. "Uh...what...what's that?"

"We need a parade permit," said Linda.

"What are we going to do with a parade permit?"

"You don't think were going to fly this thing with no one around to see us, do you?" said Linda.

"I hadn't thought about it, actually..." said Barbara, "I just assumed we would go over to the Schultz place and be more ambitious."

"Hell no," said Linda, "haven't you seen people stopping by the side of the road just to watch us test this thing? Even the kids at school are pestering me to see our first official flight. Too bad they don't have science fairs

anymore.   Then   we   could   be   really
famous."

"Maybe we shouldn't show off."

Barbara never finished her thought.
Linda   made   an   exasperated   face   and
swatted Barbara upside the head.

"Come on, girl! Stop walking around
with your head stuck up your ass! Even
at   school   you're   a   goddamned   legend.
Time to strut your stuff."

"Okay.   I   guess   so,"   said   Barbara
somewhat reservedly, "we should probably
find Sheriff Norton and see what we
need."

"He'll   be   at   Jake's.   He   usually
downs a few before he goes home to The
Wife. Let's close the shop and ride up
there."

Jake's   Mule   Barn   was   the   only
business in Milton that stayed open at
night. It was a beacon of sorts for all
of the benighted souls who needed a
little liquid solace before braving the
darkness again on their way home. The
girls rode up to the front entrance and
parked their bikes along the row of
carefully   parked   motorcycles   that
generally adorned the place with a
subdued glow on any given night.

Pausing on the threshold, the girls
peered   through   a   fog   formed   and
sustained by the cigars, cigarettes,
pipes,   and   joints   whose   incessant
burning turned the place into a giant
censer dropped from the heavens by a
clumsy god.   Its tarry incense poured
from the windows and doors in stringy

plumes that rose into the sky and dispersed as part of some gargantuan worship service whose altar was the earth.

The girls were used to this. It did not take them more than a few seconds to locate Sheriff Norton. He was sitting at a table toward the back of the bar, playing poker with Richard, Herb, and Sarah. Linda and Barbara made their way through the jumble of tables, picking up a couple of stools along the way. Seating themselves just outside of the circle of players, they remained quiet. Very few sins were acknowledged as such within Jake's Mule Barn, but breaking a poker player's concentration was one of them. Five minutes or so had passed when a very friendly, very pregnant waitress, approached the table with a tray of drinks — three shot glasses filled with straight whiskey, two tall Cokes with a handful of maraschino cherries in each, and, of all things, a pot of Earl Gray Tea. The poker players were almost autistically oblivious to the waitress as she placed the drinks around the table and slid the tab under the teapot. This evidently was Richard's round.

The game flowed uninterruptedly despite the waitress's intrusion. Richard removed the wallet from his sport jacket with one hand and, with the same hand, removed the bill, handed it to the waitress, mumbled something about keeping the change, and returned the wallet to its hiding place in his jacket all in one sleight of hand movement. The bill's denomination would have induced labor had the waitress not sputtered a protest about the overpayment. This relaxed her diaphragm just enough to discharge the pressure within her abdomen. The baby kicked once and sank back into its wet amniotic bliss.

The game was a study in concentration. The players often scrutinized each other furtively, looking for any facial movements or body language that would betray their opponents' standing in the game. It was an oddly self-orchestrated set of movements. No two people ever looked up at the same time and no one made any sudden movements. It was a silent symphony of tics and twitches whose ciphers were difficult to decode.

Sobriety, or the lack of it, was another facet of a player's style. Herb, Sheriff Norton, and Sarah each imbibed their whiskey with slow, tiny sips calculated to keep them relaxed but not drunk. Richard, on the other hand, stayed sober. Tobacco and tea maintained the sparkle in his otherwise inscrutable eyes. The only commentary on the game was provided by the little man carved into the bowl of Richard's meerschaum pipe, who found occasions for laughter in everything that he surveyed.

A few discards and mumbled requests to the dealer for replacements from the deck broke the studied stillness. Everyone except Sarah folded. After a quick glance at the table, Sarah smiled smugly and laid down a winning hand. Judging by the little piles of beer nuts that they were using as chips, this was not the first round that Sarah had won that night. Herb stuck his hand down Sarah's blouse, looking for hidden cards. One stinging slap on the wrist and Herb "withdrew" his accusations and his hand.

The little man in the pipe just laughed.

"Hey, Sheriff Norton!"

He looked up. "Oh, hi Linda. What can I do for you?"

"Barbara and I need a parade permit."

"A parade permit?"

"That's right. A parade permit."

"But there aren't any holidays coming up."

"We don't need one. Barbara and I just want to put on a little air show. We only need an hour. Maybe less."

"Does this have anything to do with that glider you two squirts have been building?"

"Uh huh."

Sheriff Norton looked at Richard and Herb.

"Is this thing for real?"

Herb answered first.

"I've been checking up on them the whole time. It's beautifully built. And the math must be all right because the girls have been testing the thing at

152

George Shultz's place. She flies. And these two know how to keep her up."

Sheriff Norton looked at Richard.

"How about it, Doc?"

Richard put his pipe down with a dismissive gesture.

"It's like Herb said. She flies. Barbara got some wind-tunnel software from a couple of very smart people at Lockheed, and it did the job."

Sheriff Norton nodded.

"So all you girls need is a few rubber cones set up on both ends of Main Street."

"That's all," said Linda. "Can we do it this Saturday?"

"Fine with me," he said.

At that, the men returned to the game and continued being slaughtered by Sarah. The little man in the pipe just laughed.

#

Saturday dawned clear and crisp. A slight breeze, drifting in from the west, fanned the flame-colored trees lining Main Street into glowing swatches of amber, yellow, red, brown, and die-hard green that would have leapt into the sky had they not been held back by the branches of trees too reluctant yet to let them go. The confluence of these opposing forces was bracing. It was a time of year when Linda felt the dust in her brain lift and blow away. For her, autumnal things were simple. They were pared to the bone, reduced to their barest forms. They held forth against the fury of winter and either lived to tell their tales or not. It was her season for clarity. Barbara's enjoyment of autumn was more benign, and more rooted in the odors of the season than she could readily account for. The autumn winds brought her countless perfumed bouquets whose scents made their way into the base of her brain and thence to the oldest archives of her mind. There, they invoked snippets of memory as ancient as the first intimations of life on the planet. What was, for most people, the smell of wet wood and rotting leaves and nothing more was to Barbara the perfume of time passing. Autumn was the season when life wrapped itself in blankets of memory and slept through winter's mock death.

The girls' opposite reactions to autumn, the one looking ahead and the other looking back, came together in a present tense of expectancy as bracing as the weather. Mid-morning found them at the western terminus of Main Street. The Phoenix sat in the middle of the road, brooding, like a pterodactyl contemplating a leap from a sheer Jurassic cliff into a dimly discerned valley far below. The metallic paint on her wings glistened with an unplumbed saurian strength. People, who had originally come to see why Main Street was closed, began lingering, their curiosity peaked by the creature that was blocking the road. Linda and

Barbara were off on the shoulder of the road, fiddling with a homemade anchor for the towline.

It did not take long for a sizable group to gather, among them being Richard, Sarah, and Herb. They made their way politely to the side of the road, looking as if they had just made the stupidest decision of their lives by letting Linda and Barbara fly their bird through the middle of town. On the plus side, the girls had revealed more judgment and foresight than the average adult would have; on the debit side there was nothing much. And therein lay the problem. The girls looked down Main Street and saw an adventure. Their loved ones, however, looked at the same thing and saw a pitiless concrete slab flanked by malevolent trees bent on snatching the Phoenix from the air and smashing her on the pavement. But they had given their word to the girls and were not going to humiliate them in public by retracting it. Her preparations complete, Linda stepped away from the Phoenix and faced the crowd. Barbara held back and hovered over the ATV, wondering what they had just gotten themselves into. Linda loudly cleared her throat.

"Ladies and gentlemen, after weeks of research, development, and testing, we..."

She was stopped short by a slap from the rear to her right shoulder.

"Linda! What are you doing?" snapped Barbara in a whisper.

"I'm getting the crowd pumped up. Think of it as free PR."

"Linda, just get into the goddamned harness so we can fly this thing," said Barbara.

"Indulge me, sweetheart." Linda turned back to the crowd. "As I was saying, after weeks of dedication and care, it all comes down to this." Linda held up a dollar coin against the sky. "Who'll attempt the first flight of the Phoenix over concrete, in a tight space? No dirt landings in a cornfield this time!" Turning to her increasingly exasperated friend, Linda said, "call it, compadre!" The coin flipped into the air. When it reached its zenith, Barbara curtly called out.

"Heads!"

The coin landed in Linda's palm.

"Tails!"

Barbara suspected that a little sleight-of-hand had slanted the outcome of the toss. They had already agreed that Linda would fly first, her low-weight providing one last safeguard. Linda tossed the dollar coin into the audience. A four-year-old girl caught it and stared into her uplifted hand. To her, it was all the money in the world. She never did spend it.

Linda slid into the harness as if it were a second skin. Barbara started the ATV and throttled the engine until it settled into its operating temperature.

She looked back one last time to make sure that Linda was secure. Wondering if she could shock Linda out of her showman's persona, Barbara shifted into first gear, throttled the engine and popped the clutch. The ATV leapt forward with the pent-up energy of a frustrated stallion. Linda's eyes bugged out, and Barbara heard a stifled but perversely satisfying "Whoa!" through the intercom. Satisfied, she accelerated smoothly until she felt the tow line stiffen. Linda was airborne.

Barbara was never nasty and Linda was flustered, to put it mildly, at the speed of the takeoff. But only for a few seconds. Undoubtedly, it was just Barbara's last word on the supposed impropriety of showing off, so Linda left it at that and yielded to the mounting thrill of speed. The wings stiffened, and then flexed as Linda's roller blades left the pavement and the Phoenix rose into the trees. She was flying through an enchanted hall with white floors and jewel-toned walls and flawless blue cathedral ceilings. Icy needles stung her face as the Phoenix continued to accelerate through the morning air. She had risen to the tree tops when the Phoenix leveled off. Linda felt the wings' strength as it moderated the supple flexions that formed in response to the increasing stresses of flight. Her sense of where her arms ended vanished. She was a bird freed finally from gravity's shackles.

Some moments later Barbara cut in on Linda's reverie.

"Great job, girl! I'm bringing you down."

Linda had other ideas.

"No, wait Barbara! Keep me up and make a tight turn at the end of the street.

"But we never practiced that. We don't know how she'll handle. Don't forget you're over concrete!"

The end of the street was only a few hundred feet away.

"Just do it!"

Barbara bore right, then cut left. At that instant, Linda reacted by banking left and matching Barbara's tight turn with a wider one of her own, much like the broad arc of a wheel matching the tight circle of its axle. The girls executed the turn well enough, but the ATV's momentary loss of speed sent the Phoenix into a free fall toward, of all places, Jake's Mule Barn.

"Floor it, Barbara!"

The ATV answered with a shriek and a tensing of the tow line that restored the Phoenix's glide path, but not enough to keep Linda from making a partial landing on one roller blade and lifting off again. From a distance however, the maneuver looked rehearsed, and the girls heard the distant sounds of applause through their intercoms. This emboldened Linda to improvise still further. With Barbara again riding down the middle of Main Street, Linda started banking the Phoenix left and right, first in small arcs, and then through broader ones, letting the wings lightly graze the trees. Barbara noticed the uneven pull on the tow line.

"Linda, what are you doing?"

"Just giving the people a little show. Don't worry."

A snort from Barbara was Linda's only answer, so the show went on a little longer, until the necessity of landing forced its end, which Linda effected with a dancer's grace. Herb and Sarah, who had evidently held their breath the entire time, exhaled and rushed into the street and hugged the air out of Linda's lungs with a mixture of pride and relief. A tear stole across Herb's right cheek. Sarah felt like a mother bird watching her only chick attempting, for the first time, to fly from her nest. Barbara smiled and held back from the crowd, biding her time.

So were the winds.

The commotion gradually faded, and Barbara took advantage of the crowd's momentary inattention to ready herself for the Phoenix's second public flight. She was tying the laces on her roller blades as Linda stepped into the street and approached the ATV.

"Give'er hell, girl! I'll bet you can't top me," teased Linda.

"We'll see," said Barbara as she climbed into the harness.

It is easy to forget the extent to which everything is connected to everything and that all of it is alive and knowing and shares a common tongue. Up to that point, the prairie winds west of Milton had bided their time, whispering among themselves. Linda's wager with Barbara was their cue to raise the stakes of the game. Winds from many places gathered to form a front that began moving east just as the tow line yanked the Phoenix into action.

The takeoff took longer than it did with Linda, but there was still plenty of road left for flying. The Phoenix took off with what Barbara could only describe as integrity. The wings were supple but strong. The control cables were tight but responsive. The lift was robust but did not overwhelm the craft's stability. Barbara looked down at the pavement. Her shadow and that of the Phoenix fused to form a flying cross. Never had she felt so strong, so confident, and so totally at home. Her body became electric, and rippled with effervescent joy. She belonged to the sky and it to her. It was not until the Phoenix was straining at the tow line that Barbara heard the whispers. At first, she thought it was just background noise coming through the intercom. But as she listened, she fancied to she could hear voices, distant but discernible, piercing the static.

"Linda, do you hear anything?

"Just you. Why? What's up?"

"Oh...nothing, I guess."

Just then, Barbara felt a gentle but mounting tailwind nudge the Phoenix into a somewhat faster, somewhat higher flight. As the wind gained strength, so too did the whispers. "Let go...let go...fly...you can do it...you are The Beloved One and you shall not fall...we are with you...you are loved...let go...fly...fly..."

Barbara looked down at the tow line's release. Doubt and suspicion flooded her mind and clouded her thoughts. Her fingers froze. But the voices whispered on, imploring her to take that one final step. Closing her eyes and forcing one hand away from the control cables, she grasped the tow line and with a jerk of her thumb and opened the catch. The Phoenix rose as the tow line went limp to and fell toward the road. Linda slowed the ATV and looked up when she felt the sudden release of tension on the line.

"What the...? Oh shit!"

The ATV lurched forward as the engine stalled.

"What are you doing! Are you nuts or something!"

"Don't worry, little one. I'm just going for a ride," said Barbara in a voice whose inflection was at once serene and exultant.   .

Shepherded by the tailwind, the Phoenix rose several hundred feet and was fast approaching the town limits. The knowing of a bird formed in her mind. It flowed down her arms and through her hands so abundantly that she forgot her human form, and whispered secret words back to the winds into whose care she had consigned her life. Thoughts of danger, doom, and death became irrelevant as Milton and its surrounding farms formed an immense quilted circle beneath her feet that faded into horizons rendered endless by the cauls of mist that shrouded them. Barbara turned about and headed back toward Main Street. It was only when she passed over her grandfather's house and happened to look down that she received a shock that would have dashed her onto the roof, had she not recovered quickly and resumed her landing.

It was one of those moments when time cracks open under the force of impressions whose vividness rivets them onto the memory with a tenacity that cannot be ignored, even after that crack has long since closed and the mind is again anchored in the present. Barbara saw the house much as she expected it to be, albeit from an unusual perspective. But at that very instant she saw something else, something that interposed itself between her and her view of the mansard roof. It was the same view of the house, but not as it was at that moment. It was subtly different. It glowed with a golden-white light that took in the root-beer stand across the street. All else blurred into obscurity. She was no longer in her body. She was instead, a ball of happy white light surrounded by others of her kind. A disembodied voice was explaining a task that she was to undertake, the task to which she readily agreed.

Hence the shock.

Barbara realized that she was reliving something that had happened to her years ago, but not in this life. It came from that indefinable place whence we fall into birth. The voice was louder this time, but she still could not make it out. It seemed to be telling her to go someplace, to undertake a journey of which only she was capable. But that was all, so she flew on and effected a perfect landing.

Amidst the cheers and applause, two suspiciously well-groomed men held back, discreetly dictating notes into tiny recorders. Barbara had been attracting the attention of some low-profile but well-placed people for a long time, and that attention was mounting. They had also begun to take interest in Barbara's pugnacious little friend.

Richard was just about to step off the curb and into the street when the two men caught his eye. He stopped and stared fixedly at them. They returned his gaze in the briefest, most nondescript way and, without betraying anything of their purpose, disappeared into the crowd. Richard turned and dashed into the street, politely forcing his way through the throng that had gathered around the Phoenix and embraced

Barbara with a most uncharacteristic bear hug.

"Jesus, Pookie! Don't scare me like that!"

"What's the matter, Grandpa? Too much excitement for one day?"

"Tell me that that little stunt was an accident."

"Not exactly, Grandpa. Let's just say that a little angel told me to do it."

Richard released his hold on Barbara and looked at her. He knew that there was more to what she had just said, but did not press her any further.

"Don't worry, Grandpa. Somebody's watching over me. I'm safe for a long time yet."

Thinking of the two men that he had just seen, Richard suspected that that was truer than any of them suspected.

"I love you, Pookie."

"I love you too, Grandpa."

Richard stepped back and let his many friends and neighbors whisk the girls off to Jake's Mule Barn for party. Two other men in the crowd had come to watch the flight of the Phoenix and they too went largely unnoticed, mostly because they had been part of the local woodwork for decades.

Walter Brown had kept a surreptitious eye on the girls during all of their test flights on his boss's land. Watching them, he had begun to feel lighter. Something inside of him had started to loosen up. There was more of a bounce in his step, and he had begun indulging his wife when she talked about finding part-time work away from the farm. Walter looked down at a dog-eared copy of the catalog that he had requested from a newly formed agricultural college, and then went home. He had some phone calls to make. George Shultz had also kept an eye on the girls as they refined the Phoenix in his fields. Now, he stood beside her for a long moment, admiring the craft's every detail, all the while fingering some dog tags in his pocket and thinking that some things were indeed worth dying for. He wiped away a couple of unwonted tears and helped Herb and Richard move the Phoenix back onto the stable's side yard.

The little girl stood alone in the middle of the road. She took the golden dollar out of her pocket and held it up to the sun, watching the light play across its surface. She wondered about the girl whose face rose from the coin in gentle relief. Who was she? And why was she so famous? A short beep from a car horn made the little girl look up. It was Sheriff Norton in his squad car. He smiled.

"Hey, Martha, maybe you should get out of the road before you get run over."

Martha smiled back. She skipped all the way home, to a trailer parked on the edge of town, and resumed her own story. But that is a tale for another day.

#

Later that night, the girls lay in Barbara's bed, reading and talking about whatever came to mind. As the darkness deepened, the bed had come to be littered with an assortment of books, pertaining mostly to flight, space travel, and science-fiction. The air outside was crisp, and the last crickets of the year beguiled the hours by composing their own dirges. Barbara had cracked open the window next to the bed, Linda's protestations to the contrary notwithstanding, the better to savor the melancholy passing of her favorite sounds. The phone rang downstairs. As Richard answered within a few rings, the girls paid little heed to it, and were soon lost in conversation again. A topographic atlas of Mars was nestled in Linda's lap.

"So where should we land first?" she queried.

"I vote for the face on Cydonia. It's in the northern hemisphere," suggested Barbara.

"I know where it is," said Linda, "but everybody knows the face is just a pile of rocks."

"I'm not so sure, surmised Barbara. "Imagine Mount Rushmore twenty-million years from now. Those faces won't look like much either, but that doesn't make them less artificial. Besides, I don't really trust the picture that NASA put out in the late '90s. It just doesn't square with those early Viking pictures.

"Well, I vote for Olympus Mons, and if I'm in charge," countered Linda, "that's where we are going. Think of it. A dead volcano four times higher than Mount Everest. How cool is that!"

"Well, if I'm in charge, we are going to the face first," said Barbara. After a moment's pause she added, "but we can go to Olympus Mons after that."

The girls laid back for a while, each fleshing out her dreams. And then they noticed that Richard was still on the phone. He sounded annoyed.

"I wonder who that is," said Linda.

"Probably an obnoxious customer," said Barbara. "Let's go to sleep."

"Okay, but Barbara?"

"Hmmm?"

"Close the goddamned window."

"All right, Princess." Barbara closed the window.

Soon after that, the girls heard Richard drop the telephone onto its cradle. He was clearly annoyed. What none of them knew at the time was that Herb and Sarah had just finished a similar conversation. They too were annoyed.

FAR BEYOND DELUDED THOUGHTS:
November 2010

The Phoenix's first public flight by
no means marked the end of her service
life. Throughout that winter, which was
almost balmy by Midwestern standards,
Barbara and Linda flew as often as they
could. With each flight, the girls
challenged the limits of their skills
and daring, all the while refining the
Phoenix to accommodate their increasing
weight. They soon became comfortable
with free flight, and even managed a few
corkscrews during high-speed tests with
the ATV.

Some of the local school-age children
took to hanging around during these
tests. The bolder among them eventually
came forward, asking if they could try
their hand at flying. After some
discussion, conniving, and arm twisting,
George Shultz's frozen cornfields became
a flight school of sorts. Barbara
discovered a penchant for teaching, as
well as an endless patience with the
more timid children whose fear or lack
of aptitude made them slow to learn.

She managed to reach them all, so much so that she could hand them over to Linda, confident that they would be airborne within the hour.

The children were not the only ones to take an interest in Barbara and Linda. Every so often, the girls noticed a couple of men parked by the side of the road. They never came within 300 feet of the girls and never spoke to anyone. To inattentive passers by, they just looked like a couple of farmhands killing time. To Barbara and Linda, they were an increasingly disturbing and incongruous part of Milton's otherwise benign scenery. Matters went on like this intermittently for two years, until the Phoenix's career was ended by the onslaught of an early, aggressive puberty. Within a few months, Barbara and Linda made gains in height and weight that outpaced any improvements they could effect on the Phoenix. Reluctantly, they separated her wings and hung them as trophies over their beds. By their fourteenth birthdays, the girls were fully fleshed women.

The two men had become a vexatious part of the local woodwork. They seemed to rise, fully formed, out of the ground at odd times. One moment they were there. The next, they were so utterly gone that they might as well have disappeared into the very same earth whence they had come. The nighttime calls to Richard and Herb also persisted, but they were much less confrontational than they had been at first, having assumed instead the character of a cautious collaboration.

Whoever was on the other end of the line seemed to have friends in high, or perhaps low, places. When, for example, the girls had clamored for motorcycle licenses on their 14th birthdays, Herb and Richard placed a few calls. Several days later, and in violation of Iowa's motor vehicle code, two licenses appeared in the mail. Each of them bore the state's approval for both motorcycle and car licenses.

Things were not as they seemed.

#

Richard's posture was typical for that time of day. Back to the window. Slumped in the heavy oak rocker. Feet on the kitchen table. Meerschaum pipe clenched between his teeth. Reading the paper. Barbara loved to sneak peeks at Richard when he read the paper. It had a lot to do with the pipe. Over the years, its laughing face had become for her a sort of moral beacon -- a constant reminder not to take things too seriously. The pipe always moved in tandem with Richard's face as he scanned the paper. Barbara imagined that the face on the pipe was reading the paper too, and laughing at everything it saw. No matter how she felt at the end of the day, the sight of Grandpa and the funny little man carved into his pipe made her smile, except on one exceptionally warm and clear night in November of 2010. Barbara was frying chicken for dinner. Her movements were abrupt, clumsy, distracted. The muscles in her face were taut. Her gaze was locked into a thousand-yard stare. She stopped paying any attention to the chicken. It was getting on towards six o'clock when the smoke from the pipe started curdling on the ceiling along with a column of smoke from the stove. Richard looked up from the paper.

"What the...Hey Pookie. Pookie! BARBARA! Snap out of it!"

Barbara jumped and for a few seconds blinked stuporously into the frying pan. Then she came to.

"Oh, shit!"

Barbara heaved the frying pan from the burner and slammed the chicken-cum-charcoal into the garbage.

"What's the matter, Pookie."

"Nothing, Grandpa. I just don't feel good, that's all. Sorry about dinner. You want me to make something else?"

"No, sweetie. Let's just go onto the porch and swing awhile."

As the sun set, the creaking of the porch swing and the chirping of the year's last crickets rose through the air and vanished into the waiting sky. Nothing more was said of dinner. Richard put his arm around Barbara, deeply disturbed that he had missed something important. He had no idea of what to do or say. For the moment, silence seemed to be the best tonic.

"What's wrong, Pookie?"

Barbara inhaled slowly, deliberately.

"I'm going nuts. Maybe I'm already nuts. Grandpa, for the longest time these two men have been spying on me. Linda too. They don't come around very often, and that only makes things creepier. Sometimes, when Linda and I are doing something, we'll look up and there they are, staring at us. First, we thought maybe they were perverts or something, but they always stay away — 300, maybe 400 feet -- and they never do anything weird. They've never tried to talk to us. When they see us looking back at they, they just pretend they have some place to go. They'll get into a beat-up truck and drive off. They never rush. We thought about telling Sheriff Norton, but then where's the crime in hanging out and looking at people? Linda's been walking around with a sheath-knife stuck in her pants. And then there are those phone calls that you and Herb have been getting. It's like there's a conspiracy or something going on. And I've started having that nightmare again. You know the one. I had it the night mother and dad died. A bunch of demons are shredding me to bits and..."

Richard raised one hand and silenced Barbara with a touch to her lips. He looked down and sighed.

"Oh God, Pookie, I had no idea they were being so obvious. We've fucked up big time."

Barbara did not know what was more shocking: her grandfather's cryptic references to "we" and "they" or his unprecedented swearing. She said nothing and waited to see what would happen next. Richard inhaled deeply and continued.

"No, you're not crazy. And neither is Linda, although Herb and Sarah sometimes wonder about that. The three of us have known for some time that you were being watched. Some very important people are very interested in you two. I guess you've never quite realized how special you are. Your parents were brilliant and they surrounded themselves with brilliant people, so I guess you took yourself for granted. Nobody else did."

Richard paused for breath and continued.

"Your parents had to rely on a lot of military money to keep the Argo's construction going. No one involved with the project trusted Congress to finance aggressive, large-scale planetary exploration. With all the hunger and political instability in the world, support for space travel is politically incorrect. You get the picture."

Barbara nodded, wondering what all of this had to do with her and Linda.

"Anyway, the project had been generating a lot of spinoff technology that the military found very interesting. Most of it pertains to high-altitude reconnaissance, analysis of electromagnetic signatures, stealth, that sort of thing. As matters now stand, completion of the Argo, and work on some kind of high-speed aircraft have become one project for all practical purposes."

Barbara was barely breathing and had altogether forgotten to blink. Her mouth had gone dry. She could barely speak.

"So...so this means that they're finishing the Argo?"

"In a clandestine way. NASA has convinced Congress to pay for so-called maintenance on the Argo against the time when the public is willing to support it. There's just one glitch, though," said Richard as he gathered his thoughts for the next part of the story.

"With the money they have and what they know they can get, they can only afford a three-man crew, and that's where you, and a few other people, come in," Richard paused and smiled at Barbara.

"Breathe, Pookie."

Barbara was barely moving. Richard poked her in the ribs.

"You're not breathing, sweetheart. Don't pass out on me. Anyway, if they're only sending three people, then they've got to be seriously smart. Each person has to be a pilot, mathematician, engineer, and planetary scientist. People like that are hard to find."

"And that's why I'm being watched?"

Barbara was in a cold sweat of expectancy.

"You guessed it. The people in charge decided to recruit candidates, children, actually, who were showing signs of extraordinary aptitude for many subjects. That was six years ago. Since then, they've had special agents combing the country for kids like you and Linda. Out of the whole country, they've only found thirty of you who may have the right stuff. You're the oldest and they want you in the worst way. You've been in their sights since the beginning, and that's the reason for those cryptic calls. They are not getting you until you're ready and I say that you're ready."

Barbara had, by then, gotten used to this sudden revelatory atmosphere.

"But Grandpa, I feel ready now."

"I know you do. But there are other things that concern me. For one thing, they'll send you to flight school. You'll become a military test pilot for a very hush-hush project. For all practical purposes, you may have drop off the map. Who knows...officially, you may not even exist for a while. You're entitled to a normal adolescence before I'll let that happen. There's something else, but I'm not sure how to put it. Maybe it's none of my business."

Barbara answered with a quiet measured voice.

"Grandpa, I don't want to keep secrets from you. I'll tell you anything you want," said Barbara.

Richard looked up and to the right. It was something he always did when mulling over a delicate problem.

"Well then, I'll come right to the point. You have visions, don't you? And I'll bet that you've had them all your life. I'll even wager that you hear voices, and sometimes you see things."

Barbara was shocked. She never discussed her visions with anyone, not even with Linda, who considered her preoccupation with crickets a little daft.

"Grandpa, how did you know?"

"Let's just say a little cricket told me," he said.

"You're right. I've had visions all my life. But the thing is, I don't know when my life started. I remember a time before I was born. I didn't have a body and I promised somebody that I would do something."

Richard felt validated, and went on. "Pookie, there used to be a saying that if you talk to God, its prayer. If God talks to you, it's schizophrenia."

Barbara laughed, but stopped herself short, anxious for Richard to continue.

He smiled. "But you're not crazy. I see now that you may have the temperament of a warrior mystic, a rare bird these days. You'll go places, see things, and do things that most people

176

can't even imagine. And you'll live to tell the tale."

He sat up straight, and slapped her on one thigh.

"Well, enough of that for one night. Let's get some burgers."

Barbara started slightly.

"Huh?"

"Dinner, sweetheart. There are laws against little girls starving old men to death."

"You're not old. You're just trying to be pitiful."

"Is it working?"

"Nope." She tweaked his beard and hopped over the porch rail onto the lawn. Richard got up and did the same, but taking care to walk behind her for a few paces. Barbara moved with an odd combination of patience and restlessness that made her something of an enigma to her friends.

As far as Richard was concerned, Barbara was not hard to understand. There she was, only fourteen years old but almost six feet tall, all legs but essentially fleshed out into a woman, a budding adult carrying intact within her the curiosity and openness of a child. Her meld of patience and restlessness was simply an enormous reserve of power biding its time until called upon.

Richard quickened his pace , and proffered an arm to his granddaughter. She nestled her hands within it and looked at him.

"Grandpa, I really want a spot in that program. Could I at least start the classroom stuff? Then, if it doesn't work out it just doesn't work out."

Richard said nothing for a few moments, but finally he nodded affirmatively.

"I'll make a few calls when we get back and set something up."

"Thanks, Grandpa."

Together, they walked silently towards the future, and to Jake's Mule Barn for a dinner that would have choked a moose.

#

As they were returning home from dinner, Barbara bounced a few steps ahead of Richard and then turned to face him, jogging backwards.

"Hey Grandpa, let's go for a ride. There won't be many nights left like this..."

"I'm a little tired, Pook, maybe..."

"Then let me go alone. Please. I need to think some more about what you told me."

"Well, all right. I guess so. But be careful. Your country and I need you in one piece."

By that time they had reached the front steps, which Barbara jogged up backwards.

"Pookie, how do you do things like that?"

"Just naturally brilliant, I suppose."

Barbara disappeared into the house and within seconds, it seemed, her motorcycle was warming up behind the cob house. A few more seconds and the two-cylinder engine was purring down Main Street.

Richard waited until the sound faded into the cornfields. Then, having thought the better about being tired, he went around to the cob house, suited up, mounted his Harley, and cruised down Main Street at a discrete distance, hoping that Barbara was as good as her word.

Once away from the lights of Milton, she had only to tilt her head toward the sky to feel awash in stars. The wind blast against her upturned helmet provided just enough lift to create the illusion of flight. Raising her left hand from the clutch enhanced the feeling. She finally felt whole, as if a long-awaited keystone had finally been set over the portal of her future.

The strength of that stone was about to be tested.

Barbara was about ten miles out of town, once again focused on the road, when she thought she saw something up ahead. It was blacker than the surrounding asphalt, and looked like a fresh road repair. Unconcerned, she rode on, not knowing that earlier in the evening two railroad ties had dropped from an overloaded truck. She realized her mistake too late. The motorcycle's front end slammed into something hard.

The front wheel bounded off the pavement while the object scraped its way under the bike's frame. When it hit the back wheel, which was still engaged in fourth gear, the tail of the bike bucked like an epileptic bronco. Barbara reflexively pulled toward the shoulder when the second collision occurred, crumpling the bike's front end, slamming it onto the pavement. She seized the handlebars and somehow stayed with the bike as it ground its way along the pavement and stopped inches from a drainage ditch.

The ensuing silence was terrible. The galaxy of stars had been replaced by a galaxy of gravel as Barbara's eyes refocused through her shattered visor and she noticed that her mouth was full of dirt. She quelled a surge of panic and remained still. First, a body check. She wiggled her toes. Then her feet. Carefully, and trying not to move her back, she tentatively flexed and extended her knees. So far so good. She wiggled her fingers, then flexed her wrists and elbows and slowly shrugged her shoulders. The peripherals were okay, but now the real test was upon her and she had to fight back tears before she could begin. Grinding gravel sounded through Barbara's helmet as she rotated her neck, slightly at first, then through ever increasing arcs. Finally, she swallowed hard and flexed her back. No pain, no odd sensations. She extended her back. Again, no pain, no odd sensations. She got up slowly and removed her helmet, spitting out dirt all the while. The visor was in shards. The knuckle pads on her gloves were torn away. The right side of one boot was sheared off. Her jacket wasn't fit to wear. Otherwise, she was fine.

Really fine. She was exultant over what had just happened without at first understanding why. But after a few moments it came to her. She was thrilled over what had not happened. At the moment of impending death, she simply shut down. Her awareness faded to grey, as did her sight, hearing, and sense of place. There was no pain. No fear. No feelings of any kind. Only a faraway calmness within which she resided while her body endured its trials.

And endure them it did. Barbara stared down at a body that should have been shattered but which was instead whole and thrilling to its own energies. She looked up at the sky again. It suffused her awareness with a simple clarity. She would soon be entering a life in which the possibility of an early, violent death was taken so much for granted that there was no use in worrying about it. It would be a life in which you prepared for the worst and then sat back to enjoy the ride. Her parents must have understood this. Barbara responded to the sky's gift of redemption by raising her arms to embrace its vastness — and any pieces of

her parents that might still be in orbit. Their deaths may not have been so very terrible to them after all. It was the survivors who hurt. And Barbara did hurt. The pain was in her fingers mostly, a   from
fighting   ering
changes i   was
that she   her
training,   and
strive us   ine.
It then   her
refuge i   oint
enabled   its
weaknesses   being
at least,

A singl   riew.
An engine   oots
trotted al   ands
reached c   face
within ea

"Are yo

"I'm okay Grandpa.   Really.   I feel fine."

Appraising   eyes.   "You   won't tomorrow.   What happened, sweetheart? This isn't like you."

Barbara gestured toward the railroad ties — black wood on black asphalt under a black sky.

"Hell's fire! Nobody could have seen that coming. Let's get these things out of the way before somebody gets killed. You up to it?"

"Sure."

After lugging the ties off the road, Richard and Barbara inspected her bike.

"Frame's bent. The insurance company will total it."

"Sorry, Grandpa. I was stupid. I should've paid more attention to the road. I..."

"Don't worry, Barbara. Nobody will hold you accountable for this. You don't have radar vision. Freaky accidents can happen to anybody. Besides, most people trash a bike sooner or later. Welcome to the survivors' club."

"I bet you never trashed a bike."

"Oh yea? I'll tell you about it sometime. Route 1 in Edison, New Jersey. Decades ago on a November night, warm like this one. It taught me not to be afraid of death. Let me call Herb to come pick this thing up. Are you up for a ride back or should I get the car?"

"That's all right Grandpa. I feel good. Let's ride back."

The old man eyed his granddaughter again. "Yea, you do look good — better than you have for a long time, actually."

"I could stand another burger, if you don't mind."

"Rolls Royce brain, Chevy stomach."

Swatting Barbara on the back, Richard returned to the Harley.

"Mount up, sweetheart, I've got some mysterious phone calls to make.

That night, the nightmare returned. She was back in the Pit again. Only this time she was climbing: climbing back toward the golden light and a gently increasing warmth. When she reached the rim of the Pit, she felt her mother's hands lift her from behind and she rose into the air to the sound of softly beating, feathery wings. The hands let her go, into the golden light, where she again lost all sense of having a body and once again became a happy ball of disembodied light.

The Book of Life appeared. It was closed until God's right hand reached down and opened it to a blank page. A quill pen took form in God's hand from the motes of golden light. Upon the blank page, God wrote:"Barbara Llandry"

She awoke with a start and moaned. Richard was right. Every joint in her body felt crushed. Her teeth even hurt. But it was all right. Better to have real pain than to be tortured by demons.

She smiled and went back to sleep.

"JUST CHOP THE WOOD": Autumn 2013

Chi Hsing Tzu was a trainer of fighting cocks for King Hsuan. He was training a fine bird. The King kept asking if the bird were ready for combat. "Not yet," said the trainer. "He is full of fire. He is ready to pick a fight with every other bird. He is vain and confident of his own strength." After ten days, he answered again: "Not yet. He flares up when he hears another bird crow." After ten more days: "Not yet. He still gets that angry look and ruffles his feathers." Again ten days: The trainer said, "Now he is nearly ready. When another bird crows, his eye does not even flicker. He stands immobile like a cock of wood. He is a mature fighter. Other birds will take one look at him and run."

Adapted from "The Fighting Cock" in The Way of Chuang Tzu by Thomas Merton, 1965.

Barbara swung languidly on the porch, mulling over the revelations of the last three years and the exotic direction into which her education and Linda's had gone. She watched Mr. Godfrey as he came by to drop off their winter's supply of firewood. With three huge fireplaces in the house, they could have had a substantial need for firewood, but Richard was mindful of trees and only used it to "create a mood" wherein he would read supernatural fiction for hours. It did not take long for Barbara to acquire the habit. Together they beguiled many a Midwestern blizzard by reading quietly and savoring the subtleties of fear artfully evoked.

Every year, Richard ordered unsplit wood and every year Mr. Godfrey offered to bring along his hydraulic splitter to make life easier for a steady customer. Every year Richard declined. It got to be a ritual of sorts, a ceremonial display of politeness. Barbara suspected otherwise.

"Cheap old bastard. The man pays a million dollars for a Remington bronze but he won't pay Mr. Godfrey a few bucks to get that stuff off the lawn."

That was one notion of which she would soon be disabused. Every year after Mr. Godfrey left, Richard honed his axe, donned his cowhide gloves and split wood for hours in dead silence, without a break. He had a system. He would load a wheelbarrow full of the unsplit wood and wheel it from the roadside to the elm stump he used as a chopping block, split the wood, and carry it into the cob house to dry. He repeated this until the wood was gone.

He never asked for help. Afterwards, he glowed with an earthy vigor that grew in proportion to the amount of wood that he split. Still, to a girl of 17 years, men Richard's age always looked like they were at Death's door and Barbara sometimes wondered if he should work that hard. On the other hand, he did make it look easy. No matter. Time to be a sport. She hopped over the porch railing and sauntered toward the stump.

"Hey Grandpa!"

"Hey Pookie."

"Let me split the wood this year. Give your tired old bones a rest."

"I'm not tired and I'm not old. Besides which I don't mind. It feels good, if you must know."

"Well if it's that much fun, then I'm jealous. Let me try. Come on."

"All right, if you want to. Just be careful and don't chop your leg off."

"Oh puhleeease! Look at me. I'm a lean mean chopping machine! I'll bet you I can split this stuff faster than you can."

"OK, you're on. Just watch yourself."

Richard leaned his axe against the first load of wood, tossed his gloves onto the stump and disappeared into the house. Barbara muttered to herself. "Men think they're so cool. I'll get this stuff chopped in half the time. How hard could it be?" She stood the first piece on end in the center of the stump, picked up the axe and swung. It missed the wood. It missed the stump. It buried itself in the ground. It barely missed her right foot.

"Shiiiiit! That's embarrassing."

Barbara turned toward the house, scanning the windows for any signs of Richard. If he had seen that, he would never let her forget it. The wavy glass panes reflected only the passing clouds and treetops. No Grandpa. Good.

She swung again. This time, the axe glanced off the stump and buried itself next to her right foot again. Visions of emergency tendon surgery passed through her head.

"What the hell?"

Again she swung. This time the axe hit the wood, but penetrated no more than an inch or so. At least it was sticking.

"That's progress, I think."

Lifting the axe with the wood snared on its blade, she hammered it onto the stump until the wood grudgingly split into two pieces hairy with splinters. Again and again the axe whizzed through the air. Sometimes it missed its mark, but usually it at least hit the wood. In an attempt to be more effective, she focussed on the middle of the wood's top surface. With increasing frequency, that was where the axe struck. And that was where it stayed. Nothing ever split on the first blow.Nevertheless, it was progress, so Barbara modified her approach. Brute force clearly wasn't working. Maybe anger would. She narrowed her eyes and saw the wood as an enemy. As her axe slaughtered the air, Barbara invoked her blood lust and chanted, "Kill, Kill, Kill, Kill."

The axe curved insanely and missed even the stump.

Back to square one.

Anger wasn't working. Maybe rage would.

Barbara again roused herself, muttering,

"IhateyouIhateyouIhateyouIhateyou."

The axe careened out of all control. It did not even pass close to the stump, but headed straight for Barbara's right leg. In a paroxysmic movement toward self-preservation, she spun around on her left leg. The axe missed her right leg by less than an inch. It was the final blow. With tears of vexation streaming down her face, Barbara threw the axe onto the woodpile, plopped onto the stump and pouted for what seemed like a long time.

#

Master Paul Yang had led a strange life. From infancy, from the moment he learned to speak in sentences, he had proclaimed to anyone who would listen that the world was alive, that he could see the wind, and that the wind talked to him. Other than that he was a normal kid. But Paul persisted. He proselytized his beliefs with such an evangelical fervor that his parents suspected mental illness as the force behind their son's queer ideas. It was when they noticed Paul tracking things with his eyes that plainly were not there — and talking to those things — that his parents took him to see his first psychiatrist.

And thus began the quest for "A Diagnosis". A battalion of doctors assessed Paul for everything from autism to xenophobia, and every time he slipped through the diagnostic cracks. In some subtle but crucial way, Paul Yang was not crazy. The real problem lay with everyone's mistaken assumption that Paul had a problem to begin with. What no one suspected was that Paul was displaying a rare and profound level of sanity that rendered him a friend to a world that lived and was conscious of its living.

Paul's alleged problem disappeared one day when he sat down to watch an old Bruce Lee movie. It proved to be an epiphany. Here was a man who danced with the wind and crushed powerful enemies because of it. He knew its language and spoke it well. Paul watched the movie twice, following every move of every fight with a fluid knowing that he had innocently nurtured from birth. When he was finished, Paul walked into the kitchen and politely asked his parents if he could take karate lessons. They agreed and from that day forward Paul never again spoke of the wind.

As he grew from childhood to adolescence, Paul invariably astounded his teachers. He seemed to be a reborn Master who was simply training a new body in the ways of the martial arts. He blossomed into a warrior mystic on the day he was handed his first sword. On his eighteenth birthday, Paul left home for China. He sought out the finest group of blade makers in the country and apprenticed himself to them. Five years later he was himself recognized as a master blade maker. By the age of thirty, Paul Yang was the most sought-after sword master in the Western world.

This put a premium on his time and he soon learned to protect the time he needed to refresh and nurture his own life. To this end, he enjoyed nothing better than renting a car and driving wherever the wind suggested. This led him, on a brisk autumn day, to the main street of Milton, Iowa. The town held within it an unusual energy flowing from a rare person, possibly a young girl. But someone else, someone very strong and not to be trifled with, was protecting her with the fierceness of a dragon guarding a treasure. Paul parked the car and began walking. He passed an assortment of Protestant churches, one Catholic church, a seedy bar, and a block of houses whose Midwestern purity of design had been muddled over the years by vinyl siding and satellite dishes. The energy was here somewhere, but not in this part of town.

He walked on.

The energy got stronger as Paul approached the center of town. He stilled his mind and moved freely among the subtle forces. Presently, he was drawn to an imposing white house whose mansard roof was frameded by hoary maple trees.

It was the source.

Paul walked toward the house and stopped in front of its main entrance. He noticed an old concrete hitching block with an intact iron ring. Judging by the rust on the metal, it had not been used to hitch horses for many decades. Paul sat down on the block and let its accumulated warmth dispel the Autumn chill. Although built on a grand scale, the house was impressive in more subtle ways. Its vast runs of ornamental iron were in perfect repair. The brackets under the eaves were intact. The windows still held old panes of wavy, bubbly glass. Lines that needed to be straight had remained true. Things, like siding and moldings, that could afford to bend had settled into the earth and adapted to it in pleasing ways, so much so that the house gave the impression of having risen from the fertile soil that surrounded it. It belonged where it was like few places Paul had ever seen. The spirit of the place was strong and stable. The obvious level of care that had been lavished on the house and its grounds by many people over the decades made it a place where the voices of the winds congregated. Their labors had bestowed upon the house a patina, a sheen of careful use, that made the house a reliquary of stories, of lives lived in one place from cradle to grave. ` The voices of the ancestors whispered from the deeps of the house and disappeared into the sky.

For all the allure of the house, it was not quite what Paul was sensing, and so he continued looking until a glint of moving metal caught his eye. That was it — a teenage girl splitting wood, or at least trying to. From the erratic swaths of the blade through the musky autumnal air, it was clear to him that the girl did not know what she was doing. Precious little wood was being split and the girl was exasperating herself. Finally, she threw the axe onto the stubborn woodpile and sat down on a tree stump, her back to Paul, sulking.

Despite her apparent ineptitude, the girl's spirit was astounding. She was an inferno whose fires shot into the sky to meet the voices of ancestors whose whispered memories peopled the heavens with countless beloved stars. Her energy also radiated in a great circle, taking in everything around her with a remarkable openness. The girl lived at the crossroads of two very different, almost opposite, kinds of energy. If she could still her mind and refine her spirit, if she could sit immovably in the midst of those opposing forces and embody the wisdom that arises from the dynamic tension between them, then she would manifest an energy that could take her anywhere she chose to go.

He rose and walked toward the woodpile.

#

Barbara was sitting on the stump, wiping stray tears from her cheeks, when she felt her back tingling. At first, she thought it was just a chill. But the feeling grew. The dancing, tickling sensations coalesced to cover ever increasing parts of her back. Finally, she felt a distinct tug at her shoulder. She turned around. Barbara found herself in the presence of a short, slender oriental man who was standing too far away to have touched her. He said nothing but continued to stare at Barbara with a frank curiosity. She stood up. At 6'3", she was almost two heads taller than the stranger.

"Uh...Hi. Can...Can I help you with something?"

"No thank you, I'm fine."

The long, appraising stare continued. Barbara looked behind the man, trying to imagine where he had come from and how he had managed to move so quietly.

"If you're lost or something, you can come inside for tea. My grandfather could get you back on your way."

"Thank you again, but I'm quite all right. You, however, don't look very happy."

"No, I guess I'm not. I made a bet with him that I could split this wood faster than he can, but all I've done is make splinters. I don't know what I'm doing wrong. I don't think I can hit the wood any harder than I'm already doing."

"That's part of your problem. Splitting wood has nothing to do with how strong your muscles are. You split wood with your chi."

"What's chi?"

"Oh, sorry. Chi is a word that doesn't translate well into English. It's an invisible life force or energy, a source of subtle strength. You see, the mind is powerful. When mind and body work together, chi moves freely."

"So how does that chop wood?"

"Very simply. Very subtly."

Paul moved closer to Barbara and pointed to a spot about two inches below her navel. "This is your 'tan-tien' or 'elixir field'. Some people believe that all the chi in the universe flows through them at this point and then travels forever in all directions to all other beings. In each of them chi behaves the same way. This means that you are a center of the universe. I am a center of the universe. And so on. All beings are centers of the universe. People who realize this can learn to point their chi in any direction they choose."

"Even into a hunk of wood?"

"Even into a hunk of wood. Let me show you. Put some wood on the stump and give me the axe."

"Are you sure? It's awfully heavy."

"Remember what I said. This is not about brute strength."

Paul rolled up his sleeves and gripped the axe. He planted his feet firmly into the ground, paused, and breathed deeply, down into his belly. He picked up the axe as if it were a feather and swung the blade through a perfect circle. It split the wood clean through to the stump. The two pieces fell softly to the ground.

"How did you do that?"

"In principle, it's simple, but in reality it requires practice. First, place your feet firmly on the ground and imagine that you are connected to the very center of the earth. Then, take a deep breath, down into your belly. When you feel centered, imagine the bottom of the wood, not the top. Imagine the axe striking through to the bottom of the wood. Then swing. With practice, the wood will seem to split by itself."

"I don't think I can do that."

"Sure you can. You have strong chi. Don't put any limits on it."

Barbara looked at Paul with a combination of willingness and lingering uncertainty. He knew her type. Like many brilliant adolescents, Barbara could become flustered when she happened upon something that did not come easily.

She reached hesitantly for the axe. Paul sensed her reticence

"Come. It's time to just chop the wood. Nothing more, nothing less. Realize this down into your bones and you will find that you need nothing more and nothing less."

Barbara did as she was told. She swung at a fresh piece of wood. The axe passed almost two-thirds of the way through. A couple more taps with the same frame of mind and the two halves separated neatly. She tried another piece. The blade passed through the entire length and came to rest on the stump. The two halves fell gently to the ground.

"See? You are more effective when you are mindful of chi. Just remember: the creative channeling of chi is the only legitimate use of power. You are a beautiful girl with intense energy. Be careful how you use it. So. Now that you understand this in your head, teach your body. Chop some more wood. Refine your chi."

Encouraged, Barbara resumed the work. Sometimes she missed the wood. Sometimes she just chipped it. But most of the time, the axe swung true and did not stop until it came to rest on the stump. Barbara was astounded at what was happening inside of her, at the things she was understanding. She paused and turned to thank the man, but he was gone.

Barbara tossed the axe aside and ran toward the street. A tiny white car was cruising to the edge of town toward the cornfields. Barbara stood in the road for a while. Finally, she thanked the point on the horizon where the car had disappeared. She was startled out of her reverie by the honking of a car horn. A man leaned out of the driver's window and shouted at her.

"Hey Barbara! What the hell're you doin' standin' in the middle of the road!?"

"Oh...sorry Sheriff Norton. I was just thinking about something."

"Yea, that's just like you and your little friend. Always standin' around thinkin' about something. Good way to get yourself killed."

Several hours later, the wood was split and stacked in the cob house. The axe was leaning against the back door frame, its immaculate blade a burning red coal in the light of the setting sun.

Inside the house, freshly chopped wood hissed and popped in the fireplace.

#

Barbara spent much of her time that evening in a trance of sorts. She felt like a shaman dancing at the edge of things, chasing her Totem through the Dreamland. She ate dinner distractedly, letting her soul's "I" roam at will. Where that "elsewhere" was, she could not really say. She stood on the brink of who she thought she was, staring into a void that was not mere emptiness, but a kind of formless place, dark and wet and pregnant with possibilities. Her Totem had flown into that void fearlessly and without hesitation, pausing only to turn and beckon Barbara to follow. She did, and all because a skinny little Chinese man, who talked in riddles and moved like a shadow, taught her how to split firewood.

Richard left her alone. Over the years, their respective temperaments had become so similar that he knew when she needed time to think. The inner space into which Barbara retreated that night manifested outwardly as a subtly protective sphere that demanded enough solitude for the shamanic magic to have its way with the young eagle that was ready to jump from her nest and learn the joys of flight by overcoming the terror of falling. Even Linda left her alone.

Later that evening, Richard came upon Barbara sitting on the porch swing, barefooted, and wearing nothing but gym shorts and a tee shirt. Her skin was flushed to the point where she was oblivious to the deepening chill. He checked the thermometer outside of the kitchen, which registered at 45 degrees. Richard put on a jacket and sat down next to Barbara, the back of his thighs protesting the sudden chill.

"Grandpa, this is <u>so cool</u>."

"You noticed."

"That's not what I meant."

"What then?"

From entrenched habit, Barbara curled up her legs and started to cuddle with her grandfather, only this time he did not return the gesture, becoming instead slightly stiff and distant. He was doing that a lot lately, and Barbara was beginning to understand why. She was seventeen. They were exactly the same height — 6'3". He loved beautiful women of all ages, fine art, and rare motorcycles. Judging by the number of boys who were practically laying siege to the house, she now fell into the category of beautiful women. She and Linda had been noticing lately that the only things on their minds were sex and motorcycles and that the two were not entirely unrelated. All things considered, it would be weird for her to persist in being Grandpa's little girl. To that end, he had been sending her quiet signals that it was time for her to find her own way among the world of men. It was a small goodbye to childhood, one of many. But the compensations were more than adequate. Both Richard and Herb were considerably freer with their bawdy language and dirty jokes when she and Linda were around. They had even taken them down to Jake's Mule Barn for a few beers. So the loss of childhood was balanced by her entrance into another world. Barbara straightened up and gathered her thoughts again.

"Did you notice anything today while I was splitting the firewood?"

"Sure I did. So did the lawn."

"Oh...yea...sorry about that. Anyway, I wasn't doing very well when out of nowhere comes this funny little oriental man. He must have noticed that I couldn't split wood worth a damn, because he started talking about energy, and breathing, visualization, and centering your chi in your...oh, what was it..."

"Your tan-tien."

"How do you know?"

"Years ago, Natasha taught me a few things about Oriental religions. Besides, that's how martial artists train themselves to split wood and bricks."

"No way!"

"Oh yes. Anyhow, I don't know if chi is real, but as a visualization it focuses the mind wonderfully. In fact, it was a Karate teacher who taught <u>me</u> how to split wood. It seems as if you've had the same luck."

"I guess so. But there's more. A lot more."

"There usually is, when these things happen."

"That's for sure. I used to think I was crazy when it came to certain things, but now I think maybe I'm not."

Barbara started reflexively to cuddle Richard again, but stopped herself. The sun had long since set and she was getting cold, now that her concentration was broken, but she persisted with her train of thought.

"Oh Grandpa, it's just that I feel so...so big inside. And you know what? I've always been that way. Mother told me once that I started talking when I was nine months old; but the weird thing is that I can remember not being able to talk at all, so I must have been <u>really</u> young. Even then, I felt huge inside, and you wouldn't believe how light and beautiful things are in themselves when they're not muddled by words and ideas."

Richard smiled. "I believe it as much as you do."

It was getting dark and Barbara was shivering, although she seemed unaware of it. Richard let her continue.

"I don't know what it is about this house, but I feel especially big inside when I'm here. Like back when before I could talk. Mother and Dad must have come here to visit. Somebody must have carried me into the kitchen, because I remember looking up into the ceiling — it was a pukey green color back then — when all of a sudden the ceiling dissolved and a bunch of golden clouds appeared, as if I were looking through a window. I left my body and before I knew it I was flying, soaring actually, among the clouds. They felt like they were made of cotton, because I could bounce around on them without being afraid of falling. After awhile, I glided down towards Milton again. I skimmed the tops of the trees along Main

Street and the next thing I knew I was back in my body staring at the ceiling again. I guess what I'm trying to say is that, ever since then, I've felt as big as the sky on the inside, right down into my guts, as if the sky's my real home, as if I <u>am</u> the sky, as if I won't feel at home unless I go back up there again."

Richard forgot the cold. He locked his eyes on Barbara's, taking in everything without so much as batting an eyelash.

"But that wasn't the end of it. I must have been carried then into the dining room because I looked at the ceiling and <u>it</u> disappeared. I saw a young man standing outdoors by a stone balustrade. It was a moonlit night and there were lush old woods in the distance. The man put his hand on the rail and looked up into the sky. It was so peaceful I just want to cry every time I think about it. He was wearing old-fashioned clothing, maybe early Victorian. How could I have seen that when I was six months old?"

"I don't know, Pookie. There weren't any Victorian pieces in the house back then. For the rest, you spent most of your time crawling around any number of aerospace labs."

"There's more. Whoever was carrying me must have been antsy because I remember passing the bookcase on the wall between the kitchen and dining room. When I looked into it, the shelves disappeared and a golden light shone through. I was looking into an endless space that was bounded only by a shiny stone floor that disappeared into the distance. There were people walking on the floor, wearing robes, or togas, or something. They were very quiet, but it seemed as if they were gods who knew everything about everything."

Barbara stared at the elm stump. Tears graced her cheeks, so clear, so like pure water that they might have frozen into diamonds had she not wiped them off. Richard was silent.

"Grandpa, I could go on about this stuff all night. The more I learn about things, the more the bigness inside of me grows to include them. It's not as if I'm just learning stuff and remembering it. I feel, somehow, that I am a pterodactyl riding the updrafts around a volcano, that I am a galaxy, that I am a Viking raiding the British Isles. Sometimes I feel so huge inside I don't know where I end and everything else begins. For the longest time, I thought I was nuts. But I'm not. This stuff is sane."

Barbara fell silent. The night deepened around them.

"And then comes this funny little oriental man from out of nowhere and he talks to me about how all the chi in the universe is flowing through my belly and how that makes me a center of the universe and things start to make sense. If everything is flowing through me, then maybe all of time is flowing through me too and I really am a pterodactyl and a galaxy and a Viking and a million other things...and yet I'm still just plain, simple little me, sitting on a porch swing with my Grandpa."

Richard looked up at the sky. It was so clear that the Milky Way spanned the roof of the house like a diamond encrusted scarf.

"Sort of like Indra's Net."

"What's that?"

"Something Natasha told me about a long time ago. It's Buddhist. It's a metaphor in which the universe is a net of precious jewels so brilliantly cut that every jewel reflects every other jewel."

"I like it," mused Barbara.

"Natasha was a wise woman."

"I wish I'd known her."

"Maybe you will someday, if what you said is true."

"Yea, maybe I will."

"Grandpa? Could I tell you some more?"

"Sure, sweetie."

"This bigness I was telling you about? Something funny started happening to it after that man taught me how to split the wood properly. Most of the time, I was really self-conscious about doing it right and the results were just so-so. But every once in a while, it was as if there was just an axe swinging in an empty sky and the sound of wood splitting all by itself. It was as if I weren't there, as if I got out of my own way and the work just flowed. That was when it happened."

Barbara paused for a moment to take a quietly exultant breath.

"At the moment when the axe split the wood, the bigness inside of me rose to meet the bigness all around me, and they met on the axe blade. Then I realized something really cool. The sharper a blade is, the better it cuts. It's as if the blade's edge is a fine line that vanishes into zero. The sharper the blade, the more it vanishes into zero. Zero cuts the wood. So it's like two infinities — the bigness inside of me and the bigness all around us — meet at the vanishing point of zero; it's as if they lock into a void, as if the cutting edge of emptiness is what holds everything together. God I love swords! I always have, especially those samurai swords that you sell once in a while. Now I know why. And there's something else. Time, the present moment actually, is like that fine edge on the axe. The present moment always seems to be with us, but it also seems to be infinitely small, because the instant something happens, it's gone. So the present moment is a zero, a nothing, a void that balances two infinities — the past and the future. The sharper the edge the finer the balance. So, a kind of nothingness binds together all of time. The present moment is the best place to be, the only place to be, really. Grandpa, are you too cold?"

"No sweetheart, I'm fine."

"Good, because there's more. I suppose you've noticed me and Linda fooling around with mirrors in Herb's side yard?"

"It's rather hard to miss."

"Do you know what we're doing?

"Pookie, when you get to be my age, you learn not to ask women too many questions."

"We're just playing with infinite reflections — trying to pair up the mirrors so that the sky and our faces bounce back and forth forever."

"Isn't that rather the height of vanity?"

"No way! It's your doing, actually."

"How do you figure?"

"When I was little, I used to think you were senile or something, with the way you sat here so much 'communing with the spirits'. Then I tried it, and everything changed. It took awhile but I got to where I could sit still and pay attention with all my senses at once. I could let my thoughts and feelings just stream through my head without thinking about them. It was wonderful. It was also really weird sometimes. Things were almost too real. Shapes, sounds, colors, smells were big. Too big to fit in any kind of normal space or time. It was like walking into a Van Gogh painting that was trying to rip space apart so it could fly into other dimensions. That's when I got the idea of playing with infinite reflections in the mirrors. It's hard to rig them just right, but when I do, it captures that feeling of other dimensions. Even Linda's getting into it."

#

It was still light out when Richard sat down with Barbara. By the time she had finished, they were awash in starlight. The house was dark and quiet. Richard studied Barbara's face for a few wistful moments. Over the last year or two it had become so beautiful that it beggared description. He looked through the lawn's dimly reflected light with the bittersweet recognition that it was time.

"Well, I guess it's time for my little eagle to fly away."

"What do you mean, Grandpa?"

"Remember that night three years ago when I told you why you and Linda were being followed and we talked about your visions?" asked Richard.

"Of course I do, Grandpa. I remember everything you tell me."

"Then you'll recall how I said you weren't ready for the life they were offering you," said Richard. He breathed deeply and said, "As of tonight you're ready. You've learned to live with your visions. Pay attention to them. Have faith in them and they'll never fail you."

By that time, Barbara was sitting bolt upright.

"Oh, thank you Grandpa! Thank you! You'll be proud of me, just..."

She stopped in mid-sentence as something dawned on her.

"And that means I have to leave. We won't be able to do things like this anymore."

Richard smiled reassuringly.

"It's not as if you won't have time off. Come home whenever you want. We'll sit here all night and croak like two lazy toads."

"I'd like that," whispered Barbara. "I'd like that a lot."

FAREWELLS: Winter 2013

Calls were placed and arrangements made accordingly. By common consent, everyone had gathered at Richard Landry's house and adjourned to his study. It was a room that Barbara seldom entered, being as it was her grandfather's office and a place where he kept his rarest art. She smiled at the site of Herb lounging on a settee that was probably worth more than his entire business, but doing it with an aplomb that would have made him at home among New York's elite. Sarah was easier on the eye, her natural beauty complementing the decor as it did -- that, plus her forehead was not dented. Linda, by nature a snoop, knew every inch of the room and the cash value of everything in it. Ironically, it was the two VIPs, one from MIT and the other from the Air Force, who seemed stunned that such casual opulence could exist in such obscurity.

The opening pleasantries were becoming a little long for Barbara's liking, but she resigned herself to them by breathing deeply and relaxing back into her seat, the better to stare at the ceiling and let her mercurial memory take her back to a simpler time, long ago, in this very room, to the day when she first entered it. It was tea time. She sat on the same settee that Herb now occupied. Richard smiled and got up from his desk. He settled into a wing backed chair separated from the settee by a small table on which he had placed a Faberge pot filled with Earl Grey tea, and an open box of Twinkies.

It was an endearing memory bud, each of whose unfurling petals held a vignette whose vividness had impressed itself indelibly into Barbara's recollection despite the attenuation wrought upon memory by time. In that moment, she became once again the six-year-old girl who was not sure how to behave in such a treasure trove, so she found herself looking up at the Russian chandelier bearing down on her from the ornately plastered ceiling, looking down at the serpentine arabesques of the Isfahan carpet beneath her feet, their curves so intricate, so bright, so clear, that they fairly danced into the air and entwined her legs, feeling not-very-grown-up because her feet dangled from the sofa, inches from the floor, admiring the ancient Greek bas reliefs — one on each wall — depicting Earth, Air, Fire, and Water. Water was over the mantel. Fire warmed her back from the opposite wall. She gingerly accepted an

Aynsley teacup with one hand and a Twinkie with the other.

"Hey Grandpa."

"Hey Pookie."

"Do I have to be extra special good when I'm here with you?"

"That would be nice."

"But why?"

"Because you're in my temenos."

"What's a te...?" The "te" sent a crumb flying onto the carpet. Barbara swallowed the "menos" along with the remaining cake. Richard smiled. He was one of those rare souls who always found amusing the faux pas of young children.

"A temenos is a sacred place. You remember those old Greek myths we read last week?"

"Sure I do. You know me. I remember everything."

Richard nodded in assent. His granddaughter had been showing signs of having remarkable intelligence and an equally remarkable memory.

"The Greeks had special places, usually groves of old trees, that they set aside for secret religious stuff. If you behaved yourself, the gods might talk to you, so the temenos was a place where you could have your own special thoughts and feelings and nobody was allowed to bother you."

"Sounds nice. So what's the Water guy doing over the fireplace?"

"I'm an Aquarian, so I thought I'd put the water symbol in the most important part of the room."

"Aquarius.   That's astrology stuff,
right?"

"Uh-huh."

"The TV preachers say that's devil
talk and anybody who thinks about it'll
burn in Hell."

"Pookie.   Why do you watch those
guys?"

"It kills time, once in a while."

"It pickles your brain, sweetheart."

Silence and long stares into the
fire.

"Hey Grandpa."

"Hey Pookie."

"Could I turn my bedroom into a
temenos?"

"Sure, why not?"

"How do I start?"

"Making your bed would be nice..."

Richard's voice disrupted Barbara's
reverie.   The blossom furled its petals
and sank back into the darkness whence
it had arisen.

"Well, I think we're all agreed that
this has been a remarkable journey.   And
I suspect that there's more to come.
Professor Penrose?"

Richard nodded to a short man with an
amiable paunch and impish eyes.

"Thank you, Dr. Llandry.   My
colleagues and I have been following the
young ladies with intense interest and I
have to say that both of you have
exceeded even our most extravagant
expectations and hopes."

Professor Penrose paused to pick up a
snifter of Armagnac.   He thoughtfully

assessed its bouquet and took a long appreciative sip.

"Wonderful stuff...my compliments, Dr. Llandry."

Richard nodded indifferently.

"Anyway," the professor continued, "my colleagues at MIT have reviewed your files and, even as we speak, are granting both of you bachelor's degree's in aerospace engineering — summa cum laude, of course."

No one broke the ensuing silence. Penrose sat back and enjoyed the moment until his sense of drama suggested that a segue was in order.

"There's more. It will be my privilege to act as your advisor while you two pursue master's degrees in planetary science. But more about that later. I should probably turn the meeting over to Major Frankel."

Penrose poked the major in the ribs. He was a taciturn man with intimidating eyes.

"What about it, Major? Can you turn these girls into spit-polished officers?"

Major Frankel looked first at Linda, then at Barbara, and back again at Linda. She returned his gaze with the unblinking confidence of someone who takes it as given that she will succeed. Satisfied, he returned his attention to Barbara. She was different. Very different. Not your usual military type. She was intensely calm. Or was she calmly intense? She could not have been more than twelve feet away, and yet she seemed to be looking down at him from a height so great that she might as well have been on another world. The electric blue of her eyes made the impression all the more vivid by affording as they did specular hints of places too remote both in space and time to be readily discerned. Yes, he could make of Barbara a fine officer. But she might be unpredictable. What else she would become was anybody's guess. Major Frankel turned to Professor Penrose.

"Yep."

"Well then, it's done," said the professor. He stopped short. "Oh, please forgive me. I assume that you ladies are comfortable with these arrangements?"

Barbara and Linda smiled at each other as if sharing the same thought, and addressed the professor in unison.

"Yep."

FAREWELLS REVISITED: June, 2034

COMMANDER'S PERSONAL LOG: June, 2034

I look back often on that day when Linda and I formally accepted Professor Penrose's offer. I can't honestly say that we were surprised. From the day that Herb and Grandpa tendered their tentative acceptance of the government's hush-hush offer, we went into overdrive. Within the week, Linda and I received high-school diplomas with every possible academic honor tacked on to them. With Herb's and Sarah's help, Grandpa converted the second floor of the house into two private studies and a library replete with everything we needed: computers, satellite uplinks, books, stationery. It was as if a genie had popped out of his bottle for the express purpose of nurturing our minds. On his end, Herb enlarged one of the service bays into a hybrid laboratory and machine shop, in which we indulged our interest in propulsion and aerodynamics. To wit, we built rockets, each more ambitious than the last. We learned that anything we could clearly conceive, we could create. It was the nidus, the seed crystal, around which our studies accreted, layer upon lucent layer. We soared.

And then it was over. Sitting among Grandpa's treasures, we committed ourselves to a future that none of us, not even our benefactors, could limn with any certainty.

I spent that evening alone, saying goodbye to things. The night was mild and still. I stepped out onto the front entrance. From there, the hoary, red-maple tree blotted much of the sky with its black tangles of unmolested growth. It was the best climbing tree in the world, its main branches forming a spiral around its trunk, and my first ambition in life was to climb to the top. I wanted to poke my head above its canopy and take my place among the leaves. I wanted to live in the light and see things as the birds did. My parents thought it was a wonderful idea.

I remember my first climb. I was too small then to reach the lower branches, so Dad hoisted himself up first. Mother handed me off to him. He set me down on the branch and held my hands in his. I felt dizzy and safe all at once and I wanted more. I reached out and took hold of the highest branch I could reach. Dad steadied me at the waist. When he was sure I had my footing, he let me go, inch by cautious inch, praising me all the while. Mother stood directly under me, alert to my slightest misstep. I knew I could fall. I knew I could get hurt. But I also knew that I wouldn't. With so much strength above and so much love below, I couldn't fail. Grandpa took over after they died, and led me higher than ever, until he was satisfied that I wouldn't kill myself. But as my climbing skills grew, so did my weight. I never did push my head through the canopy. But it's all right. That's what dreams are for.

Without quite realizing it, I had wandered off the front porch and was looking up at the tree. It's branches, seasonally bereft of their greenery, gestured imploringly to me. I don't know what impelled me to do it, but I stepped forward and hugged the poor thing. I found myself whispering words of comfort to it, promising it that the cold never lasts forever. I was never so sane as I was that night. The tree returned my gesture with a friendly gratitude that few people in my life have matched. Then I laughed. If my mentors knew that I walked around at night talking to trees, they might have taken a second look at my file. I patted the tree and wandered off.

The hitching block caught my eye next. Within spitting distance of the maple tree, its lone iron ring and the rusty halo that had spread from it bore mute witness to time's leprous power over our days. All mankind's history lay in that ring, from our domestication of the first horses to the dubious blessings of the internal combustion engine. I sat down on the block. It was still warm with the day's clement weather. Leaning over the ring, I tapped it a few times. Beneath its hundred-year-old mantle of rust, the metal rang true. Many years would yet pass before the last molecule of iron yielded to rust. I wondered what the world would be like on that day, but not for long. I'm not into making predictions. It's a fool's game.

I got up and looked at the house. No farewells possible there. The place was so much a part of me that it might as well have been a vital organ. I could journey to the far side of forever and it would still be there, inside of me. And all because of a tall, soft-spoken, slender old man who occasionally commanded the attention of powerful people the world over, and who at that moment was enjoying a smoke on the porch of a house in the middle of a sea of green, gold, brown, and white, depending on the season. Him I would die for.

But not just then. I had one last chore, one last goodbye to make.

I gathered all the trash in the house and carted it to the makeshift fieldstone enclosure behind the cob house that served as the fire pit in which we burned it. When I was little, the fire pit was my favorite place in all the world. I always insisted on being the one to burn the trash, regardless of the weather. Boxes, milk cartons, and cardboard tubes were the best. With these in hand, I built no end of imaginary cities and fortresses, each a city state waging war on the others. As their stratagems unfolded, one or another of the buildings caught fire and vanished into the sky and bursts of moribund sparks. Civilizations rose and fell within the confines of that ashen world. The smoke from those fallen powers assumed delicate, evanescent forms before the breeze carried them off to places I had never visited but longed to see. That night, I dumped the trash into the enclosure, lit a match, and dropped it in randomly, letting the fire find its own way among the scattered shapes.

I stood back from the flames and watched the rising smoke curl into Rorschach blots of memory that curtsied and smiled and danced away into the night. I waited until every ember yielded its secrets and collapsed among the ashes of its brethren. That done, I walked back into the house.

As I read these passages again, they ring with a finality that I didn't quite intend. Linda and I had to wait a couple of months for the right semester and round of Air Force ROTC training to begin. And of course I visited Grandpa as often as I could. I would burn many more loads of trash. I even climbed the maple tree a few more times and read poetry to it.

But there was a difference. Never again would I be the Pookie whose Grandpa cuddled her on a squeaky porch swing and read to her on stormy nights. She was a ghost that would soon take her place among the whispering shadows in Jake's Mule Barn. For me to have clung to her world would have made of me a hungry spirit, wandering among the possibilities of tomorrow, unable to shake off the dust of yesterday. I had acquired my first coat of rust, and had plenty of mettle yet to test.

#

The next four years passed like the flight of an arrow toward a distant target. Linda and I completed our course work, fell in and out of love once or twice, finished our flight training, and undertook theses on a couple of problems related to gravitational theory. These quickly assumed dissertation proportions, and so we graduated as Air Force captains with PhDs. Along the way, Linda found the time to get married.

And then the work really started. But not without a poignant segue. The afternoon of graduation day found me standing by the window of my dormitory room, standing in shocked disbelief at the gift that Grandpa had just handed me. It was a set of folded-steel Samurai swords. The scabbards alone were stunning. Each was finished with 40 seductive coats of hand-rubbed red lacquer that begged to be touched and stroked and caressed. I donned the traditional white cotton gloves that came with the swords and unsheathed the katana. It shimmered with the blue of the early afternoon light. The blade's undulating temper lines belied the remorseless edge that lay just beyond them and for whose sake they existed. The wakizashi and tanto were no less exquisite, and I shuddered to think what he must have paid for them. As a rule I'm not a weepy person. Hell, I didn't even cry when I got jilted. But at that moment my eyes started leaking and there was nothing I could do about it. I reverently sheathed the blades, sniffling all the while, and embraced Grandpa with a gusher of gratitude for everything he had ever done for me. His capacity for love and guidance was so vast and so freely given that I could only blubber my thanks. The shoulder pads of his sport coat were pretty well soaked by the time I got control myself. I returned the swords to their case. Locking the door behind me, we walked slowly and in an intimate silence toward a party that lasted for the rest of the day and well into the night. I'll never forget the sight of Linda sitting on her husband's shoulders, whipping him with a riding crop and chugging a bottle of champagne all the while.

Such talent.

#

I first saw them as if in a dream. Curtains of mist from an early-morning fog had draped the runway, turning it into a phantasmal stage on which brooded several dark forms. As the sun rose, the curtains lifted, revealing three austerely beautiful aircraft. They were SR-71 Blackbirds, old but well maintained. They were well named. The mounting sun was powerless against their relentlessly black surfaces. If anything, they became darker under the increasingly brilliant sky. They swallowed light. Scores of hours in flight simulators, to say nothing of my expertise in flying the newer subsonic stealth aircraft, did nothing to prepare me for that moment of first contact with the Blackbird's combination of thundering power and tea-cup delicacy of form. It stood on the runway begging to be flown.

The brainchild, or perhaps the love child, of the Lockheed Martin Skunkworks, each Blackbird was equipped with a pair of Pratt & Whitney axial-flow turbojets. Their combined thrust of 65,000 pounds easily pushed the Blackbird to speeds exceeding Mach 3.2 and cruising altitudes over 85,000 feet. After 30 years of service involving aerial reconnaissance and research, the Blackbird had taken its place among the classics of aviation. By the time that Linda and I finished our training, the Blackbirds had been reborn as experimental platforms for research into propulsion, body design, high-altitude atmospheric studies, and pilot training for future generations of hypersonic aircraft.

The Blackbird was the sort of plane that rewarded her pilot's efforts. Willful on takeoff and ornery at subsonic speeds, she shuddered at the threshold of Mach 1 — as if afraid of her own thunder and fury — and then passed into a supersonic silence that left sound far behind. It was here that the Blackbird ruled. Burning up Mach 1 and Mach 2, she punched her way through Mach 3 and thence to a classified maximum speed before leveling off and cruising 17 miles above the Earth — high enough to see the Earth's all encompassing curves. The Blackbird afforded her pilots a thrill denied their more timid colleagues.

It was my privilege to become intimate with more than one Blackbird before I breached even their far limits to the rarefied realm of Project Dark Star — the government's most secret of secret projects. Evidently, I was not the only one to be inspired by those black angels. I subsequently learned that several major aerospace companies had convened under the aegis of NASA and the Department of Defense to reinvent the SR-71 Blackbird from the wheels on up. Their idea was to create a hypersonic stealth bomber with modular weapon and reconnaissance arrays that could easily be interchanged to accommodate any number of tactical scenarios. A world in which four guys in a rowboat had once crippled a $1 billion destroyer was one in which the military had to be strong, swift, and subtle.

Hence Project Dark Star.

By the time I joined the project, several prototypes had been tested. The Blackbird's original Pratt & Whitney engines had been replaced by smaller and lighter linear aerospike engines whose combined thrust trebled that of the originals. The prototypes were the same size as the Blackbird, but their fullerene-based carbon-fiber bodies permitted weight reduction without compromising strength, flexibility, and transparency to radar. And then there was the skin. It was described technically as an "optically chromoplastic film" that mimicked ambient light to blend into its surroundings. In other words, the prototypes were chameleons. Viewed from above they shifted color to blend with the surfaces over which they were flying. Viewed from below, they blended with the sky. If the aircraft was damaged during combat, the pilot had the option of ejecting and remotely detonating the fuel. If captured, enough of the plane's classified technology was booby-trapped so as to incinerate any fool with the temerity to tamper with it.

They were a real hoot to fly.

The prototypes were close to perfection. But their designers, who

I'm sure had watched too many Star Trek reruns, still yearned for an innovation that bordered on fantasy. As Fate, or Chance, would have it, Linda's dissertation and mine afforded intimations of a solution. Within a few years, a lot of smart people did what no one else had even thought possible. They learned how to build an aircraft that was lighter than the sum of its parts. Put another way, they designed a primitive gravity shield. The irony of it all was that the solution to the problem was far simpler than any of us suspected. It reduced the weight of an aircraft by 12 percent, and that was enough for our birds to take off from and land on surfaces that the laws of physics would otherwise have rendered too short. During limited tests of the shield, we easily broke Mach 5.2 at an altitude of 100,000 feet without breaking a sweat. The engines ran cool and purred like the happiest cats on earth. A little more tinkering was all we needed to create an orbital space plane. The fleet was duly commissioned and put into service. For these and other deeds, I was promoted to Wing Commander of the Dark Star stealth fleet.

And none too soon. Too many starving rogue states had been taken over by too many religious and political fanatics whose arsenals included decaying nuclear warheads smuggled from the former Soviet Union. As one would expect, these luminaries hadn't a clue as to the maintenance, deployment, or disposal of their new toys. The terrorist threats of these rogues were being met by constant saber rattling on the part of their otherwise stable but fearful neighbors. The slightest misstep, the slightest misunderstanding amidst all this brinkmanship could have sparked a nuclear war, and I had a feeling that we would be called into action before I finished training my people.

Sometimes being in charge really sucks.

THE ART OF WAR: winter 2022

Barbara found herself poised on the cusp separating vexation from boredom. Under the circumstances, neither alternative held any particular charms, so she focused on her breathing and pretended to be poring over the latest intelligence reports. The only thing that betrayed her labile mood was her persistent tapping of a pencil on a table around which sat the President, Vice President, the Secretary of Defense, the Air Force Chief of Staff, and mutually mistrustful emissaries from India and China. Barbara mused that a bomb well placed in this room could destabilize the government and the rest of the free world. As it was, the tension and mistrust in the room would have served just as well, and she fancied that the minute seismic waves spreading concentrically from her restless pencil could set off an earthquake guaranteed to bring them all down. She wondered if anyone on the outside would hear it.

Probably not.

And that was because they were 500 feet beneath the Pentagon in a war room impervious to nuclear, biological, and chemical weapons. In retrospect, the designers of this place were not as paranoid as they may have appeared at first. As is the case with all senescent empires, the collapse of the British Empire and the Soviet Union in the same century, within decades of each other, in fact, unleashed the power voids and ethnic instabilities that had brought them to this room. There seemed to be no end to the ideologues and fanatics who were more than happy to appropriate pieces of the wreckage. In recent years, the rogue states that rose from these ruins were becoming increasingly shrill, aggressive, and otherwise dangerous. Now that she thought of it, the war room was probably one of the safer places on earth to be hiding, especially in light of recent intelligence reports.

Well armed and powerful, the various political and religious factions in Pakistan, Tajikistan, Kashmir, and Nepal had formed a clandestine federation that comprised two sides of a triangle wedged between India and China. Enough threats and guerrilla attacks had been inflicted on both nations that they were massing troops along their common borders with an ill-defined plan to search out and destroy the offending parties. Where that would lead no one cared to predict.

Barbara set aside the reports and opened a copy of Sun Tzu's Art of War. It was her Bible and she took it with her everywhere. Opening it, she read randomly.

"TO OVERCOME OTHERS' ARMIES WITHOUT FIGHTING IS THE BEST OF SKILLS."

They were way beyond that. Every conceivable diplomatic and political solution had been tried and all of them had failed. The heads of state in these regions were clearly unable to control their own people and the status of women was again plummeting in the face of renewed radical fundamentalism. And yet the talking droned on. It had even infected this meeting. No one, it seemed, was willing to risk the first active step toward aborting a major war. Barbara had brought her best pilots and tactical officers with her on the increasingly unlikely chance that they would leave the meeting with a plan. The troops were getting restless.

She wanted to stand up and shriek at every politician in the room. It was all she could do to stay seated. Her backside was as numb has her brain. She looked up at the satellite-telemetry monitor that formed most of the wall opposite her seat. It displayed continually updated reports on the status of the disputed territory along with coded intelligence that only a few people in the room could decipher.

It also showed mountains. Lots of mountains. Much of the political wedge that had interposed itself between India and China spanned territories that were largely mountainous. It was a mixed blessing. Routing the insurgents from such terrain would be as dangerous as it would be difficult. But if they did fail, at least the mountains would form a natural barrier between India and China, making it difficult for the two nations to engage each other on the ground.

Barbara looked down at the book.

"ATTACK WHEN THEY ARE UNPREPARED, MAKE YOUR MOVE WHEN THEY DO NOT EXPECT IT."

The insurgents were moving leisurely through circuitous and remote mountain passes. It made them hard to attack. Hard but not impossible.

"WHEN YOU KNOW THE SKY AND EARTH, VICTORY IS INEXHAUSTIBLE."

It was her job to know the sky. She and her people were learning the earth. They could boast of being able to blow up a mailbox and back it up with pictures.

"TO UNFAILINGLY TAKE WHAT YOU ATTACK, ATTACK WERE THERE IS NO ATTACK."

A few more weeks and they would be able to do that.

"THOSE SKILLED AT THE UNORTHODOX ARE INFINITE AS HEAVEN AND EARTH, INEXHAUSTIBLE AS THE GREAT RIVERS. WHEN THEY COME TO AN END, THEY BEGIN AGAIN, LIKE THE DAYS AND MONTHS; THEY DIE AND ARE REBORN, LIKE THE FOUR SEASONS."

She and her people were nothing if not unorthodox. Down to a man, each pilot, each flight engineer had a streak of the devil in him. You could see it in their eyes. It was one of the secret criteria she used to recruit people.

Barbara looked up at the screen again and smiled at an irony that had just occurred to her. The people in the room were concerned about a clash between powers that were only a few decades old. But they were wrong. The conflict they were worried about had not been mounting for a mere a few decades. In a way, it had begun much, much earlier than that. One could argue that it had begun 225 million years ago when forces deep within the earth broke the primordial supercontinent of Pangaea into several continent-sized slabs whose wanderings have persisted into the present. India, with its 2 ½ billion-year-old bedrock foundation, was the first land mass to break away from Pangaea. It began traveling north, moving about twenty seven feet per century and dragging Sri Lanka haplessly behind it. One-hundred and eighty-five million years later, India rammed Eurasia and met its match. Neither yielded the fight. Thirty-million tortured years passed as the two Titans ground against each other. Then the rules of war changed. The ancient rock of India slid under the newer rock of Eurasia, undermining its crust. Casualties mounted as one stony warrior fell upon another, forming the five-mile-high Himalayas. It is a war that continues to this day and, as with the struggles among men, there is no end in sight.

Barbara smiled at the cosmic Trickster that had placed so many belligerent nations atop such piles of death. She found comfort in knowing that her concerns, as well as those of the people in the war room, were no more than dust devils flitting across a careworn land.

It was just a matter of perspective.

The fact that an irresistible force had just met an immovable object need not be overwhelming. It all came down to strategy and Barbara had long known which one would work. She knowingly riffled the pages of Sun Tzu's book until she found the passage that described perfectly what they must do.

"BE EXTREMELY SUBTLE, EVEN TO THE POINT OF FORMLESSNESS. BE EXTREMELY MYSTERIOUS, EVEN TO THE POINT OF SOUNDLESSNESS. THEREBY, YOU CAN BE THE DIRECTOR OF THE OPPONENT'S FATE."

Barbara looked up when she noticed a heavy silence crushing the room. The President caught her eye and nodded discreetly. Taking this as permission to assume control of the meeting, she rose and walked toward the telemetry monitor.

"Gentlemen. Now that we all understand the political crisis, we need to move on and assess our strategic options. Our operatives in the field, as well as our aerial intelligence teams, have detected clandestine movements among known terrorists toward the borders of Nepal. Thus far they have confined their movements to the high Himalayas between Tibet on the north and Nepal in the south. This makes them hard, but not impossible, to track."

Barbara walked toward the left end of the monitor.

"Insurgents have been entering Nepal from the northwest by two routes: from India by way of the Valley of Flowers National Park and the Lipu Lekh Pass; and from Tibet through the Namsê Pass. They are also crossing the northeastern borders from Tibet via the Ragba Pass."

As she spoke, Barbara tapped the monitor screen over the points of interest. Each time she did this, the view shifted to high-resolution renditions of the mountain passes.

"Judging by their movements, the insurgents suspect nothing. They are traveling at their leisure just south of the Northern Highlands and converging at a common point in the middle of the northern border, roughly here."

Barbara tapped the monitor over Annapurna. It revealed terrain practically inaccessible by overland routes. Its remoteness notwithstanding, the area hosted a cluster of buildings that looked like an obscure village. To knowing eyes, however, the buildings were far less benign.

"We have evidence that these buildings conceal an arms depot and manufacturing facility. It's all very crude, but it functions well enough for the terrorists to assemble biological, chemical, pyrotechnic, and tactical nuclear weapons from contraband components. The wonder of it all is that they haven't blown themselves up.

Barbara paused.

"Any questions?"

No one spoke. The delegates' renewed anxiety tacitly strengthened their brittle alliance against this faceless enemy. Barbara continued.

"We can destroy this facility. We can kill the insurgents en route. But this does not solve the problem. We still do not know who commands the operation and that is a serious liability. As long as that person is alive, he is a threat. We do, however, know that personnel and shipments of weapons are converging on Kathmandu. Thus far, none of this has left the city. We suspect that the staging area for the operation is somewhere within its environs."

The Chinese delegate spoke.

"Commander Llandry. We assume that you will neutralize the threats with which you are familiar. How do you propose to accomplish this?"

"That is classified, Mr. Ambassador," said Barbara.

The Ambassador pressed his point.

"But Commander, you're asking us to permit the passage through our air spaces of a secret military force whose lethality is unknown to us. Surely you understand that this is unacceptable."

The Chief of Staff, who had been quiet for most of the meeting, broke in.

"Ambassador, we certainly understand your concerns, but there are additional factors to consider. We are facing a threat that could easily escalate to an international conflict. We must therefore eliminate it with the utmost discretion. To this end, and for the sake of your own national security, the less you know, the safer you will be. No one must know how, when, or where the attacks will take place."

The delegates were only somewhat mollified. The President sensed it.

"Gentlemen, you have my word that we will make no unauthorized incursions within your respective territories. We will confine our actions to those goals enumerated up to and including this meeting. Those of you know who know me will also know that I never give my word on anything unless I know that I have the power to keep it."

The delegates murmured their assent.

"Well then," continued the President, "if there are no further questions or comments, I suggest that we all adjourn for today. Commander Llandry, I believe you have some work to do."

#

The weather over Nepal was dismal when the attacks began and stayed that way for the duration of the mission. This made high-altitude directed-energy weapons attacks imprecise and ineffectual, as the weather would have attenuated the weapons' outputs. The Spirits therefore had to effect low-altitude attacks, often barely skirting the mountain peaks that hid the terrorists so well. There were also times in which the pilots had to descend into steep valleys in order to kill their targets. The entire campaign resembled a high-speed video game written by a lunatic.

The SR-72 Spirits flew their sorties in groups of four each, and at no time was the entire fleet in the air. Each Spirit was equipped with side-looking radar, laser cannons, and directed particle-beam weapons. The flight crews maintained continuous contact with spy satellites parked in geosynchronous orbit over Nepal. The sorties confined their attacks to the western half of the country. Operatives on the ground were still tracking known suspects as they moved east in the hopes of locating the staging area within Kathmandu. Barbara led each sortie herself. When her superiors objected, she replied that she would not order inexperienced flight crews into the air on such intricate combat missions by themselves.

Most of the air strikes were impeccable. One moment a target was there and the next it was gone, its disappearance betrayed only by a few puffs of smoke and some scorched earth. No one heard or saw the Spirits approach and there was no one left to hear or see them leave. If nothing else, the attacks were in remote areas where rapid communication was somewhere between nil and nonexistent. Judging by their unharried movements, the surviving terrorists seemed clueless for the time being. In effect, Nepal was under attack and no one knew it.

But not all of the attacks were clean. There was the occasional hamlet, a remote farm, a rural market, that was mistargeted and vaporized by that most heartrending of oxymorons -- friendly fire. These deaths made themselves at home within Barbara's conscience and, like the proverbial man who came for dinner, had no intentions of leaving. Despite the fact that the civilian casualties were, by any military standard of reckoning, remarkably low, Barbara could not help but wonder whose parents-sons-daughters-friends-lovers-wives-husbands had been snuffed out by her mistakes. She had no qualms about killing the terrorists. But she shuddered to imagine people returning to their homes and families after an attack and finding instead patches of scorched earth where once they had built their lives. Their's would be the faces of shock, horror, denial, fear, mourning, desperation, and confusion. She wondered where they would go, what they would do, or even whether they would survive prolonged exposure to their unforgiving climate. It was not long before she realized that this guilt came with the burden of command.

They were two weeks into the campaign and the flight crews had yet to sustain any casualties worse than a paper cut. The Spirits outperformed themselves and morale was high. But any given crew only flew every three or four days. The only person in the sky every day was their commander and the Spirit she had nicknamed Tinkerbell. Barbara was the first to begin the unnervingly low-altitude strafing runs and the last to leave a target. She shepherded every Spirit back home, until the fifteenth day, when a shorthanded ground crew neglected to perform a few trivial maintenance checks on Tinkerbell's engines. The sortie was approaching a target 60 miles west of Kathmandu when a red light appeared on Tinkerbell's systems console.

"Hal, check out my starboard engine. I've got a fire light on," said Barbara.

"You look all right from here. No, wait! I see smoke," he said.

When in stealth mode, the Spirits were hard to see even at close range. At best, they were blurs. Their pilots got used to this and eventually became comfortable flying in tight formation behind the leader. When Hal looked out of his port window, all he saw was a black contrail coming from nowhere.

"Hal, I'm leaving you in charge. I'll shut her down and limp home," said Barbara.

"But Barbara..."

Hal never finished his objection. The Spirit's crippled engine ruptured its housing, ripping the starboard wing away from the fuselage. Tinkerbell plunged into an uncontrolled corkscrew dive.

"Major to Ground. We have..."

The ground people broke in.

"We're on it. Proceed to the target."

The sortie regrouped behind its new leader and flew on. Barbara reacted instantly and ejected at a point in the downward spiral where she would be assured of moving up. Otherwise, she would have hit the ground with the speed of a bullet. The ejection pod began transmitting a homing beacon that proved to be unnecessary, as rescue teams had already mobilized themselves and were making their way to the crash site. Barbara counted to three and transmitted a self-destruct signal to the dying Spirit. Tinkerbell disintegrated into pixie dust that soon dispersed among the foul-tempered winds. For perhaps a millisecond, she was amazed at the force of the shock wave that slammed her into a hillside and oblivion.

#

Barbara did not know if she was asleep or awake. Her sense of time, of place, of duration, had been trampled insensate by confusion. She was aware only of being in a tunnel. A long tunnel. Or maybe many short tunnels. Or maybe a labyrinth of short and long tunnels in some netherworld. The tunnels were black. But blacker still were the shadows that slithered everywhere around her, shadows that oozed pustulently from the walls, shadows that were obscene with cruelty and malice. She was groped. And beaten. She was forced into lewd postures. And beaten some more. Somehow she was forced into performing salacious movements. And beaten yet again. Fingers that could only have been playthings of the Devil felt their way along every part of her body, lusting in the darkness for access to her form-fitting flight suit. Finding none, the fingers seized her with bone-crushing hatred and tossed her like so much garbage into a windowless chamber. She tried to stand. She was trying to speak when a kick from a steel-toed boot to her diaphragm made the effort moot. She doubled over, suffocating, instinctively rolling into a fetal ball. She retched. She vomited. She gasped. She choked in a desperate attempt to breathe. All the while, a renewed hail storm of kicks and punches mocked her will to live. It no longer mattered whether she was asleep, if she was awake, or whether she was in a limbo somewhere between the two. Consciousness was a luxury she could no longer afford. She stepped off into a void whose remorseless nothingness swallowed her so completely that she might as well never have existed.

The hours passed — how many Barbara never knew. But eventually she heard a voice. A man's voice. Or was it a demon's? No matter. It was shrieking at the malicious shades who had so lavished her with their uniquely dubious brand of hospitality. The owner of the voice was making it abundantly clear that if the prisoner died he would personally flay each of them alive. And slowly. Judging by the cowed and obsequious murmurs of apology that fouled the air, she got the impression that he had made good on that threat in the past. She again sank back into the dark.

When next she was aware of anything, Barbara found herself resting on a bed of angel wings in an empty white space. Beings of golden light tended her wounds. She settled deeper into the bed and was falling into a healing sleep when something poked her in the shoulder. She shifted in the bed and felt another poke, this time in her ribs. Everything around her faded to black, and again the same dilemma presented itself. Was she awake or was she still asleep? Again the point seemed moot. Whatever the answer she

could at least try to move. She did and
was rewarded for her efforts by salvos
of pain from every part of her body.
She fell back to the floor. Or was it a
floor? Groping around, her hands closed
about a hard, curved object that felt
for all the world like a rib. She felt
around some more. Another rib. A
fractured pelvis. A thigh bone. And
finally something smooth and bulbous and
with a piece of somebody's face attached
to it. She dropped the thing when she
realized that she had been tossed onto a
pile of bones. Fortunately or not,
Barbara did not have much time to assess
her situation. Two pairs of arms
emerged from the darkness and wrenched
her upright by the shoulders. They were
not kind arms.

#

He lived in the darkness. Or rather,
as he often mused, he lived for the
darkness. He traveled in it. He
forever sought new dark places in whose
deeps he could orchestrate his campaigns
of random terror. He also coveted dark
places because in them was he best able
to nurse his contempt for essentially
everything. Hate was his religion and
Satan his only god. His was a gospel of
chaos and fear and he their most fervent
evangelist. Tyrants and fanatics the
world over were but his lieutenants in
an invisible holy war. He rewarded them
lavishly for their efforts and loyalty.
And he punished them just as lavishly
when he saw the need.

He had no name, or at least none that anyone knew of. His most intimate co-conspirators — he had no friends as such — were always at a loss as to how he should be addressed, so they fell back on the usual pronouns: you, he, him, his, and it, the latter being studiously avoided in his presence. It was a clever ploy. People with no names are hard to track. They have an annoying habit of leaving no records behind them.

He especially loved his current lair. It was perfect in so many satisfying ways. Considered only as a point on a map, it could not have been more obvious. It was in the busiest part of Kathmandu, just under the Baudhanath stupa in fact, and radiated from there in all directions. But it was deep. Very deep. The engineers who, centuries ago, laid the stupa's foundations never unearthed it and neither, it seemed, had anybody else. The place had lain unmolested for more centuries than he could count, had he been so inclined, which he was not.

And best of all, the place was a mass grave, a catacomb fashioned from a vast network of caves by a civilization so antique that, were it to be discovered, would push human history further back than anyone would have thought possible. The entire complex was replete with inscriptions and statues, all of them intact, but he was not interested in them. Instead, he relished the irony of all the Tibetan Buddhists directly overhead of him worshiping at the stupa, oblivious to the fact that Death had established its kingdom right beneath their feet.

He received few visitors, which under the circumstances was not hard to explain, and so he was understandably curious about the giant woman who his minions had pulled from an odd piece of wreckage. Upon hearing that she was more or less awake, he ordered that she be brought before him. The chastised shadows were only too anxious to comply.

#

Barbara did her best to bear up under the dead weight of her pummeled body, but pain eventually got the better of her. By the time she was dropped onto a stool, she was little more than a lurching corpse. She staved off unconsciousness by repeating to herself, as if it were a mantra, that the typical interrogator needed to keep his captive confused to the point of psychosis — but not so confused that useful information could not be culled from him. So important was the maintenance of this useful torpor that its subtleties have been elevated to high art in certain low places. Barbara still knew that she was confused, and this gave her at least one advantage. But she was so thoroughly drained that keeping silence was the only stratagem that she could devise. If she were dreaming, her silence would make no difference; if she were awake that selfsame silence could literally make all the difference in the world. The challenge was to play the game long enough for her people to complete their mission.

Barbara was startled into something like wakefulness when she heard someone address her in the hissing whispers of what could only have been a cultured snake. She squinted through the charnel air and saw a pair of lips attached to a skull. They paused in mid-breath and then resumed.

"Well, Missy, you're awake. I trust that our amenities are to your liking?"

Barbara started to say something sarcastic but thought the better of it. He continued.

"We receive so few visitors here that your unannounced arrival is quite surprising. And mysterious. Might I prevail on you to enlighten us?"

Despite the torpor that muddled her every thought, Barbara realized that the talking skull was affixed to a living skeleton of a man. His clothes hung from him like funeral shrouds. His eyes were two guillotines that she dared not engage for too long. She shrugged her shoulders diffidently.

"I'm not all that interesting," she barely said through her cut and swollen lips.

"Ah, but I beg to differ. I'll wager that you know all kinds of interesting things. The very fact of our meeting like this has raised more eyebrows around here than mine. Here you sit in a pressurized flight suit. To my knowledge, high-tech women's wear is passe this year. And then there's the matter of the ejection pod in which we found you. Its design is unlike anything we've ever seen. We don't even know what it's made of. And it's so light!"

As he spoke, he scrutinized Barbara minutely, alert to the slightest hint of affirmation or denial in her demeanor. Finding none, he went on.

"And if all this were not sufficient cause for curiosity, there is the matter of why you were in an ejection pod in the first place. There was no wreckage in the vicinity of your crash site. We have no intelligence regarding low- or high-altitude flyovers. There is no military activity in this region beyond the massing of ill-equipped troops along the Sino-Nepalese borders, but we have been aware of that for some time. And yet here you are, fallen from the sky, an enigma to us all. We have disassembled your ejection pod, hoping to find a clue as to where you and it have come from, and again we have come up short. Why, even your flight suit has no indication of who and what you are. This means to me that you and your superiors have something to hide. Please, at least tell us your name, so that we may address you properly during our next meeting."

Barbara for the first time looked directly at him. He instantly detested her eyes. He hated their blueness, their quiet intensity, their mute proclamation of intelligence. He hated her. She mustered as much composure has her pain, hunger, and exhaustion would permit and spoke for a second time.

"I have no name."

His obvious surprise at this response embarrassed him. No one had ever answered him that way. For the briefest of moments he was off-balance. It seldom happened to him and he had to take a long, deep breath to regain his center.

"Our guest has spoken yet again! And despite herself she has told me something. She is an American. An American pilot flying a mysterious aircraft on a secret mission over an unstable part of the world. She has obviously been sworn to the utmost secrecy. Otherwise, she would not be willing to endure our hospitality. And best of all she has no name! People with no names know many valuable things and invariably know many important people. This suggests that our guest is herself a very important person. Perhaps she is a first-rate engineer. Or maybe a mathematician. Or a scientist. Or maybe all three. This is not important to us. What is important is that she is invaluable to her superiors. They will spare no effort in retrieving her. They might even be persuaded to make substantial concessions to this end. Their need for secrecy will make them easy to blackmail. I thank you so very much, mystery woman! You have given me no end of things to think about. By the way, are you offended by my referring to you in the third person?"

No answer.

"I'll take that as a no."

He rose to leave and then stopped himself, as if suddenly remembering something.

"It just occurred to me that you'll want some facilities for attending to your private feminine needs."

He nodded to one of the many shadows that always seemed to hover around him. It disappeared briefly and returned with a bucket.

"Please, feel free to relieve yourself."

Humiliation, especially of women, especially in that part of the world, was a common psychological torture and Barbara knew it. She also knew that her bladder was about to rupture. Taking the bucket, she set it on the floor and began loosening her flight suit. The shadows gloated over her every move. She had become the subject of a peep show. The sickly light which, a moment before, had invested everyone in the room with a safe, dusty obscurity, now brightened obscenely to tease the eyes of the shadows that swarmed around her with their prurient malice.

Barbara had to peel the flight suit down to her thighs before she could sit on the bucket and urinate. With each patch of skin revealed, the more the silence in the room festered. When finally she was able to start a stream, it pounded against the sides of the pail like the wrath of God, so total was the stillness around her.

No one moved. No one dared break the spell that held them in its salacious grip. No one, that is, except Barbara. She stood and dressed faster than she ever thought possible. Her tormentors rose.

"Well, Missy must feel like a new woman! How about some water? A pretty thing such as you must be desperate to spruce herself up. At the risk of being indelicate, I suggest that you do something about your hair. A good rinse perhaps?"

So saying, he nodded at the shadow who had brought the bucket. It padded its way to Barbara's side, at which point it picked up the pail and dumped it over her head. While she sputtered and clawed the hair away from the eyes, her nemesis rose and bowed with consummate aplomb.

"I look forward to our next appointment. But I must leave you for now. I have many things to accomplish before then."

So saying, he slithered from the room.

#

Barbara was dragged from the room and tossed onto the pile of bones on which she had awakened earlier. She lay still, not daring to move. From out of her festering confusion rose the image of a night many years ago when she lay sprawled on her back, the bones of a dead motorcycle strewn along the asphalt behind her like a giant smear. Looking up at the stars that night, she realized that death was a cakewalk, a mere stepping-off point. Barbara held onto that thought and somehow fell asleep.

Hours passed. How many she could not know, there being no way to mark time in a place that detested the sun. When finally she awoke, it was to a fit of hacking, choking, and retching. Something was swelling in her throat. In the space of a breath, it sealed her windpipe, quietly, but with the charnel finality of a tomb being sealed for the last time. She propped herself on one elbow but collapsed with the effort. A darkness deeper than anything she had ever imagined closed around her. She saw her own body rotting into anonymity. Skeletons rose from the bones scattered about. They joined hands and clattered around her in a macabre dance, all the while mocking her agony with their cynical pantomimes. The last of them had danced its way into the moldering darkness when Barbara's will to live gathered itself for one final assault on death. Her fractured ribs ground against one another with spasms that ejected a blood clot from her throat with the fury of a cannon. She devoured the air even as she hacked up no end of phlegm and blood.

When finally the ordeal subsided, Barbara noticed that someone had left a small loaf of bread and a mug of foul-smelling tea beside her. Her hosts evidently did not want her to starve to death. At least not yet. She was reaching for the loaf when the usual assortment of arms materialized and grabbed her with a malevolence unusual even for them. They shackled her hands and feet and hoisted her onto their unkind shoulders. After the usual labyrinthine journey, she was set down on a chair in front of the ghoul that inspired no end of fear among his minions. Barbara hardly recognize him.

Gone was his veneer of mock civility. The real man lay exposed to her in all of his necrotic rage. He rose from his desk and lurched toward her.

"Well, Missy, it seems that secrets are drawn to you like flies to shit! My people have exhausted their considerable talents in trying to find out who you are. And guess what? As far as they can tell, you do not exist. And need I add that whatever it is that you fly doesn't exist either? But I'm sure you know that. And many other things."

He paused to take a long, malicious breath.

"And there's more. Oh yes! So much more. All our operations west and the northeast of here have stopped. My observers tell me that entire facilities are gone. All that's left of them are scraps of scorched earth. There have been no signs of violence. No unusual aircraft sightings. In fact the skies are quiet. And yet we are under heavy attack."

He bent over until his face was inches away from Barbara's.

"Who are you?"

No answer.

"Who are you?"

Silence.

"Damn you, woman, who are you!"

This last he articulated more as a threat than as a question. He rose and walked back to his desk. He motioned to someone in the shadows who strode calmly into the light.

"There's someone here that I want you to meet. Missy, this is Mr. Homng. Mr. Homng, this is a mystery. A mystery that I want you to crack open."

The stranger looked at Barbara as if she were already dead.

"Mr. Homng is an artist — an artist much in demand in our circles. By way of introduction, let me just say that Mr. Homng has forgotten more about the art of inflicting pain than you or I will ever know."

Homng walked up to Barbara and began probing her right shoulder. Within seconds, she was paralyzed from the waist on down. The probing continued. When he found what he was looking for, he twisted her arm in a way she would have thought to be anatomically impossible and neatly dislocated it. Barbara was so shocked at what he had so unceremoniously done that it took a few seconds for her to register the pain. By then, he was working on her left shoulder. Again he twisted her arm out of joint, only this time with an added yank. For the first time since her capture, Barbara screamed. Homng nodded as if satisfied with his work. He produced a length of crude hemp rope and lashed her arms to the back of the chair, all the while watching her intently. The renewed onslaught of pain beggared her capacity to scream. Homng loosened the rope slightly when she showed signs of blacking out. Barbara had to be conscious or there would be no point to the torture. He secured the rope with a knot contrived to dig through her wrists every time she struggled. Homng stepped away from the chair.

Her host, in the meantime, had settled himself behind the desk, gloating all while as if watching a strip tease. When his colleague was finished, he rose and addressed Barbara.

"Well, Missy, I trust that you are now as impressed with Mr. Homng's skills as I am. But should you be entertaining any doubts to this end, believe me when I say that you haven't seen anything yet. There is so much more yet to come."

He paused for dramatic effect.

"So what shall we talk about? Hmm? You might introduce yourself. It would put us on a more cordial footing. How about it?"

No answer.

"You are proving to be the rudest excuse for a human being that I have ever met. I am a patient man, Missy, but even I am getting sick of you. Perhaps this will loosen you up."

So saying, he produced a glass object from his robes.

"This is no 3-minute egg timer. This is an honest-to-god hourglass, and you are about to experience just how long an hour can be, grain by bitter grain. And to make your experience as complete as possible, Mr. Homng will provide you with a visual aid. Mr. Homng?"

The man bent over Barbara's face. Two large safety pins nestled in one corner of his mouth. And then, with the professional detachment of a tailor marking alterations to a new suit, he pierced each eyelid clean through and then secured them to her eyebrows. Tears of blood flooded her cheeks, pooled in the corners of her mouth, formed rivulets down her neck and, like so many probing fingers, disappeared into her flight suit, a fact that was not lost on her captor's salacious fancy. He inverted the hourglass and placed it on the desk in front of her.

"Enjoy, Missy. Thank you, Mr. Homng. You may leave for the next hour." Homng withdrew to wherever it was that persons of his ilk passed their free time in that mass grave. "He" then went about his business as if Barbara were not there. People came and went. He issued orders and held conversations in languages she did not recognize. Occasionally, he screamed at someone. She was left in a rictus of pain that made screaming irrelevant. The pain that was rooting its way cell-by-cell through her body made the effort of screaming an extravagant waste of energy. The point was moot anyway, there being nothing that could begin to voice her agony. And then there was the forced contemplation of the hourglass. Each hateful grain took its time passing through the strangled neck of the hour glass and fell, as if in slow motion, to a bottom that seemed never to fill.

The hourglass captured her thoughts and held them up to her mind's eye. It forced memories, the wrong kind of memories, upon her. Such as the time she first learned about bounded infinities — two points in space connected by a line of infinitely many intervening points. The endpoints are there. They can be measured. But once within the chasm separating the two there is no way out when the closest of points themselves become maws that swallow the points between them ad infinitum. Pain was a lot like that. Only worse.

There was nothing left but to yield and wait. Let time dilate to the limits of her endurance. Let it go beyond them. Nothing was to be done until her captors saw fit to release her, which they did after the specified hour had passed. She felt Homng enter the room. At a nod from "him", Homng removed the safety pins from Barbara's eyes with the same unnerving detachment that he had displayed before. He released the nerve block to her legs and reset her shoulders. Had she not been shackled to the chair, she would have been tempted to kill the man with the same detachment that he was using to ruin her body. The exquisite irony of it all would have been worth her probable death. Her captor looked up from the desk.

"I see that we are as good as new. A penny for your thoughts?"

Barbara looked at him as best she could through her bloated eyelids.

"You'll have to do a lot better than that," she said.

He laughed, if the howling of a jackal can be so construed.

"The poor child! She labors under the misapprehension that she is in a position to bargain with me. I suggest that she check and see who is in shackles and who is not."

He was cut short by a lackey who entered the room with the air of someone who expects to be beheaded as the bearer of bad tidings. The man spoke furtively to him for several minutes. As the man conveyed the apparently bad news, "he" took his eyes off Barbara's face and stared through the walls as if scrutinizing something 1000 miles away. A slight trembling around his mouth was the only thing that betrayed his rage at the news. Dismissing the man, he returned his attention to Barbara with a renewed sense of menace. He got up from the desk and stood before her. She was shocked that what he did next.

He extended his dead hands and, for another seeming eternity, caressed her face with fingers whose studied incapacity for feeling mocked everything they touched. The ordeal was as humiliating in its own way as everything that had gone before. And if the experience were not surreal enough, he started crooning over her.

"...pretty girl...such a pretty, pretty girl...her face...so smooth, so soft, so nice to touch...your fancy soldier boys must swoon over you...but my pretty baby must be grouchy today...won't even tell me her name...bad girl...naughty girl...bad, bad, naughty little girl...she must be punished." So saying, he stepped back and slapped Barbara in the face, over and over again, with a fury that would not be slaked until he had ripped her face off. Checking himself, he stepped aside and motioned for Homng to take his place.

"Missy, your life is about to change irrevocably. And for the worse, I might add. Among Mr. Homng's repertoire of skills is a little-known ordeal called

"The Death of a Thousand Cuts". It was practiced in China hundreds of years ago, but has fallen into disuse in these enlightened times. It is always a special treat for me to watch Mr. Homng display this facet of his craft. Mr. Homng, considering our subject for today, might I suggest that we begin with Missy's face?"

Homng bowed and opened a leather pouch filled with an array of finely machined steel tools. Each of them was designed to cut through skin and muscle in ways calculated to heighten both the victim's agony and the pleasure of any suitably predisposed onlookers. He forced her head back and began with her cheeks. Blood pooled in her eyes and puddled on the floor around the chair. It was not until Homng changed instruments and set to work on her forehead that Barbara came to a sickening realization.

She had no idea of how long she had been a prisoner. For all she knew, it might have been days. If the mission's security had been breached and public disclosure was imminent, then the President might be forced to disavow her existence in the interest of aborting a major war. If that were the case, she was expendable. Her life, with all of its striving and all of its aspirations, would have amounted to nothing but a shred of cannon fodder trampled underfoot. If her captors also suspected this, then they were just amusing themselves with her. She prayed to her guardian angels, imploring them to come and lead her to that stepping-off point where she would never have to suffer again.

Barbara was in too much pain to realize that she was mouthing the words of her prayers, and that the words themselves were spattering blood into the faces of her tormentors. Homng paused in his work so that "he" could hear what she was saying. He soon rose in contempt.

"The bitch is praying to her pitiful little gods! We're getting nowhere with her. Raise her head so she can see me." Homng complied.

"You've reached the end of the line, Missy! I have no more time to waste on you. You've one last chance to tell me who you are or I'll leave you to Mr. Homng's tender ministrations. Well? How about it?"

Barbara looked up with the last of her strength and started to speak. She stopped and resumed her prayers.

"Fine! I leave you at the gates of Hell! Mr. Homng, I suggest that you begin the execution by pulling the wretch's eyes out."

He paused, as if struck by a novel idea.

"Indulge me, Mr. Homng. It might be easier to pull her eyes out if the lids are first removed. May I?"

Homng handed him a suitable blade. He bent over Barbara with the starving malice of a spider preparing to suck the life out of its hapless prey. He had begun the first cut when a series of queer popping sounds distracted him and he stood up, the better to hear what was happening.

Just then, a door off to one side of the room splintered under the force of a battering ram. Men wearing the black fatigues of the Marine Corps special forces flooded the room. "He" had barely realized what was happening when a wet red dot formed between his eyes. He seemed surprised, but only for a moment. Blood spewed from the dot. He slumped onto the ground, motionless, and never hurt anyone again.

Among the soldiers was a team of medics that stayed behind while the others pressed on with the attack. They freed her from the chair, laid her on a stretcher, and implemented emergency life-support, all the while trotting down the maze of corridors that ended in some abandoned sewers outside of the city. Another escort awaited them. Amid a flurry of whispered orders and rapid-fire consultations, Barbara was handed over to another team of medics who took her to a waiting helicopter. The first team re-entered the maze with a fresh escort. They had reason to believe that the catacombs held many hostages who had suffered at least as horribly as she.

Overhead, the citizens of Kathmandu went about their business, unaware of the legions of demons who had perpetrated so many horrors for so many years just beneath their feet.

#

Barbara had sustained too many assaults on her mind and body to be at all lucid during the hours that followed. Occasionally, she caught a word or phrase from the Babel of voices that seemed always to surround her: morphine...blood loss...shock...vitals ...fractures...ruptured spleen...God, look at her face...These shards of awareness did little more than ruffle an otherwise healing rest. Some hours after her rescue, Barbara felt herself being lowered into a warm bath. Kind hands washed away the filth of her imprisonment and bundled her in a soft bed. All the while, the drone of aircraft engines soothed her with their white noise into a sleep deeper than any she had ever known.

When next she was aware of anything, Barbara heard voices — voices that seemed to come from the far end of a tunnel. She knew one of them, but was too exhausted to place it with a familiar face. It was a voice that belonged to someone accustomed to giving orders that were instantly obeyed.

"Wake her up."

Barbara felt the sting of a needle in her shoulder, followed shortly by an awakening that she would always remember as a second birth. She looked up. The voice belonged to the President.

"Uh...Mr. President?"

"Welcome home, Barbara."

"Where am I?" she asked.

"Out of harm's way," he answered, "in Walter Reed Hospital."

From the moment she first met him, Barbara liked her commander-in-chief. He was, in her judgment, the only leader in the Free World with a spine and the integrity to keep it straight.

"I won't keep you, Barbara," he said. "A lot of people have been holding vigils by your bed ever since you got here. They're anxious to see you. But before I go, there are some things you need to know. First off, your mission was more successful than any of us dared to hope. Your crews performed brilliantly. Other than you, there were no casualties. Our security is still intact. No one anywhere suspects anything. And then there's the matter of your capture. You were a prisoner for four days. If you had snapped at any time, we would never have completed the mission and you would be dead now. The terrorists who held you were better connected than we suspected. We're finally in a position to break some of the most lethal insurrectionists in the world."

The President paused and removed a small box from his suit.

"Here's a little something you can wear around your neck for Halloween or whatever."

He placed the box in Barbara's hands. As she opened it, rays of golden light dotted the walls behind her bed. She removed the Medal of Honor from the box and held it up to the light. For the first time in her life, words failed her. The President stepped into the breach.

"I wish we could be more public about this, but at least the people who count know what you've done."

"But Mr. President, I didn't even finish the mission," said Barbara.

"Your people finished it for you. And I don't mind saying that you've trained some of the finest pilots we've ever seen. They've all received commendations commensurate to their accomplishments," he said.

"Thank you, sir, that means a lot to me," she replied.

"You're welcome," he said. "There's one more thing. We are relieving you of command and sending you on an extended leave."

Barbara looked at him guardedly, unsure what to say.

"Don't worry," he assured her, "we're not sending you out to pasture. You've taken a beating and we'll need some time to put you back together. You'll need to be better than new, actually. We're offering you a job."

"What kind of a job?"

"How about commanding the Argo on her first manned mission to Mars?"

The President made the offer so casually that Barbara thought he was kidding.

"How...how did you know about work on the Argo, sir?"

He laughed.

"It's the biggest goddamned thing in orbit! Besides, I've been helping your bosses with their creative bookkeeping for most of my career," he said.

"You're behind us?" asked Barbara with a mixture of disbelief and joy.

"Yes, but don't tell anybody. My feeling is that if we don't get our sweet asses off this planet soon, we'll all die one way or another," he confessed.

"That's how my grandfather sees it," said Barbara.

"I know," said the President, "we've often spoken of it."

"You know him?"

"You bet. He's the smartest man I've ever known. We've been doing business for years. I have a passion for fine cloisonne, and as far as I'm concerned he's The Man."

"It's funny," said Barbara, "he's never mentioned you."

"Richard Llandry is the heart and soul of discretion. That's why he's so well-connected. People know they can trust him with anything."

The President rose.

"Speaking of your grandfather, he's first on the list of people waiting to see you. I'll be off for now. Thanks to you I have a few dragons to slay before dinner."

The President walked toward the door, and then stopped.

"By the way, Commander, you haven't formally accepted our offer."

Barbara smiled. "Sure."

The President nodded and, surrounded by a flurry of Secret Service agents, left the room. Barbara closed her eyes and settled back into the pillow. She inhaled deeply, relishing the simple pleasure of breathing without pain. She went on like that until a quiet voice lent its cadence to the rhythm of her breathing.

"Hey there, Pookie, you're looking well today."

Barbara tried to rise from the bed, but collapsed with the effort.

"Hey, Grandpa!"

The familiar whisper of velvet curtains rustling in the breeze was soon followed by the settling of a well-loved presence onto the mattress. Richard reached out and stroked her hair exactly as he had done countless times during her childhood. It was a balm that soothed the worst of wounds; it was a warm bath for the heart.

"Don't get up, sweetie. Your hosts were somewhat less than hospitable."

Barbara looked up at her grandfather. His face bore mute witness to the anxiety, relief, pride, love, and fatigue that had held him in their thrall during the last week.

"How long you been here, Grandpa?"

"Since they brought you hear a couple days ago," he replied.

Barbara started to speak, but Richard silenced her with a touch to her lips.

"Don't talk. I just wanted to be here when they woke you up. Get some rest. I've arranged to have dinner with some friends. I'll come back later. If you're awake, we can commune with the spirits."

"OK," said Barbara. But before you go. I didn't know that you and the President were tight."

"Let's just say that I have some dear friends in," he paused, "in strange places. I should be going now, so I'll turn you over to someone who's managed to keep her mouth shut for an impressive span of time."

Richard kissed the bandages covering Barbara's forehead, rose, and left the room.

"Hey, girl, you really know how to piss people off."

Linda's disobedient blond curls filled Barbara's field of view.

"Hey there, Captain! Don't you have something to bomb?" said Barbara.

"Nope. The world has had enough of me for the moment. Besides, you left Hal Major in command. Don't you remember?" said Linda.

"Oh yeah...I guess I did. How's he doing?" asked Barbara.

"Well, he hasn't started any wars that I know of," replied Linda.

"That's a relief," said Barbara.

"I'd say it's stinkin' wonderful," said Linda. "He picked up where you left off and led all the remaining sorties himself. You'd have thought that the-son-of-a-bitch was on a holy war. He didn't call off the strikes until every last target was toast. If you want my opinion, the man was avenging your capture. In his own shy away, Hal's really very gallant."

"What's that supposed to mean?" asked Barbara.

"Oh God, girl," exclaimed Linda. "Are you stupid <u>and</u> blind? The man's got a serious crush on you. He's just too honorable to come on to a superior officer. That's your job."

"I guess I am a little dense," said Barbara, "he'd be just what the doctor ordered right now."

Linda became serious. She shook the hair out of her face and looked squarely into Barbara's eyes.

"OK. The dust is settled and you're a hero. Now how do you feel? I mean really. Come on, 'fess up," said Linda.

"I feel like shit," replied Barbara. "And I don't want to be in charge of everything for a while. What I really need is to snuggle up with a warm body and be fussed over."

Linda smirked. "I could make a few calls..."

"Don't you dare," exclaimed Barbara, "I don't want him to see me like this!"

"Darlin'," said Linda, "you could be a hunchbacked troll and Hal Major would still want you."

At that, Barbara touched the bandages on her face. Linda instantly regretted her faux pas. Tears welled in her eyes.

"Oh Jesus, Barbara! I didn't mean it that way."

Barbara pulled Linda down and hugged her.

"It's all right Linda. Your mouth has been outwitting your brain for years. Everyone who knows you knows that."

Linda sat up. Her cheeks were soaked. Barbara handed her a box of Kleenex.

"Here. Your eyeliner's bleeding all over your face."

Barbara lay quietly while Linda pulled herself together.

"Uh, Linda...now that we're on the subject, have you heard anything about my face?"

"You mean are you going to be as ugly as you always were?" quipped Linda.

"Something like that," said Barbara.

"Well, the word on the street is that they brought in the best of the best to put you back together," said Linda, "and I hear they even went ahead and made a few improvements. You'll be fine."

"That's good," said Barbara, somewhat relieved. "I hate to admit it, but I've always been a little conceited about my looks. I tell myself that it's just an accident of birth...but I just can't help feeling smug about the way men look at me."

"Well kid, it's like they say: make hay while the sun shines. If I had your body, I'd have gone straight into modeling. I'd rather have guys with cameras shooting me than guys with bullets."

They sat quietly together for some moments. Linda spoke first.

"Barbara, did you know that you were being held in a catacomb?"

"I figured it was something like that," answered Barbara. "I slept on a pile of bones for four days. What about it?"

Linda moved closer to Barbara and spoke in a conspiratorial stage whisper.

"Well, it took a long time for the Special Forces guys to flush all the low-life out of their holes. It turns out that the place is huge. The rooms were hollowed out from the chambers of a network of caves. They still haven't reached the end of them. The terrorists used only a few of the rooms."

Linda shifted her weight on the bed.

"So anyway, after the bullets stopped flying, the guys noticed that a lot of the walls were covered with inscriptions and weird artwork. And then they noticed the bones. They looked human enough, but they were a little weird too. A few of the guys rummaged around until they found a few decent skulls. After the mission, they passed the stuff along to the forensics team. Last I heard, the eggheads in the lab flipped out. They've sealed off the catacombs tighter than a crab's ass. Teams of geologists, spelunkers, anthropologists, archeologists, and historians have been sworn to secrecy and sent to explore the place. Since then, there's been a news blackout. There isn't even any reliable gossip."

Does Grandpa know anything about this?" asked Barbara.

"Nope. At least that's what he says. I used all my womanly wiles on him to get some gossip but nothing worked," said Linda.

"Well," surmised Barbara, "if it's that important, you can bet we're not going to hear anything about it for a few years yet."

"No, I guess not," admitted Linda. She chortled and added, "Only you could fall ass-backward onto a major discovery."

"I don't see that I had any choice in the matter," said Barbara.

"Maybe you did and maybe you didn't," countered Linda. "I guess we'll never know."

BUTTERFLIES IN THE RAIN: summer 2022

The months that followed more than vindicated Linda's confidence in Barbara's physicians. June found her running ten miles a day and excelling in a body building program. It was a sweaty, locker-room life that helped her, for a time, to forget that she had been violated. The subsidence of those days into forgetful waters had their tonic effect. The filth of her torture and molestation lifted away from her spirit and moved on to places where it could be dealt with and left behind.

Richard wrote often to her. His letters revived memories of when life was good, and assured her that life would again be good. Without intending it, his gossip about Jake's Mule Barn, his news about Herb and Sarah, and his musings about art, beauty, business, and money gently convinced her that evil is simply a phantasm arising from greed, hatred, and ignorance. But his letters also disturbed her with their intimations of a fatigue that had settled into his bones and had no intention of leaving. And then one day, early in June, came a letter in which Richard confessed that he had been diagnosed with aplastic anemia some months earlier. It had stymied every attempt at treatment. He asked if she could come home for a while.

#

Barbara paused in front of the house. To her left stood the maple tree that had so challenged her childhood. To her right the cob house and the well-tended garden were as they had always been. The grass retained its springtime sheen. And in between stood the house, perennially fresh and strong. To look at it, it could have been just another summer day in Milton, Iowa. She would not have been surprised to see a couple of motorcycles parked on the grass. She half expected to smell bacon frying on the stove. But this was not an ordinary day. There were no motorcycles parked on the lawn and there was no bacon frying on the stove. The spirit that had made it all so real was preparing to take leave of the life that it had so munificently lived. With a clarity that brooked no rebuttal, Barbara knew that her first step onto the front porch would consign all that life to memory and dust. She stood on the grass. She implored her feet to sprout roots and anchor her in that moment, in that morsel of time in which the memories could still be revived and made to move

273

on with her to the future. But that was a delusion and she knew it.

Barbara climbed the steps to the front porch and opened the screen door. It yielded with its usual creaky protests, and she stepped into the parlor. She let go of the door. It closed with a thunk that she knew intimately, only this time it had the character of a coffin lid being sealed for good. At that moment, she felt another of her ghosts peel away and make its way to Jake's Mule Barn for a very long poker game.

The musk of fine old furniture, of leather, of wool, of silk, of old paintings had been sullied by the cheap cologne of an unnatural cleanliness. A day nurse greeted Barbara with a plastic smile and led her to Richard's office. He had converted it into a sick room. The Isfahan carpets lay rolled up against the walls. Rare art was jumbled in odd corners. Everything had been obliged to make way for disease and death. Even Richard's desk had been pushed aside to accommodate a hospital bed.

All of this became trivial compared to Barbara's shock upon seeing the figure in the bed. Her first impression was that Richard had gotten up to bathe or something. But what she at first mistook for crumpled sheets and blankets resolved itself into the forms of legs, torso, arms, hands, and feet — all of them so emaciated it was hard to believe that they could sustain themselves, let alone the life that somehow persisted in clinging to them. Worst of all was that the figure had no head, or so it seemed to Barbara's flustered eyes. Again, what she had first mistaken for wrinkles in the bedclothes organized themselves into disheveled hair, a neglected goatee, and the contours of a handsome face whose starving skin was as white as the linen around it. The figure breathed slowly, so slowly that Barbara herself felt faint just watching the barely perceptible undulations of the sheets.

Barbara sat by the bed and settled down for a patient vigil that proved to be unnecessary. The figure quickened, as if responding to a subtle perception. It's breathing deepened. The contours of the blanket shifted to accommodate the figure's movements. Everything became human when the figure opened its eyes. They were lucid, and kind, and blue in a way that belonged only to Richard Llandry.

"Hey, Pookie! Glad you could stop by."

"Hi, Grandpa. You know I wouldn't be anywhere else."

Richard moved again. A whisper of color suffused his face.

"Hot damn, girl! I haven't felt this good in days. I bet you have this effect on all the boys."

"No, Grandpa, only you," said Barbara.

Richard chuckled.

"Oh, I bet if you looked around you'd see more than one heart start racing when you walk into a room."

Barbara looked down and smiled.

"Will you look at that! I made the High Commander blush!"

"You did not! And that's Wing Commander, not High Commander," said Barbara in the sassiest voice she could muster under the circumstances.

"Whatever," said Richard dismissively. "All I know is that you fly the biggest, baddest combat birds in this or any other world."

Richard had not talked so much in several weeks and he had to catch his breath. Barbara started to apologize, but the old man stopped her with whispered assurances to the contrary. She sat quietly while Richard took a nap. She felt the house waiting forbearingly with her. As the day waned, so did the house's grumbling against the heat. It settled into another summer night's rest, awaiting the dreams that haunted its many rooms. Barbara dismissed the nurse, intent on looking after Richard herself.

It was not long before the only sound in the house was the well-worn chiming of the grandfather clock in another room as it intoned the passing hours. Richard awoke when the chimes pealed six o'clock. He saw that Barbara was still beside him. She had dozed off under the subdued light of the reading lamp. To look at her, one would never suspect the troubles she had seen. The only thing that belied her composure at that moment was a tangle of fine white scars that covered her face like the web of a mad spider. Their grotesquery, seen against Barbara's unaffected natural beauty, made her all the more ravishing. Richard's reflections ended when Barbara somnolently twitched her nose and pawed at it. She twitched again and awoke to the sight of Richard staring at her.

"Oh man, I must have fallen asleep," she muttered.

"So it would seem," said Richard.

"How long have I been out?" asked Barbara.

"I don't know. I just woke up myself, but I did hear the clock ring six."

Barbara stretched and sat up.

"Is there anything I can do, Grandpa? Are you hungry?" asked Barbara.

Richard gestured toward an empty can sitting on a tray table.

"They only let me have that high-protein, high-calorie sludge," he said.

Barbara walked over to the table and sniffed the can.

"Yuck! They call this food?"

"That's the prevailing wisdom," said Richard, "but since they're not here and you are, there's a pound of bacon in the fridge. Fry that up for me and I'll die a happy man."

"Oh Grandpa! Don't talk that way! You'll make me cry," said Barbara.

She left the room and disappeared into the kitchen. Richard settled back onto the pillow. It had been too long since he had heard Barbara puttering around the kitchen, and he enjoyed it as much as he looked forward to the meal itself. The bacon was almost done when she called out from the kitchen.

"What do you want to drink, Grandpa?"

"Just some water, I guess...no...make that orange juice."

"OK."

A few minutes later, Barbara returned to the office with a platter of bacon and a pitcher of juice. She set them on a tray table.

"Pookie, take at least half of this. You haven't eaten since you've been here," said Richard.

They ate slowly and spoke of whatever came to mind. About halfway through the meal, Richard paused and looked at her.

"Barbara, I've been settling my affairs and there are a couple of things you need to know."

Barbara stopped in mid-swallow. She knew they would have to have this conversation, but she dreaded it nonetheless, as it signaled another farewell that could never be retracted. To her surprise, Richard smiled.

"Swallow, Pookie. You can't croak before I do. It'll mess up the paperwork."

Barbara swallowed.

"I'm keeping things simple," said Richard. "You get the house, its contents, and all my financial assets after expenses. Those will include some cash gifts to the family and a few friends, but the lion's share goes to you. I'm leaving you all of the art because you're the only one in the family with the taste and the yearning for it. Herb and Sarah will live here until you've finished gallivanting around the planets. My lawyers will settle my clients' accounts and execute the will. You don't have to worry about anything."

Barbara could barely bring herself to look at her grandfather. She picked up some bacon, nibbled on one end like a nervous rabbit and muttered, "OK, Grandpa, whatever you say. Thanks. Thanks for everything. But I'd spend it all in a flash if it meant you would be cured."

"Pookie, sweetheart, everybody dies. Don't spit into the wind. And don't worry about me. I've had my time in the sun, and let me tell you it was glorious! I've lived well and I'm going to die well."

"I'll see to it, Grandpa," promised Barbara.

"Good! Now go over to my desk and open the center drawer. You'll see two sealed letters. Bring them over here."

She moved quietly toward the desk. Everything suddenly seemed unreal, as if she were the main character in a play and did not know her lines. She returned to the bedside and handed him the letters.

"This one is my will. Read it at your leisure. I don't want you to open the other one until I'm gone," said Richard.

"OK, Grandpa, I won't," she said in the plaintive tones of a lost child.

"Good. Now help me out onto the porch. I need to commune with the spirits."

"Communing with the spirits" had always been for Barbara a figurative statement. That night however, it assumed an eerie reality. She helped Richard out of bed and into his favorite dressing down. He had become so frail that his every move threatened to be his last. He declined a wheelchair and seemed to derive great comfort from having Barbara steady him as he hobbled toward the porch under his own power.

Every step tired him more than the last, but in time he made it to the porch and collapsed onto the swing. She sat beside him. He looked up at the sky and mustered the last of his strength to stay awake. Neither then spoke for a long time. They watched the sunset behind the tassels of that year's early corn while fireflies winked into existence and crickets began their nocturnal love songs. This they had done for millions of years and would continue millions of years hence. The old man and his granddaughter were nothing more than transient onlookers to a slow dance whose rhythms were metered by the beat of planetary epochs.

Night had fallen when Barbara stiffened with an aching realization.

"Grandpa?"

"Yes?"

"This is it, isn't it? When you go to sleep tonight you aren't going to wake up, are you?"

"That's what the spirits are telling me," said Richard. His voice was serene, fulfilled, peaceful.

Barbara wanted to grab the moment, stretch it, pull it, lay it out before them so that the night would go on forever. But it was a fool's delusion and she gave it up. Richard looked at her. Despite the darkness, his blue eyes shimmered with the light of a spirit taking leave of its crumbling temple.

"It's time, Pookie."

"OK, Grandpa."

Rising, she helped Richard to his feet, but it was no use. The old man was spent. Barbara picked him up and carried him back to bed, her every step fading into the darkness. She set him down on the mattress and turned on the light. Even at death's door, Richard was handsome. She kept his dressing gown on and laid him on the bed, taking pains to assure his every comfort on this, the night of his long sleep. Her preparations complete, Barbara sat on the side of the bed. To her surprise, Richard was awake and looking at her.

"Thanks, Pookie, I feel good."

There was nothing left to say or do.

"Goodbye, Grandpa. I love you."

"Goodbye, Barbara. Live well. I love you."

Richard closed his eyes, but opened them again, as if remembering something.

"Oh,...and Barbara?"

She leaned over him.

"Good bacon. Thanks."

Those were his last words. He fell asleep and continued breathing for a long time. The grandfather clock, having outlived every resident of the house, continued its inexorable ticking and ringing as if itself marking time on a journey all its own. Barbara settled into the easy chair, more exhausted than she realized. But the moments were still too precious and she lay awake for awhile, listening, until sleep came and everything faded to black.

#

The night was well advanced when Barbara had a dream, a vision actually, as she later surmised. She awoke in a field of light. Beings of vaguely human form hovered near the ceiling of the sickroom. They were waiting for something with the patience of those who know they have all the time in the world. She looked at the bed and knew that Richard was dead, in a manner of speaking. As she watched, his body began to glow. The light was fluid and subdued, and floated onto the floor. It gathered itself into a mass that rose as a column before her. It was Richard. He smiled at her. He was both young and old, much like the man and woman she saw floating in the sky when she was an infant. He bent over and stroked her hair. He rose and, joining the other beings, dissolved into the light. The light disappeared and Barbara again fell asleep.

She awoke at the first glint of false dawn. Everything was as she had left it the night before. The spirits that had peopled her dream had vanished and things were once again ordinary. She looked at Richard's body and thought it odd that she did not feel like crying. If anything, she felt peaceful, unruffled. She knew, somehow, that he was off on a journey that would more than satisfy his boundless curiosity.

Barbara had fallen asleep with the sealed letters in her lap. The will she set aside. Picking up Richard's posthumous letter, she paused to admire the wax seal that he used to secure all of his personal documents. The seal embossed the wax with the letters "RL", unembellished and set in a style that conveyed his understated self-confidence.

She broke the seal and began reading.

Dearest Pookie:
If you are reading this, then I am dead.

Poor love, you've pestered me so many times over the years to tell you where

Natasha's antique shop was, but please believe me; after you've read this letter, you'll understand that there's no point to it. Her shop was so weirdly out of place that many people more or less just stumbled on it. If curiosity ever drives you to find the shop and its current owner, don't bother. Things change so. The shop is long gone and its owner is very dead. It would appear that the bearings of my life have not been as constant as your stars.

But not to worry, my Planetary Puppy. When you return several years hence with your Martian souvenirs, my collections will be yours as a backdrop. You <u>are</u> planning on slipping a few trinkets up your space suit sleeves, <u>aren't</u> you. You do, after all, control the ship's manifest. I mention this, as I sometimes despair of your ever learning the fine points of "discretionary clandestine acquisition".

This brings me, ever so obtusely, to the subject of this letter. You've known for years that shortly before her death, Natasha gave me something that she came across by accident, although I have since come to suspect it was the other way around. It proved to be her nemesis. In all the years since, I have shown it to no one and no one knows that I have it. Now I want you to have it, and for a purpose that only you can accomplish. If Mars once hosted intelligent life, as you seem to think, and if that life left signs of its sojourn among us, then for the love of life, please leave Natasha's gift among their ruins. Let it come to rest in a quiet place, where things neither laugh, nor cry, nor pass judgement.

Please believe that this is not the caprice of a moribund old man. I hope I'll live long enough to see your lift-off. I'll definitely be dead when you get back, so this is my last chance to tell you what you need to know about Natasha. It's fragmented, but much of what she and others told me over the years is internally consistent, so I will do them the honor of assuming that they were not liars or conspirators, whatever else they may have been.

I met Natasha in 1974, when she was 69 and I was 24. Her shop was in an old building that was apparently not for sale at any price when the surrounding office towers went up. In fact, it was so vindictively hemmed in that Natasha could only maintain the building's facade. So she didn't bother. Amidst all of that bird-killing Bauhaus plate glass, Natasha's place was positively waifish -- the more so because the business didn't have so much as a name or street number on it, not even anything old and painted over. Natasha was one of those rare dealers who didn't pander to money. Penniless browsers were as welcome as regulars who paid for everything from anonymous Swiss accounts.

On the day I first entered the shop, what struck me the most was not the Old Master paintings or the Louis IV furniture, but simply the odor of the place. It smelled old. In a city of obsessive activity, the shop smelled of things that had lain unmolested for generations. I could smell time in this place. As I wandered among the Persian rugs and Ming dynasty vases, half-remembered shapes formed themselves among the odors and drafts. I could almost see the long-dead owners of these treasures beckoning me to enjoy what they once adored.

One odor subtly dominated all of the others. I finally traced it to a case of antique books and realized that I had been drawn to the creaturely smell of old leather. It occurred to me that I had savored books with my mind, but never with my senses. How would a book taste? I couldn't help myself. I picked up a late seventeenth century copy of Paradise Lost and licked the binding. Just then a garbled voice from nowhere asked, "May I help you?"

Triangulating toward the sound, I turned and stifled a shriek over what I thought was a disembodied head propped on a pile of blood-red cloth. This impression was strengthened when the face shot me a Cheshire-cat grin and a disembodied hand drifted up to remove sundry needles and pins from its mouth. I was saved from psychosis when my brain finally registered a body connecting the

head and hand. Natasha was wearing a
burgundy satin dress, sitting amid piles
of new curtains made of burgundy satin,
and sewing an ottoman cover made of
burgundy satin.

I subsequently learned that Natasha
was frugal in the midst of opulence.
She had survived the Russian revolution
and both world wars, as well as the
centrifugal impoverishment of the world
caused by the Great Depression, and so
she used everything and wasted nothing.
Natasha could have suggested novel uses
for buffalo parts to the Indians. Her
love of fine fabric often impelled her
to make clothing from the remnants of
material used to make drapes and re-
upholster old furniture.

Natasha introduced herself and
apologized for causing a fright. She
invited me to sit down and nodded toward
a gilt sofa that looked as if it had
coddled the butts of French kings. She
started making small talk about how
artists and their studios were being
squeezed out of the city in favor of
corporate raiders and office towers.
All the while, I could feel her eyes
taking my measure, as if she had enough
scraps to make me a burgundy satin suit.
After a while, Natasha asked what I·
wanted.

Ah yes, to be young and stupid again.
I replied that I had inherited some
money — enough to set a budget for
investing in some art, hopefully in
order to become a discerning collector.

Howard L. Enfiejian

I'm grateful that Natasha was in a mood that day to suffer fools gladly. She smiled at me as if I were a cute but slow child, and said that investing in art was vulgar and that art is not purchased on a budget because art objects have destinies like people. If it is an object's fate to find somebody, then that person will be able to acquire it.

I felt foolish in her presence and was rising to leave when she touched my hand and said, "If you want to see the blind leading the stupid into bankruptcy, then by all means go to some pretentious auction house and invest to your heart's content. Shop here and you might learn something." Having said this, Natasha suddenly lowered her eyes and pulled back slightly. But her fingers lingered on mine, and after pursing her lips for a moment, she said, "Will you trust an old woman to play teacher with a promising pupil? I'll try to <u>show</u> you what I mean. People <u>talk</u> about art too much anyway. You can't impale beauty on your teeth and then expect to spit it out alive and well at gallery openings. It has to slide down your throat and burn your guts."

She locked the front door and then cast about the shop for a moment before finding a small abstract painting and a yardstick. Placing the painting in front of me and herself behind, Natasha held the stick with both hands, raised

288

it above her head and said, "What do you see?" Up to that time, I had never cared much for abstract art. This piece looked as if the "artist" had swallowed a few tubes of paint and vomited onto the canvas. The painting had an undercoat of lumpy gesso applied indiscriminately with a coarse brush. The "top" of the painting consisted of coarse swirls of bluish-white paint that blended with uneven gradations of color and texture into a lower mass of blues, greens and blacks. It was chaos frozen in time.

"This is either a psychology experiment or I'm on Candid Camera." I thought I was being cute.

I heard it before I felt it — a distant snap that sounded like a gun shot outside. It was when the base of my skull exploded that I realized Natasha had hit me between the shoulders. The bitch was crackers. I had walked into a Hitchcock movie and I was going to wind up as fish food in the Hudson.

"What do you see!"

"A Rorschach blot — could be anything. Bat shit. That's what it is. Moldy bat shit." Still clinging to cuteness.

Again the stick. This time, my brains started leaking out of my nose.

"WHAT DO YOU SEE!"

"NOTHING!"

"<u>EX</u>CELLENT!"

Suddenly this chatty antiquarian turned Gorgon was a chatty antiquarian again."Good. Nothing worthwhile can be known unless the mind is first emptied of trite ideas. Now I'll give you a name. Naming is serious work, as any Old Testament Hebrew could tell you. To speak a name requires breath. The breath is spirit, the spirit is of God — the breath of God. So to name something is to invoke its essence. YAHWEH. "I am that I am". You can look it up. It's in the Old Testament somewhere. This painting is called 'First Snow on Bear Mountain'. It was made by a monk after a period of contemplative prayer. So now, tell me what you feel deep down. No attic noise from you head. Just gut-thoughts." I looked at the work and suddenly realized that what I thought was a pile of sloppy gesso and crude brush marks actually evoked a mood.

"On the bottom: cool, moist black; still, quiet, massive; old, very old. Feels safe, comforting. On the top: shrill, busy white; all frenzy, movement. Cold. It bites, shrieks. Hurts. The brush strokes have character."

Natasha turned the painting upside down. "Now tell me what you feel. Don't think."

"On the top: soft black, green, blue, cool, packed white on the bottom. The white is quiet now. Motion's gone. The hurt's gone. The brush strokes have the opposite character."

She pursued, relentless. "Now hold those feelings inside of you, both together. Don't let go of either one. How do they feel? One word. Only one."

"Contrary."

"But they came from the same painting."

"Yes."

"Is that a problem?" she asked.

"No."

"And you. You held within your mind those opposite feelings."

"Yes."

"So you were able to remain still between the opposites?"

"Yes."

Natasha lowered the stick and her eyelids in one motion, smiling.

"Don't try to figure it out. At least not until you've sat in a cave for fifty years and meditated on it. Just know that opposites hold tension. Tension creates energy. So does Mystery. And all of it is the stuff of life. Just embrace the opposites with your stillness."

Through all my years of training, I had never met anyone who could teach so vividly. Ten minutes had passed and no money had changed hands. At the risk of being bludgeoned again, I asked if 'Bear Mountain' was for sale.

"No."

I started to apologize when Natasha said, "Let me finish. I was going to say that the painting was given to me, and now I'm giving it to you. You've made it yours, which is probably its fate. Pay for the frame if you want."

Thus ended my first purchase at Natasha's.

To say that Natasha was beautiful is trite. She beggared description. Suffice it to say that if Odysseus had known Natasha, Penelope would have become the love slave of a Greek army battalion. More objective minds might have suggested that this hyperbole was simply the projection of a puerile romanticism onto a passably attractive Jew. My biker friends would have said that I was just horny for an old broad.

The reason that I am regressing to puberty on this matter is that Natasha restored and maintained an impressive inventory of old picture frames in her shop. Since space was always at a premium, the frames were used to display whatever art was at hand, as well as old photographs of herself and various acquaintances over the years. My favorite was one of Berenson, an art historian before your time, gesturing expansively at a "newly discovered" Old Master painting in front of a group of fawning collectors. Natasha was visible in the background, apparently trying not to pee in her pants while thoroughly enjoying a private joke at Berenson's expense.

My apologies for the delectations of an old man and his memories. What I mean to say is that watching Natasha age in these pictures was like watching

Olivier age.   It was an epiphany of
sorts to see a face which never decayed
with age, but which instead continued to
reveal nuances of beauty that were
immanent but not expressible within its
youthful forms.

Over the years, I deduced that
Natasha was well, if privately, known to
some very important collectors in New
York and elsewhere. Their reluctance to
admit any connection with her was
usually so extreme that I always
wondered if she had something on them.
Nevertheless, the Muse will, on
occasion, rip open lips that have been
stapled shut and inspire even the most
mediocre minds to extravagant flights of
gossip.

And so, stories about Natasha
abounded — if you knew where to listen —
and her indiscretions, such as the time
she got drunk at the Yale Club and
started regaling some business
executives with The Wasteland, did
little to dispel them. She was, for
instance, rumored to have fashioned a
bikini from some ruined Medieval chain
mail in order to satisfy the archetypal,
if goatish, passions of an Arthurian
scholar. After he had sheathed her to
the hilt, he begged for a repeat
performance at Stonehenge at midnight
during the summer solstice. He had
connections, he could get them in after
dark, he...

Happily, most of the less amusing
stories about Natasha turned out to be

sniper fire that missed its mark. There were, however, enough internally consistent fragments, garnered from disparate sources, to provide a sketch of Natasha's youth in Asia and Japan, and to justify your little errand on Mars.

Beyond the fact that she was Russian and Jewish, I never deduced much about Natasha's birth or childhood and she never talked about it. The earliest clues of my inspired gossips hint at a savvy art student who was sardonically amused by one of the first official acts of the new, and brutally egalitarian, Russian communist government: seizure of the Czar's collection of Faberge eggs.

Natasha's dark amusement soon turned into an obsession when she realized the implications of this ideologic lapse within the revolutionary leadership: that there might be a class of art dealers who specialized in salvaging the collections of fallen aristocrats, or other privileged persons, and who catered to tight-lipped customers. Why should she starve trying to crank out politically correct socialist scribbles on cheap canvas when such markets might exist? After this, Natasha'a life recedes into a fog of conjecture and misinformation. When next the stories coalesce, we find her in Japanese-occupied Manchuria. Her intuitions are correct: within the ranks of every revolution since at least the French, a few enterprising revolutionaries have mastered the art of discretely looting the homes of despots prior to provoking their patriotic, but woefully naive, confreres into sacking and burning the victim's real estate. Incriminating tracks are thereby combusted and the trinkets are passed on to customers in faraway lands who, as a rule, are privately thrilled that their rivals have been so inconvenienced by the ravages of politics.

Such is the company that Natasha now keeps. She is part of an underground art business that variously involves the Jewish survivors of Czarist pogroms and Stalinist purges, Soviet apparatchik middlemen who know the value of a free, if black, market, and tight-lipped Chinese and Japanese distributors with access to wealthy Western customers. The Byzantine complexity of this leaderless network is matched only by its secrecy.

But there are problems. Apparently no one in the network quite anticipated the speed with which the extremist Japanese government would establish their empire, and that their blitz on Pearl Harbor would alienate customers on three continents. Natasha's decision to become the mistress of a well-connected, but suddenly displaced, Manchurian nobleman was evidently part of this colossal miscalculation. So was the child that she purportedly had by him. When a rival art dealer once confronted her with this, Natasha replied that her wartime indiscretions had no place in a peacetime economy.

Once again, my sources falter, fog arises, and our story fades to black.

For the next piece of my story, all I need do is penetrate the vapors of my own mind. Gossip has served its purpose for now.

Natasha and I are having lunch in Windows on the World. We are facing the Brooklyn Bridge and contemplating the millennium. It's 1998. She's undiminished at 93, still a statuesque beauty, and I'm less pretentious, if not less stupid, than I was 24 years previously. It's her birthday, and the waiter approaches with a bottle of Cristal champagne and a plate so full of caviar that it wiggles like Jell-O. My motive for inviting her to this place, aside from friendship, was to scratch an itch that I'd been harboring for years.

I never really understood how Natasha made so much money. She ignored trends, fads, and inflation or deflation in the art market. She specialized in nothing — the shop was as likely to offer Medieval broadswords as it was Satsuma ware. She never took advantage of the feeding frenzies that seize art collectors now and then. But she always made money. In fact, for someone who never tried to make a killing, Natasha was obscenely wealthy. And it all came from the shop. The gossips agreed uniformly on that.

All I knew up until then was that I had seldom seen an inventory of work that so purely embodied the passions of its creators. Natasha had icons dripping with the blood and tears of Christ; renderings of St. George and the dragon that stank with the beast's breath; Safavid Persian carpets that could fly into paradise, and all this in a city that encouraged trends like few places on Earth. She never cultivated the mercenary edge that would enable her to pimp fads.

For instance. During the early eighties, tribal oriental carpets were all the rage among collectors and interior decorators. Prices soared out of all proportion to the long-term realities of the art market. Dealers were even going so far as to buy late 19th century rugs whose wool contained cheap aniline dyes which were so pathetically faded that the patterns looked like sun-bleached camel carcasses. Yet these abominations were touted as having astoundingly subtle pastel palettes that blended uncannily with contemporary interiors. Truly, pieces that were ahead of their time. Blah, blah, blah.

Anyway, one afternoon in '81 or '82, I forget exactly when, an impressive pile of Turkoman rugs was being auctioned off. At the time, I wasn't especially interested, so I didn't go. During the time slated for bidding, I happened to be strolling along the waterfront in Battery Park City when whom do I espy but Natasha sitting quietly, staring at the Hudson.

This was odd. Natasha worked assiduously and seldom left the shop during the day on anything other than business errands. If nothing else, I thought she might descend like a Harpy on the bidding. Her good word would have quadrupled the price of anything she chose to carry away. I stood there watching her for a while. To say that she was sitting quietly is an understatement. She was so quiet that she became invisible. For minutes at a time, not so much as an eyelash flickered. Panhandlers looked right through her. A troupe of gyrating Hare Krishna kids practically trampled her. At one point a squadron of mosquitos hovered around her face and flew off without biting.

But her stillness wasn't total. Every so often she would either write something on scraps of paper and toss them in the water or take manly swigs from a bottle of saki. To compound the mystery, I eventually noticed that she did this whenever a piece of trash floated by her on its way to New Jersey. Long ago I had learned to love Natasha's deceptively intelligent eccentricities, but even this was more than a little strange. Curiosity eventually got the better of me and I began to approach her from behind.

"Hello Richard. Have a seat." Still staring at the Hudson.

"How did you know it was me?"

"You walk like a cat with a limp."

"Huh?"

"When you sit this still, you learn to let your body sense everything. I heard your footsteps following the Hare Krishna kids and then stop after they passed on."

"What are you doing?"

"Something I read about when I lived in Japan. During the eighteenth century, in a place called Korakuen, a stream was routed through an open pavilion and allowed to gather in a small pool just beyond. Once inside the pavilion, the water flowed through a straight channel with a black bottom. Rocks were placed along the bed to punctuate an otherwise restful black background. Feudal lords and ladies would sit on the banks and compose haiku while cups of sake floated down the stream. Anyone who failed by the time a cup floated by had to drink its contents. It sounded like fun. When I got to the States, I had to improvise. In New York I have to settle for floating garbage instead of sake cups.

"Are you any good at it."

"I get drunk a lot."

"Even so, why throw your writing away?"

"Because it's all right to let go."

"But why? What if it's good stuff and you're too crocked to know it?"

"Because creation is endless. Infinitely many haiku to write. Infinitely many paintings to make and sell. Infinitely many children and animals to care for. Infinitely many lives to know. Infinitely many agonies and deaths to pass through. When you learn to let go of little things, you start to see how much there really is." At that she pointed to two unopened sake bottles and patted the seat next to her.

"Come on. Let your mind drift with the garbage. You should've seen it. About an hour ago, a giant plastic Jesus floated by..."

I looked at Natasha and then at the river, and the scraps of junk occasionally floating by.

"This could work," says I to myself. Letting things come and letting things go. I wondered how far up river Rip van Winkle was when he wandered into the Catskills for his twenty-year snooze. All those years, just lying quietly in the woods, amidst the passing seasons, letting thoughts and dreams float for a while on the still, black waters of his mind, and then letting them drift soundlessly back into the void whence they came. And every so often a distant and muffled rumbling would roll through the moist darkness of Rip's nest whenever the ghost of Henry Hudson played ten-pins with the elves — something that the local merchants on the Hudson probably dismissed as thunder while they poured over their accounts.

Vast amounts of time and forgetfulness flowing down both shores of the city that never sleeps. It wasn't Korakuen, but it had its charms. I sat down. She handed me the paper and pen.

"Okay Tash. How do we do this?"

"You probably know that the Japanese form requires three lines of 5, 7, and 5 syllables each. In English, 10 to 14 syllables, or fewer, in any arrangement will do. So relax and pick a piece of garbage upstream. Treat it like a timed chess game where every wrong move is punished with a drink."

About ten o'clock that night, we both threw up in the river and fell asleep in each other's arms in the back seat of a cab on the way home.

Memories of sake bottles on the pavement drop off as the Natasha of 1998 refills my glass with a hesitancy suggesting that she thinks I'm drunk.

"I'm not drunk. Just distracted. Come on sweetheart, how do you manage to be the envy of everyone with any taste?"

"I suppose I could tell you, especially since I'm considering a change of venue for the shop. The strategy is absolutely dead stupid simple, really. I'm amazed that no one else does it."

She orders another bottle of Cristal and settles in.

"You probably know from the gossips around here that the network was badly constipated by the war. The collapse of Czarist Russia and Manchuria freed up no end of first-rate stuff, but we couldn't move any of it. What with Hitler in the west, Japanese war mongers in the east, and Stalin being paranoid in the middle, we couldn't reach any of the markets in Europe or America. Even Yang, my liege lord turned opium runner, couldn't get anything out. So we just stockpiled stuff until the war ended. With diplomatic relations more or less restored, I was able to come here and set up shop. Me and about a hundred other people, placed in the most lucrative centers of our respective markets."

"For a long time, things were simple. I just moved what was sent to me and sold it at fair prices. But then, as time went by, I got fed up. My sources were so obsessed with making up for lost time that they started sending all kinds of shit my way. That I couldn't tolerate. So I started phasing them out, which was just as well, because I was starting to feel like a whore again. I'd had enough of that with Yang. And then I got my idea."

"You don't deal art the way I deal art without crossing paths with lots of -- shall we say -- highly motivated wannabe immigrants to the States. So I started making deals. I'd sponsor people to come here — arrange for a visible means of support and all that immigration stuff — in exchange for the best pieces they could bring over with them and access to their connections.

In effect, I said, 'You show me how badly you want to come here and we'll talk.' After that, the rest started taking care of itself. Once people realized that they could count on me for the best of everything, I started gaining privileged access to the best contemporary artists, to very private estate sales, whatever."

At that she raised her right hand and touched her thumb to her pinky finger."What am I doing?"

"Calling the waiter?"

"No, twit. I am moving my thumb into opposition with the digits of the same hand. Incredible engineering. We are the only species on earth who can do that so well. It means that we can create anything that we can fully imagine. Why else would Michelangelo show God and Adam touching hands on the Sistine ceiling? With your hands you can spark divine fire. So if you have talent and somebody offers to teach you how to use your hands, don't screw around. Reach the top of your form and make it clear that you don't tolerate shit. That's how I make money."

Crafty old broad.

When Natasha mentioned a change of venue for the shop, I thought she was specializing — Native American fetishes or something. So I was totally unprepared for what I saw when I dropped by shortly after our birthday lunch.

Scattered among the paintings and bronze age weapons was an assortment of stuff that looked like the detritus from an old engineer's attic: Lucite paperweights depicting the early TIROS and TOS weather satellites; Telstar bookends; scraps of Mylar from the Echo satellites; Ranger TV subsystem reports complete with photos of the actual moon shots; photo cells from the Lunar Orbiters; original photographs from the Gemini missions; Viking photographs of Mars; slide rules (slide rules?). The more I looked, the more I saw.

"Tash, tell me you're not becoming an engineer."

"Nope. Just cashing in on the next generation of collectibles — spacecraft memorabilia. Sotheby's made a start with their auctions of Russian astronaut stuff in '93. I want dibs on memorabilia from the winning side of the space race before somebody else realizes its market potential. You wouldn't believe how much treasure is moldering in attics. A little while ago I just got to thinking about how people love old trains, cars, planes — even toys of old trains, cars, and planes. And then the light bulb, or should I say the solar panel, went off in my head."

"Tash, you're 93. Isn't a gracious retirement in order? Why don't you buy France and charge admission?"

"No way. I'm starting to get good prices. Imagine an auction catering to collectors with near complete sequences of photos from the Orbiter moon-mapping missions. Think of the bidding wars for pictures that would complete the sequences. I can't imagine what these people might pay for negatives. And if I could get some moon rocks..."

As usual, Natasha was right on the money. Before long, she had started a trend. The collectors of antique scientific instruments were especially ravenous. But with time, she started losing her Valkyrian presence. She started staring into space for unnervingly long periods of time, and was startled easily. Her face became a death mask.

Finally, on a slow day, when the shop was empty and I had stopped by to visit, I found Natasha slouched on a sofa, staring at the ceiling with the look of someone who has just had their brains sucked out. After a while she leaned forward and buried her face in her hands. Her loins shuddered, if that's possible. Finally she realized she wasn't alone and looked up.

"After 40 years, the network sniffed me out and made a delivery."

Outwardly, the business didn't change much, except for the erratic deliveries of some massive crates, all of which disappeared into the basement. This went on for months without swelling the inventory on display. All that changed was Natasha. To those of us who knew her well, her behavior became uncharacteristically robotic — outwardly gracious but inwardly void and rote. I started wondering when this histrionic and affectionate old Russian Jew was, going to explode.

In this I was wrong. Natasha imploded instead and undertook a sad, withdrawn literary catharsis. She read all of the love poetry she could find. She also stopped her game of letting her writing mingle with the garbage on the Hudson. She wrote a lot in the shop and just let it fall. I took to collecting the verses furtively. Eventually the bits of writing seemed to be telling a story. I don't know if Natasha's verses were any good, and I loved her too much to care. Here is some of the writing, and a glimpse into the lingering passions of an old woman. Please judge them, and her, kindly.

> Bangkok:
> everywhere,
> monks and prostitutes.

> dark.
> door closes softly.
> our teeth touch.

> in the foyer,
> our shoes
> up against each other.

> late night storm.
> fitfully,
> you turn in your sleep.

vomiting on floor,
blood in toilet:
the bloom of motherhood.

if I had fangs,
they would shine
as once more
they tell me to push.

waking up,
having to start it
all over again.

moaning.
sweat dries
between sheets.

morning:
among vanishing stars,
a white butterfly.

...cauled within skin
and passing through a world
so loved by God...

clutching my finger
and a cherry:
four of her steps
for each of mine.

the autumn tree
can't shelter us
from the rain
anymore.

snowflakes on eyelids
melt to tears
on frost red eyes:
sad salt flows.

'til death
do us part:
soul murder.

pulling the marker
from the book —
it doesn't matter
where i am.

rippling in my tea:
the moon overhead.

   Natasha called me late one afternoon
and started talking as it we were
already in the middle of a conversation.
   "I can't do this anymore. No. I
won't do this anymore. I'm dissolving
the business and liquidating the
inventory. All except for one thing,
which is too precious to sell, and I
want you to have it. Please come over

when you can. That's code language, Richard. Get your sweet ass down here so that I can make my confession before I die." At that, Natasha hung up the phone.

I reached the shop around 5:00 p.m. It was locked. Natasha must have been watching out for me, however, because the instant I tapped on the glass a cadaverous arm opened the door and pulled me in. The place felt like a mausoleum, and for the first time, Natasha looked old. Not old in the sense of being decrepit, though. She was tired, as if fatigue were a terminal disease.

She gestured vaguely toward a wing-backed chair, slumped into a divan, and bundled herself within a tapestry. The arch art-dealer was letting all of this go.

"I'll start with Yang. It's not important for you to know how we got together or why I was in Manchuria to begin with. I was a fallen angel in love with art, and a liaison with Yang seemed to promise a union with my beloved. A well-connected Chinese aristocrat coupled — excuse the pun — with a cagey Russian Jewess. Profitable, to put it mildly. And then we discovered that we could satisfy each other in ways that one doesn't discuss in polite society. It seemed too good to be true. And it was. The Japanese invasion of Manchuria saw to that. Within days, the scion of an ancient

Chinese family was conscripted as a houseboy on the estate of a Japanese rayon manufacturer. His round-eyed concubine went with him."

"In the beginning, it wasn't too bad. This rayon mogul, I forget his name, had a house above the Koi district of Hiroshima with a view of the city. The work was easy and we were left alone. And then I got pregnant."

"That was when Yang started to get ugly. Late at night, when everybody was asleep, he often got drunk in the garden and peed all over the master's bonsai collection. Then he would start crying, and after awhile would fall to his knees and start punching the ground until he was too tired to move or cry. Yang was a small man and I could usually get him into bed by myself. There he would cling to me, trembling. There was nothing for me to do, so I just held him until he fell asleep."

"Nobody knew what was happening, and it wasn't long before the trees — some of them were 300 years old — yellowed and died. To say that the gardeners were horrified was to describe them on a good day."

"Late one evening, the master himself wandered out to take in the night. And wouldn't you know it but Yang staggered out a moment later and peed on him. Yang waffled onto the ground, blubbering apologies, shielding his head with his arms. Incredibly, nothing happened. The old man simply shook the loose drops off his pants, turned around and searched Yang with his eyes. I didn't sense any anger from him. Not even pity. Possibly a little empathy though, as if the master knew that the only things separating them were the grace of God and fortunes of war. For the rest of the night, Yang cowered in the garden and wouldn't let me near him."

"The next morning, we were escorted off of the grounds and deposited in the Hypothec Bank in downtown Hiroshima. The master must have taken pity on us and found other work for Yang. I was always grateful for that."

"And so Yang became a janitor at the bank. I was pretty ripe by then, but nobody seemed to care if I did odd jobs with Yang. Pretty soon the dam burst, and out came Assha. It was summer 1941. Well, almost everything came out. She was missing her left hand and forearm. Years later, I found out that Assha probably suffered something called a spontaneous amniotic amputation. Big words for a little girl's misery."

"Assha. The last half of Natasha with an extra 's' thrown in for sinister — the Latin word for left. Such was my stream of consciousness when we named her. For a baby who was half Russian, Assha looked completely oriental and I just wanted her to have a little piece of me. Hence the silly name. Silly me. Silly war."

"Fast-forward the tape: this is the abridged version of my life. We got by.

My Manchurian nobleman continued to clean toilets at the Hypothec Bank for rich Japanese asses while his whore nursed their bastard. Cute little bastard. When she was two, she would kiss flowers and say, 'Is cute!' She could say 'Workers of the world, forgive me!' in Russian. She..."

"The war went belly-up for the Axis powers. The Allies were bombing everyplace in Japan except Hiroshima and Nagasaki. People started obsessing over what the Allies were saving for them. Let's just say it was no fun being a Chinese menial for the losing side. And having a Russian mistress around didn't exactly put Yang on the fast-track for anything."

"Through it all, the network managed to find us. They wanted us back. I was getting itchy feet, but Yang was getting comfortable in a self-pitying kind of way. So one night in July of 1945, we fought. Big time. He got drunk. I stayed sober. He beat the shit out of me. After that, he got even drunker and passed out. So I left him. Forever."

"But not without making one last stop. Assha could sleep through anything and that night was no exception. While Yang was drooling onto his blanket, I knelt beside Assha's futon and drifted back to when Japan seized Manchuria. To memories of dead civilians stacked like firewood in cratered fields. To the stench of body parts blasted beyond recognition. To

the sight of people fleeing the invasion
like autumn leaves scattering before a
tornado. To my own terror as I ran with
them. I contemplated the prospects for
a Russian woman living in enemy
territory in the twilight of a lost
cause. It wasn't a pretty picture. I
was a mistake. I wasn't meant to be
there. I wasn't married, I wasn't
wanted, I wasn't worth anything to
anybody. I knew the Allies weren't
barbarians and they were especially kind
to children. And then it occurred to me
that Assha wasn't my shame. I was her
shame. I was tired of how people looked
at her when they realized that I was her
mother. She'd be better off without me.
Yang was almost psychotically in love
with her and would see to it. Besides,
the cities were teeming with casualties.
Nobody could afford the luxury of
shunning a crippled child. So for a
long time, I stared into Assha's face
and memorized it between fits of
crying."

"The three of us were supposed to be
in the Land of the Rising Sun. So I sat
with Assha until the sun rose and turned
her face pink. She had dimples like
cherry blossoms."

"A few weeks before, I had finished
making a rag doll for her. I had some
spare cloth, so I made a tiny kimono and
dressed it like a geisha. It was
supposed to be a surprise. I tucked it
under her good arm and left."

"An hour later, I slipped into a service entrance behind the Museum of Science and Industry and disappeared. I surfaced in Manhattan."

"The tape speeds up. Return to now. A few months ago, actually."

"Just after I got into the space business, the network sniffed me out again with a proposition. Incredible. I thought I was shrewd. They got the jump on me by 50 years. Those guys were slime bags, but they saw the big picture."

"Here's how they put it to me: No civilization has ever refrained from using its ultimate weapon. You can tick off the list. Bronze-tipped spears, chariots, body armor, armor piercing crossbows, the Spanish armada, the Gatling gun, mustard gas, rockets. A relentless evolution of innovative offense and defense. And always the stakes of war got higher. But no innovation in warfare has ever been decisive. Always a defense has arisen."

"Until 1945. The Allies invent The Bomb. And they road-test it in Japan. So now comes the gamble for us venal types. Will the Allies refrain from using their ultimate weapon on each other? If so, might not the relics of its first and final use become premium collectibles? Don't laugh. Just remember how much of the Berlin wall was sold off. In fact, it was the collapse of the Soviet Union that inspired the network to start moving this stuff."

"But there was a problem at first: what to collect and how to do it discretely. And here is where the rumor mill paid off. Soon after the Hiroshima bombing, people started talking about the 'shadow prints'. Apparently, the heat at the bomb's hypocenter was intense enough to instantly scorch otherwise durable building materials. Concrete turned light red. Granite surfaces flaked off. This meant that the bomb could leave prints of the shadows cast by the light of its explosion on durable materials. The roof of the Chamber of Commerce building held the shadow of its water tower."

So now the network knew what to collect — the smallest shadow prints they could find. The problem was how to find them. And this is where the Japanese government unwittingly helped. It wasn't until mid-August that President Truman revealed what sort of bomb had been used. Once the Japanese knew what they were dealing with, they sent people to Hiroshima to locate the bomb's hypocenter. They did it by triangulating the scorched sides of telephone poles and seeing where the lines converged. This turned out to be roughly the torii gate of the Gokoku Shrine. The only buildings left in the immediate area were the Chamber of Commerce, Hypothec Bank, Chugoku Electric Supply and Gokoku Shrine. They were fried."

"The rest was simple. People posing as refugees or scavengers discretely followed the investigators and removed all of the small shadow prints they could find."

Natasha stopped and started staring into space again. It was dusk by then and her face faded into the shadows. I thought she had fallen asleep when she suddenly convulsed and tossed the tapestry aside.

"All of this is germane to your inheritance, dear. Follow me. "We descended the basement stairs. Natasha kept one hand on me and the other on the rail. When we reached the bottom, she flipped on the light. The room was a war zone. The walls were studded with ruined religious implements: a crucifix whose bloodied Christ had his ribs and loins scorched away; a mutilated golden monstrance that looked like an exploded star; gilt Buddhas with their faces melted into masses of tears; a smashed chalice that still held somebody's fingers. You could feel the heat. You could hear peoples' screams as they vanished into a thermonuclear Hell.

Everything was tagged to indicate its origin within Hiroshima. Nothing had a price on it.

The shadow prints were on the floor — fragments of everyday life, burned onto masonry rubble:

a gas pump handle
the back of a chair
branches of a tree

the rungs of a ladder
a teapot.

All of them were neatly tagged. Again, no prices.

"This is your's now. I have to let it go before I die. Send it down the river for me when you think it's time."

Natasha led me toward a large shadow print. It was a thin concrete slab, about four feet tall, leaning against the wall under the monstrance. The figure of a child at play was burned into it. One hand held what might have been a rag doll. The other arm faded into nothing.

It was tagged "Hypothec Bank".

All my love, dearest heart, as you dance among the stars.

Grandpa

#

The rising sun infused the sick room with its impartial light. Barbara set the letter aside. Despite the morning's warmth, her hands were tremulous and cold. She got up and went into the kitchen to make some tea. The day nurse arrived just as the kettle began whistling. Setting the kettle aside, Barbara greeted the woman and told her about Richard. The woman started making the requisite telephone calls while Barbara returned to the kitchen. She brewed a pot of Richard's favorite tea and took it out onto the porch. She sat on the swing, savoring the warmth of the tea and the sun, and contemplated many things.

COMMUNION: June 2034

Barbara's dreams swirled and tumbled among themselves in a kaleidoscopic cascade of visions, each teasing her with glimpses of worlds too distant, too eldritch, too beyond imagining to have hailed from the universe we know — or think we know. But dreams are timid fawns, easily spooked. They are glittering, ghostly dancers who quit their dark stage at the slightest provocation and, in a burst of fey colors, disappear into the black forests of Possibility. She heard voices, distant at first, that soon commanded her somnolent attention. Someone, a woman, was calling her name between' bursts of laughter and the sounds of play.

"Hey Barbara," shouted Linda," you just got some sort of eyes-only message from Mission Control!"

Barbara groaned and slipped out of her sleeping pod like a grouchy butterfly forced too early from its cocoon. Pulling herself along the floatway toward the command module, she wondered what could have prompted NASA to encrypt a message to the commander of a three-man crew trapped in a tin can in the freezing middle-of-nowhere. Secrets here were unnecessary, impractical, and unethical. She entered the command module just as Hal claimed he had won some sort of game. True to form, Linda was contesting the point.

"What are you two doing?" asked Barbara as she glanced at the flight simulator.

"We've reconfigured the virtual reality software to run dogfights," said Hal. "You want to try it?"

Barbara smiled.

"I think somebody and his evil twin have too much time on their hands. Let me check this message first."

Barbara sat at one of the communications consoles, swiveling it away from general view. The screen bore one line of text: "Encrypted message. Commander's eyes only." She entered her clearance code and began studying the message. When she finished, she slumped back in the chair, looking like she had just been gut-punched.

"Guys, you've got to see this."

Hal and Linda looked up from the new game they were setting up and walked over to the console. Barbara moved it so they could all see the message.

"So. Any ideas as to what that thing is?"

For a few long moments, the three of them looked at the screen. The image before them showed one side of a heavily weathered slope. At ground level and set into the hill was a bright bluish-green object. Hal spoke first.

"Where is it?"

Barbara zoomed out to a view of the entire planet.

"Here it is, on the western scarp of Olympus Mons."

"That's one hell of a trek from the base camp," said Hal.

"We have six months to figure something out," said Barbara.

"Okay, zoom us back in slowly," said Linda.

Barbara complied, but the additional information left them as clueless as before, so she elaborated the message.

"Mission Control has been tracking a dust storm in the northern hemisphere for about a week. It's turning into a monster and they expect it'll cover half the planet by the time we arrive. This blue thing was an accidental finding. If the imaging technician on duty at the time had so much as gone out to pee, they would have missed it. A few minutes later it was gone. It reappeared a half-hour later, only this time it was bigger but almost out of the Argus orbiter's sensor range. So the ground people parked her in a synchronous orbit over the thing. What they sent us is a cleaned-up composite."

Barbara paused to let the others speak.

Linda asked, "Are they sure there's actually something there? It could be a fluke."

"They've had the Argus perform every kind of spectral analysis on board and a few more that have been developed on the ground since she was launched. It shows up every time."

Hal started to say something when the Argo lurched as if being forced into a new trajectory. Everything that was not tied down, including the crew, continued on its way to Mars and slammed into the port bulkheads while the ship herself plunged toward the Sun. Unanticipated torque along the hull rent the air with the shrieks of tortured metal. Shipwide alarms sounded. Multisystem failure lights littered the command and control console. The force of the incident kept the crew pinned to the walls until the Argo lurched again, releasing its centrifugal hold on them. The groans and shrieks from the ship tripped even more alarms.

Barbara dove toward the console. So numerous were the active alarms that it was easier to see what was wrong by looking at the few intact systems. She knew that they were as good as dead without power. The electrical power grid was unstable but more-or-less functional. Propulsion was a mess. The VASIMR engine had shut down improperly. Worse yet, the rocket's hydrogen injector had disengaged and was venting gas into the access corridor. The slightest spark from anything near the engine room could turn the Argo into a torch visible on Earth.

"You two stabilize the power grid. I'm going down to propulsion."

Barbara looked up from the console and saw that Linda was bleeding profusely from a scalp wound. Drops of weightless blood formed perfect spheres around her blond curls, creating the unnerving impression of a bloody halo.

"You all right?"

"I'll be fine. Go on down to propulsion," shouted Linda. To herself, she muttered, "If we weren't half way to fucking Mars I'd swear we were just hit by a train!"

Barbara pulled herself along the floatway, oblivious to the accumulating cuts, bruises, and abrasions forming from her chaotic collisions with unsecured objects and, she realized to her horror, wreckage. She was thirty feet from the engine room when the shock wave from an explosion up ahead slammed her back onto a girder. A piston of onrushing air from the opposite direction hurled her forward until she struck the airlock leading to the engine room.

Willing herself not to black out, Barbara assessed the damage around her. The airlock door had been warped out of its frame by the two concussions. This must have created enough sparks to ignite the hydrogen gas that had already been escaping the fuel injector. The engine room had become a torch that was feeding itself on the ship's air. She knew what had to be done — and quickly. She barked into her headset.

"Hal, Linda! Seal the aft air locks now!"

"But Barbara, that puts you in a vacuum!"

It was Hal.

"JUST DO IT!" She screamed.

The sound of the airlock door engaging its mechanism mumbled a death knell along the passage toward the engine room. Barbara leapt through the flames toward the opposite wall. Thoughts of Hell flashed through her mind as she slammed into a storage locker housing some emergency tool kits and pressure suits. She ripped one off its hanger and struggled to get inside of it. The fire died as it consumed the last traces of oxygen. But no sooner did the one danger pass when another took its place in the form of fresh hydrogen gas escaping the crippled engine. Already short on breath, Barbara began choking. Her limbs were heavy and seemed to stretch out forever as she fought her away into the suit. She could not think and was on the verge of forgetting where she was when at last she snapped on the helmet and fresh air began flowing. Barbara sucked it in desperately until her mind cleared. She looked around.

What she saw appalled her. The VASIMR engine laid dead before her within a floating confusion of ruptured conduits and shredded electrical cables that were undoubtedly hot. Barbara picked her way to the hydrogen injector and closed its intake. Next, she approached an outer airlock. The atmosphere inside the room had to be vented carefully. She could not afford to blast any parts or supplies into space.

Before doing anything further, she spoke into her headset.

"Hey! Is anybody alive up there?"

"We were wondering the same about you," said Hal.

"A little singed and battered, but otherwise okay. How about you?"

"We're good. Ms. Linda's managed to bloody up everything, though. She has a gash in her scalp right down to the bone."

"Linda! Take a break and let Hal sew your head back on. And keep the airlock sealed. I've got to vent the air down here. How's the power grid?"

Linda answered. "We've got it stabilized for the time being. We can patch it up after we've checked out all the other messes up here."

"Do you guys know where we're headed?" asked Barbara.

"Don't ask me how, but we're back on course. We're not moving very fast though, maybe one-tenth normal," said Hal.

"Then we'll have to recalculate our energy reserves when we get the worst of this mess cleaned up," said Barbara.

She heard some mumbled conversation through her headset.

Linda spoke next. "Uh...Barbara...as things stand now we have the resources to abort the mission. Do you want to bug out?"

"Not yet," said Barbara, "how about you two?"

"No way," came the unhesitating reply.

"Good. Let's get to work," said Barbara. We'll reassess the mission when we've fixed everything we can."

She stood back from the engine and prioritized the tasks ahead of her. The hydrogen fuel was safely contained, so repairs on the fuel injector could wait, but a VASIMR engine was essentially scrap metal without its magnetic containment fields. If these could not be reestablished, then they were as good as dead. Barbara inspected the electrical power couplings. They at least had snapped cleanly away from the body of the rocket and could be repaired. Shutting off the main power switch, she renewed the air, opened a tool kit and got to work. She was well on her way to restoring the engine power when she noticed a rustling sound overhead. Barbara looked up to locate its source.

She froze when she saw what was happening just over her head, and everywhere else in the engine room. The Argo was putting herself back together. Pieces of wreckage flowed purposefully past her, as if under the direction of one mind, and rejoined the structures from which they had been torn. The power couplings finished repairing themselves. They even plugged themselves back into the engine, as if nothing had ever been amiss. Barbara spent a few minutes watching the wreckage repair itself. After a while, she noticed that the objects around her were folding in on themselves along lines — impossible lines. They made no three-dimensional sense. Their target surfaces did the same thing. Barbara thought of her early childhood vision of strange people walking along impossible lines in a vast white space. She stopped herself. She had to assume that she was hallucinating. To put it mildly, she needed a reality check. She spoke into her headset.

"Hey guys...how are you making out? Is everything okay up there?"

Linda answered. She was unnerved. She could barely speak.

"Uh...yeah, I guess so...how about you..."

"I'm good. By the way, have you noticed anything strange?"

"You might say that," said Hal tentatively. "Come see for yourself."

Barbara pulled herself along the floatway. There too, everything was putting itself back together. She had a good idea as to what she would find in the command module, and was not surprised when she came upon Hal and Linda staring at the power-grid schematic. Unless they were all somehow sharing the same delusion, the Argo was repairing its own power grid. Systems came back online as if awakening from a nap. The spell was broken by a loud snap from the centrifugal axle. The crew gradually regained their footing as the Argo re-established the false gravity created by spinning the command and work modules around the centrifugal axis.

"Jesus..." said Hal. "Those bearings were fused! They couldn't have loosened themselves."

As he spoke, the ship reverberated with the sound of the VASIMR engine as it went through a textbook-perfect ignition sequence. Something was throttling the fuel injector just enough to induce a gentle acceleration. The hydrogen reserves were replenishing themselves. Barbara grasped a piece of wreckage that was still floating around. It behaved as did all the others.

"What do you two make of this?" she asked.

Hal and Linda approached the object.

"Beats the shit out of me," said Linda. "It's like it's here and not here at the same time."

As the three of them watched, the object moved, as if under its own power, and attached itself seamlessly to its mate.   The   Argo   moved   on   to   minor repairs and sundry housekeeping tasks. They watched as a splattered cup of coffee poured itself back into the cup. That done, the cup floated back to a workstation and landed neatly on its surface.   The liquid was still hot.

"Well, Toto, I don't think we're in Kansas anymore," said Hal, hoping to break the tension.

The Argo was quiet once again, except for   the   sound   of   something   rattling around in the cargo hold.

"I'll go see what's going on down there," said Barbara. "You two check out the rest of the ship," she continued, gesturing vaguely in the air.   "Make sure we're not nuts."

At that, Barbara slid back into the floatway.   The noise persisted as she made her way to the cargo hold.   Nothing along   the   way   seemed   amiss. Nevertheless, she approached the cargo hold   carefully.   Closing   her   helmet visor, she opened the airlock slowly, entered the hold, and vanished into thin air.

#

For eons, she had drifted among the interstices   of   space,   weaving   and reweaving   with   her   mind   the   ten dimensions   in   what   passed   as contemplation among those of her race. They called her a Shtatàam, a Wise Woman, first among the order of the Nath Kadir.   She simply thought of herself as a woman.   It was simple.   Obvious.   She had done the things that women do. She had loved, been loved in return, born children, worked, and become wise in the ways of loss, for she was exceedingly long-lived and had seen the passing of much that she had cherished. In her aloneness she held and adored the memory of many a dying eye filled, until its very last moments, with an undying love for all things born of the Creator whom she now sought.

She did not have a spoken name as we understand such things. Her name, such as it was, was not borne 'by the breath. Her kind had long ago shed their lungs, as we once did our gills, for the sake of a life in places as incomprehensible to us as dry land would have been to our water-bound ancestors. To the extent that we could know her name at all, it would be an essence issuing from deep within the mind, capable of distilling her uniqueness. This the Nath Kadir required of their Shtatáamin and encouraged among all members of the race.

At one time, her race actually had much in common with Man, and lived not so very far away in the same solar system. However, that was part of a remote past that had almost faded from their ancestral memories and fragmented records. Of this time, they remembered only their home planet. It was the fourth out from a middle-aged star situated in one of the arms of a spiral galaxy. For a while, it was lush with water and rapidly evolving life, but with the passing eons, the water disappeared, and with it most of the life. This, plus an apocalyptic meteor barrage, left behind a cold, red, dusty cinder of a planet whose molten core was little more than a sullen ember. Of the beings' life on this small red planet there were few signs, save for one thing that had remained pristine millions of years after its creation.

Well before this slow death, the beings sensed their own potential as sapient life and embraced their destiny through a patient manipulation of their own speedy evolution into forms capable of traveling among the Universes. The last of the beings left their home planet just as life was exploding across the third planet -- a warm, watery, blue gem of a world with interior fires adequate for billions of years to come.

The journeys of these beings among other races would be too vast to chronicle were it not that they uncovered so many common patterns in the evolution of life and mind. One of these, and perhaps the most poignant, was the appearance -- and persistence -- of gender in places where life was even remotely possible. In some form, Yang always craved Yin. Among all the races in the Universe, flesh took on flesh in an ecstatic embrace whose issue assured that Creation would continue to be aware of itself.

Other common patterns had a particular bearing on this particular Shtatáam, who was so adept at weaving space with her mind. Among the earliest patterns in the evolution of sapient races was their discovery that mastery over the fundamental forces of Nature changed irrevocably the course of a species' technology and thus its destiny. Species who advanced this far generally found that their theories became simpler and more elegant when expressed in four or more spatial dimensions. Light, for instance, could be described simply as vibrations within a fifth dimension, and matter became another type of vibration ruffling the fabric of spacetime. Ultimately, if the Universes were viewed as clusters of bubbles, then outside of the bubbles space and time lost their meaning.

These latter considerations interested creatures such as the Shtatáam, formed the substance of their quests, actually. In effect, the more one's conception of space grew, the simpler the Universe revealed itself to be, until regions of Creation could be conceived of in which space and time fell away, and what remained was...

...the Hub of the Wheel. The changeless Void around which revolved all change. The field of infinite potential. The field of infinite being. Possibly the Creator's home.

The realization by most races that the apparent structure of space and time are, in part, projections of consciousness raised the possibility that the evolution of mind into an awareness of other dimensions would enable it to exist in the Universe at deeper and simpler levels.

The Shtatáam found it fascinating that members of all races -- call them mystics for lack of a better word -- always sensed that the evolution of being required a life of voluntary simplicity for deep realization to emerge. How like the Universe itself. The deep understanding of spacetime leading one into great simplicity. It was as if life is the Universe's way of being aware of itself, and that this awareness has a structure parallel to the stuff of Creation.

Becoming an exemplar of all this is a lot of work, and all races have recognized the need for a retreat into Wildness to do it. What exactly comprised Wildness was invariably dictated by a creature's biology. In the course of weaving herself among the many dimensions of spacetime, the Shtatáam befriended beings who had retreated into lava pits, the metallic hydrogen of gaseous giant planets, the coronas of stars, the pitted interiors of comets, in order to fold space, to understand it, and in so doing see the Cosmos as it truly is. There were times when the Shtatáam needed her own retreats from the demands of being a wise woman and so she formed the habit of orbiting her race's home planet as a kind of third moon. There, her meditations on the past and those she loved centered her, renewed her energies.

And then one day...

...she sensed that creatures from the third planet were making their way to her home planet. This was a matter of some curiosity to the Shtatáam because she sensed that one of the beings in the vessel was herself on the verge of becoming a weaver of time, space, and mind. This invariably was a benchmark in evolution. It meant that the species in question was on its way to becoming co-creators with The One. It augured well for their future.

She collapsed herself into a bioplasmic semblance of her native form and entered the vessel's hold. She was not at all used to the claustrophobic density of three dimensions, and for a few long moments staggered under the weight of an unwonted confinement, which resulted in her banging into a bulkhead and tripping over things. This wrecked the creatures' vessel and endangered their lives. The Shtatáam cursed her clumsiness and immediately began reweaving spacetime so as to set the vessel right.

#

Hal and Linda were two hours into their inspection when Linda noticed something.

"Hal! Listen!"

"Huh...to what?"

"To nothing, that's what!"

"Well that's good isn't it? I'd say it's goddamned wonderful."

"No. I don't like it. The hold's quiet. The ship's quiet. Everything's back to normal and we haven't heard anything from Barbara."

"If you're worried, just page her."

Nothing.

Barbara was the sort of person who would stop peeing in midstream to answer a page. Hal started to share Linda's concern.

"Okay, Fearless Leader, let's go."

#

Barbara threw on the lights the instant she entered the hold.

Nothing.

Nothing was amiss. All the equipment was strapped into place. Natasha's time capsule was resting in its cradle. The air was still and free of clutter or fumes. The bulkheads were sound and breathing was easy. The airlock's failsafe mechanism checked out all right.

So what had she heard coming so unmistakably from the hold?

Barbara was about to leave the hold when she turned and cast one last look around. That was when she noticed something, a bluish something, behind the time capsule. At first it looked like light reflected from an unknown source, but then it began shifting in ways that rendered simple reflection impossible. Intrigued, Barbara shut the lights and saw the thing glowing with a light reminiscent of the blue skies of her recent dreams wherein ancient, nameless caravans silently made their way to places they could only half-imagine.

Barbara felt no threat from the thing. Rather, she felt a soft tug at her shoulder that drew her again into the hold. An intuitive trust impelled her to within arm's reach of whatever it was, during which time the thing assumed a thin, humanoid form somewhat taller than she. They stood facing each other, motionless, until the thing moved. It extended what might have been an arm to touch the time capsule with what might have been seven fingers, such ambiguity arising from Barbara's inability to fix the thing in space, or in time for that matter. It seemed to flow in and out of both in ways she could see but could not articulate.

Then it moved towards her.

#

Momentarily taken aback by the creature's confusion, a feeling she had long ago forgotten, the Shtatáam collapsed herself behind the time capsule until the being, a female, calmed down. During the moments it took for the creature to do this, the Shtatáam turned her mind to the cylinder, specifically to the thing within it. Its fate, at least for the next hundred years or so, was fixed and easy to read, unlike the female's, whose destiny lines were a maelstrom of energies remarkable for her species in their variety and intensity.

The thing in the cylinder was much the same as the female in some ways, save that the forces behind the thing's unintended creation were dispersed among many individuals of the female's race. Within the cylinder was the consummation, not only of greed, hatred, and ignorance, but also of great love, great death, and great sacrifice. All of these energies had come together in a flash of thermonuclear chaos that would have rendered trivial these creatures' worst visions of Hell had it been prolonged by even a few more moments. This was by no means unique. The thing in the cylinder was testimony to a birth by atomic fire that delivered most races into a time of confusion for as long as it took to bring the forces of this infernal birth under control.

Most races succeeded.

A few did not and were now ashes drifting among the stars, awaiting rebirth within any infant star that happened to cross their aimless paths.

Had she assumed her fully enfleshed form, the Shtatáam would have shed tears over the time capsule. As it was, she was more interested in Barbara, hopeful that she could Meld with a being so primitive yet so promising.

The Martians discovered the Meld millions of years ago as a kind of spiritual lovemaking that satisfied their craving for erotic communion. Before long, the ecstatic union made possible by the Meld also proved to be the gateway for bending time and space, and for insinuating the soul into ten dimensions of our Universe. Twenty-six dimensions actually existed, but sixteen were as yet impervious to the Meld. Even within ten dimensions, the Meld validated the proclamations of lovers among all the sapient races that their passions took them places beyond the time and space that they knew. The Shtatáam sometimes mused, with a sadness almost unbearable, that her skills as a lover with a husband long since departed led her to become a Meld Master, that this in turn had opened her to the ten dimensions, and to communion with a Creator who itself provoked a desire for communion that in many ways was its own consummation.

The Shtatáam could have lost herself in this reverie had she not resolved to Meld with Barbara and unfold a small amount of space within her. She ascertained quickly that a human's bioplasmic energy flowed much as did a Martian's -- from the base of the spine up through the crown of the head. Fusion of their energies into parallel streams -- the Meld -- at first established the communion and then, if the partners were strong enough, a launch into the transcendent dimensions and the unfolding of mind and space.

The erotic partners, the Jiddashin, typically remained entwined as male-female pairs and made the journey together. The Shtatáam could go beyond this and Meld with energy that the Nath Kadir believed flowed from the Creator. All she needed to do was bound along Its energy in search of any unfoldings for which she was ready. Analogously, Barbara might be able to move along the Shtatáam's energy and do the same thing on a small scale.

To this end, the Shtatáam drew Barbara into an embrace that aligned them for the Meld. Barbara's fusion points were easy to find, and communion occurred readily. When it happened, the Shtatáam realized that they could have become fast friends, in other times, in other places. For now, she had to be content with the stability of the Meld and attenuated her bioplasmic form into a blue halo around Barbara's free-floating body.

It was simple. Within the darkness of a cargo hold, in a frail and primitive vessel leaping the void between two planets, two strangers, two aliens, became one, each not knowing where she ended and the other began.

#

Barbara did not move as the Shtatáam approached, she felt no need to, until something enfolded her into an embrace filling everything in her awareness with the blue light of her dreams. She knew then, in that moment, what it was like for her skin -- all of her skin -- to be an organ of pleasure as the light worked its way along her body, touching, tickling, stroking, scratching, caressing, deeper and deeper until even her bones were thrilling to things never conceived in even the most exotic pillow books. For perhaps a millisecond it occurred to Barbara that anything capable of causing this much delight could also inflict pain in equal measure. The thought lasted but a millisecond because something feathered its way into her awareness, replacing fear with a longing for fusion with, what?

Then the whispers began.

Barbara's mind had become quiet to the same proportion that her body was effervescing with delight. Within the deeps of this solitude she heard two voices murmuring between themselves, their words sliding over each other much as would two lovers rolling in a field on a sultry night. She had no idea what the voices were saying, even though one of them was hers. She was speaking from a place to which she had never been to someone who lived there all the time. Confusion fell away when Barbara realized she was listening to those whispers between lovers that can never be told in their proper form to another, being, as it would, an intrusion into things that must remain untold and kept forever inviolate. The whispers suffused the space around them with their intimacies and then faded to black, but not before she heard a voice urging her to find the mysterious blue object on Mars, at which time she would know what to do with it.

#

Hal and Linda pulled themselves along the floatway until they reached the hold's darkened entry. They tumbled over each other when they heard a series of increasingly stertorous, gasping breaths that soon subsided into an unnerving silence. Cautiously, they peered inside the hold, looked everywhere, and saw nothing. No damage, no floating equipment, no debris, and no Barbara. They ventured inside.

"Hal, did we hear that right?"

"Beats the shit out of me..."

Hal never finished his sentence. He cut himself short when a misty, blue light shimmered into existence less than a foot from his face. He stepped back just as the light assumed a vaguely human form. Before either of them could speak, the form condensed into Barbara. She was asleep and breathing calmly. Hal shook her shoulder, tentatively, half-expecting her to again disappear.

"Barbara...Barbara...wake up."

She opened her eyes slowly, as if reluctant to leave behind the blissful sleep of the unborn. Somewhat disoriented, she looked up at Hal.

"Hal, where am I...why are you two staring at me like that?"

"We're hoping you could tell us."

340

Barbara righted herself so as to face her friends.

"I...don't know," she said looking around the cargo hold. "I remember coming in here...I saw a blue light in one of the corners. I approached it...or maybe it approached me...and then I fell asleep. That's it."

Barbara shrugged her shoulders. And then she remembered something.

"Somebody told me that we have to find that blue thing on the surface at all costs, that it would be the most important discovery in human history."

Hal and Linda looked nervously at each other and then at Barbara.

"Barb, today's been weird enough but this is really creeping me out," said Linda. If we report this to Mission Control, they'll think we've gone nuts."

"And what are they going to do? Put a tractor beam on us?" said Barbara. "We've been sent on a mission of discovery. We discovered something, or something's discovered us. I'll report what we saw and let them deal with it. How's the ship?"

"You'd never know that anything happened," said Hal.

"Go figure...," mumbled Barbara.

At that, she pushed herself into the floatway. Linda followed. Hal stayed behind and sealed the mystery within the airlock.

Barbara made a full report and transmitted it to Mission Control. It took them a long time to answer.

341

TRAJECTORIES AND DESTINIES:6,000,000,000 B.C. to 2034 A.D.

By most measures, "birth" is an arbitrarily defined event that has no discrete beginning. At most, it acts as a gatekeeper for events that unfold by infinitesimal degrees into an "afterbirth", also arbitrarily defined. This being the case, then all existence can be seen as a continuous birth, with space being a midwife to the ceaseless labors of time.

Such was the case for a piece of rock and ice that was born, along with billions of its kind, in a cloud that was forming some ten trillion miles around the center of an accretion disk that would eventually form our sun, the nine planets, and the asteroid belt.

But we need not begin here. We can go back still further in time, along the continuum of birth, to the molecular cloud that would coalesce to form the objects just described. It was a place whose temperature was so close to absolute zero that its very molecules were still. Not so much as an atom could whisper its presence into the void. The place was so quiet it almost was not there.

This was fortunate, at least for us, because it meant that the atoms and molecules of the cloud could coalesce under the influence of gravity without being dispersed by their own heat, given the proper stimulus. This was provided by a nearby supernova, whose shock waves passed through the cloud and caused part of it to collapse into what would eventually be the protostar in whose its middle the sun would form.

The gravitational collapse of atoms within the protostar intensified over millions of years, as additional gas and dust fell into it. It started to get hot. The core temperature of the protostar soared to eleven million degrees. The heat-driven expansion so created loosened the vise of the protostar's gravitational collapse, and the thermonuclear fusion of hydrogen to helium began. The protostar ignited and became our Sun.

All of this was invisible to the fragment of rock and ice as it formed from carbonaceous matter within the cloud, because our infant sun was so heavily shrouded in dust. Likewise the rock. Its surface was so utterly nonreflective that it was blacker than the surrounding space. Innumerable collisions and gravitational interactions during those dark times conferred upon the rock a stable but exceedingly long-period orbit around the sun of about 30 million years.

Things continued in much this way for the next 4.6 billion years. The rock was so far from the sun that the solar wind was the merest whisper on its surface, and not nearly intense enough to evaporate the ices that had accumulated on it during the solar system's formation. But there came a time when the sun attracted a partner — a dark star. They began waltzing around each other once every 26 million years. There came a point in this dance when the dark star came close enough to the sun to disturb the rock's orbit and send it toward the sun.

Once within Jupiter's orbit, solar warmth was strong enough to soften the water ice and loosen the dust on the sunward side of the rock. After some months, the resulting jet of water and dust preceded the rock by several thousand miles, turning this lump of carbonaceous matter into a faintly visible comet.

The rock's life as a comet was short lived, however, because it contained very little dust and ice, as these things go. By the time it crossed the orbit of Mars, the rock had been purged of all volatile substances and had become nothing but a black meteor preceded by a long cloud of dust. It went unnoticed by otherwise meticulous observers on Earth.

The sojourn of this rock through the solar system is worth mentioning only because of a singular event which occurred as it dove toward the sun. Shortly after crossing the orbit of Mars, the rock encountered a living being. The encounter was singular in the extreme. The probability of these two objects crossing each other's paths at this point in the solar system was so remote that a similar event never had and would almost certainly never occur again anywhere in the galaxy.

The rock was perturbed very little by its encounter with the being. ` It, however, was shattered by the encounter. Large parts of it dispersed into space. The rest infiltrated the surface of the rock and briefly formed a crust of organic ice that, over time, was degraded into simpler molecules by the solar wind.

Although the rock was largely unchanged by its encounter with the life form, its orbit was altered just enough for the sun's gravity to act as a slingshot, hurling it out of the solar system toward the galactic core at 47,000 miles per hour. A suitably placed observer would have noticed something peculiar on the surface of the rock facing the galactic core, which was also the surface that encountered the life form. An oval lump of organic matter, with five slender appendages extending from one side, had formed a small crater on the surface of the rock, which was actually quite fragile and porous as rocks go. A small piece of gold had fused onto one of the appendages by the force of the impact.

At its present speed, the rock, along with its speck of gold, would reach the galactic core in another 385 million years, provided that nothing else interfered with its trajectory.

#

Barbara was practicing a landing simulation, when a worried Linda floated in and tweaked her commander's fingers. This had the effect of crashing the virtual shuttle into the shoreline of Cydonia Mensae, which got the commander's attention. Barbara opened the visor, and flung a few choice words squarely into Linda's frown.

"Why the puss."

"We have a problem."

"Imminent?"

"I think so. The sensor nets on the forward hulls have been registering more micrometeor impacts than normal. A lot more. And all of a sudden. A few have already pierced the hull. There's nothing on the charts, but we must be passing through a dust cloud. I made some assumptions about particle size and density and ran a simulation. If this keeps up there's a sixty percent chance of a forward outer hull breach within the next five hours. Not a big one, but we should do something about it. There's no sense in letting the hull integrity slip so early in the mission."

346

Barbara's frown now matched Linda's. She called down the floatway. "Hal, are you listening to this?"

"Yep. We both worked on the simulation."

"Do you agree?"

"Yes. If you want, we might transmit the data to Mission Control and see if their simulation matches ours. If it does, we could discuss repairs."

"That would take too long, said Barbara.

"Then why don't I just go out and make a few spot welds. That should hold us for a while," said Linda.

"Yea, but anything that could breach the shield could pierce your suit." Barbara was starting to experience a sick sense of foreboding.

"Impacts on the hull sides are only two to three percent above baseline. We mustn't be creating too much turbulence. I could do the whole thing manually," said Linda.

"OK, but take a jet pack and keep your butt behind the forward shields. And don't stay out any longer than necessary. Hal, inform mission control of our situation. Do your best not to bruise their egos over not being consulted first."

#

Within the hour, Linda was effecting repairs under the shield. Sections of it were more battered than she had expected. The three of them would have to repair it in shifts. If nothing else, the work would relieve them of the tedium of simply maintaining the ship's systems, exercising, and sleeping.

About two hours into the repairs, Linda noticed an increase in the impact noise that Hal was piping through her headset. The benign sound of dust bouncing off the shield was suddenly punctuated by the random pops of micrometeors large enough to dent it. Linda thought the better of staying out and was packing the tool kit when Barbara's voice cut through the noise.

"Come on back in, Linda."

"I'm one step ahead..."

Faster than anyone could react, a pea-sized meteor slashed one flank of the jet pack. Outgushing fuel sent Linda tumbling along the hull and out into the void. Some moments passed before she could close the damaged fuel cell and stabilize herself with the remaining maneuvering rocket. She came to rest about one-hundred feet from the Argo, moving abreast of her at the same relative speed. For the first time in her life, Linda Maddock muttered a prayer - a prayer of thanksgiving to Barbara's parents for designing so much redundancy into the Argo and her equipment.

"Jesus, Linda, are you all right?" exclaimed Barbara over the headset.

"Yeah...I think so," muttered Linda, more flustered than she cared to admit."

"Do you want Hal to come out and get you?"

Linda checked the jet pack's monitors. Except for the ruptured fuel cell, it was intact. She inhaled deeply and replied.

"No, I can make it myself."

"Well, then, take it slow. And no heroics," said Barbara.

Linda nudged herself toward the Argo, her gaze alternating between the nearest air lock and the jet pack's monitors. This disinclined her to pause and take in the silence of space and the brilliance of the stars around her. Had she done so, she might have looked toward the outer planets and noticed a small, irregular patch of black blotting out a few stars. If she had lingered to study this curiosity, she would have seen it grow.

Hal monitored Linda's telemetry, as well as the sensor nets in her suit and the hull shields. Barbara hovered over him. The audio channel of the monitor emitted occasional beeps as micrometeors hit various sensor nets.

"Hal, how're we doing with the impaction rates?"

"Still about five percent above baseline. No significant dips. Linda's suit pressure is stable."

"Then why can't I stop feeling sick about this whole thing?"

"Beats me, sweetheart. It's your stomach. Maybe it's trying to tell you something."

For the next few minutes, Hal continued his vigil over the monitor, while Barbara stared at Linda, who was visible through the cabin's starboard porthole. Suddenly, the audio channel squealed an increase in impaction activity.

"Linda, get back in here!"

Linda didn't need to be told. As Barbara watched through the porthole, Linda throttled her jet pack, her voice overriding the noise on the audio channel. "Guys, this is seriously weird. You should hear it. It's like rain..." For a moment, Barbara thought she saw something blot out the stars. The instant they reappeared, Linda's telemetry went dead, and she was nowhere to be seen. The impaction rate quickly dropped to baseline, and things got awfully quiet.

As Barbara peered through the porthole, an arm tumbled into view and bounced off the glass, spattering it with blood that quickly boiled down to a terra cotta smudge. A sickening realization turned her bowels into water. She spoke in a cracked whisper.

"Sweet Jesus! We've been sailing our asses through a comet tail! What are the chances of that?"

Hal did not answer.

#

An observer suitably placed on the comet would have seen Linda's face smash into a death mask. For a few moments, tears of blood flowed down her crushed cheeks before boiling off into space, where the solar wind would eventually

350

degrade them into simple organic compounds. As the comet began its journey toward the galactic core, Linda's face froze onto the surface and shadows began to fill her unblinking eyes as the Sun shrank to a point of cold light. Several meters away, cupped within a small crater, a tiny piece of gold shimmered feebly in the dying light before fading into the eternal night of interstellar space.

The paralysis of thought and feeling that ensued had to be broken. Barbara straightened herself and moved toward the porthole. She ran her fingers down its glass, as if wanting to caress something forever beyond her reach. Another face had taken its place among the others in the night sky of her heart. Mother. Dad. Grandpa. And now Linda. Forever gone. Forever watching over her. She felt a hand on her shoulder.

"They say you two went way back."

"Yea...way back...two cocky kids on motorcycles," she said. "Nothing was going to stop us."

Shuddering with grief, Barbara turned to face Hal. She hesitated a moment before placing her head on his shoulder. He returned the gesture with an embrace. Feeling safe for the moment, Barbara brooded over the thought that the radio transmission informing Mission Control of Linda's death would reach the galactic core in 27,000 years. What she did not know was that Linda's gold wedding ring was also on its way to the galactic core and would reach it in another 385 million years, provided that nothing else interfered with its destiny.

Barbara placed her hands on Hal's chest and pushed away from him.

"I have a report to write."

#

Linda's remaining body parts assumed stable orbits around the Sun. Over time, the solar wind reduced them to desiccated lumps of dust, and they remained as such for the rest of the Sun's existence. But these lumps of dust that once comprised the vehicle for a being called Linda Maddock were many things and were called by many names before they came together and were called Linda. They were the binding of a book; they were the eye of a horse; they were the rust on a Viking's sword; they were the teeth of a dinosaur; they were the shell of a trilobite, and so on ad infinitum back to a time when the body of the universe exploded from a point in virtual space smaller than an atomic nucleus. The improbable sojourn of Linda's dust as satellites of our Sun was simply that: an interlude before the Sun's eventual supernova would hurl them back into deep space, whence they first came, where they would eventually accrete again to form pieces of other stars and planets, and perhaps find their way again into another sentient being.

It was the same with Linda's commander and friend on the Argo. Her dust had been many things before it became part of the being named Barbara Llandry, and it would become many other things before its ineluctable expulsion into deep space would make it a part of other stellar systems.

What no one could ever know is that a whisp of Barbara's dust would coalesce with a whisp of Linda's dust and be hurled together into deep space during the Sun's death throes five billion years hence.

HARD LANDINGS: July 2034

"This really sucks," said Hal. "You'd think someone didn't want us to land."

He and Barbara stood in front of the Argo's main viewing screen, appalled at the scene unfolding beneath them. The storm that the Ground Control people were tracking had grown malignantly over the last few days and engulfed the entire planet in a rusty shroud. Even the Tharsis volcanoes, which straddled the equator like three giant boils, were invisible. The final insult came when Olympus Mons — at 80,000 feet the tallest volcano in the solar system — disappeared under the blanketing winds as if it were being put to bed for a very long nap.

Linda's death had forced a radical revision of the mission and the deferment of certain tasks for future landings. Now, they faced the prospect of effecting a controlled landing while flying blind through a hurricane whose dirty winds would confound readings from the navigational computers. The meteorologists at Mission Control had determined that the storm had stabilized and that there was no predicting when it would relent. Whether they landed now or a few days hence was Barbara's call. She saw no benefit in waiting. Once they were stable, Martian dust storms were known to last upwards of a year.

"Well, Hal, let's rock-and-roll," said Barbara.

"I hope you don't mean that literally," said Hal.

"Just think of it as a chance to do some fancy flying. You're not scared, are you?" said Barbara teasingly.

"Hell no," said Hal.

Barbara relayed their plans to Earth while Hal parked the Argo in synchronous orbit over a base camp that had been established on the planet's equator, some 50 miles east of the Tharsis volcanoes. Telemetry from the camp had gone dead several hours after the storm first thundered through the region. For all they knew, they were setting their sights on a trash heap.

The shuttle had been readied some hours earlier. After securing the Argo, Hal and Barbara stood hesitantly in front of it. The original plan required that the Argo be manned at all times. The person on board would coordinate the mission, effect maintenance and repairs, and supervise the stowage of geologic specimens once every two months. This would have permitted one full crew rotation aboard the Argo. But that was history. Henceforth, they would have to monitor the Argo remotely. Any onboard emergencies would likely scuttle the mission and subject them to a slow death through exposure. Barbara stepped into the shuttle first. Hal followed and closed the airlock. It occurred to him that the 'hisss-thunk" of the pressure seals marked either the start of mankind's greatest adventure or its most appalling blunder.

"Hal? You all right?"

"Uh, yeah, Barbara, I was just thinking."

"Well stop it. You know how much it hurts your brain."

Barbara smiled at him and patted the copilot's seat.

"Let's make history," she said.

Hal strapped himself into the seat. Barbara began the launch sequence. Within minutes they were set to go. At a nod from Barbara, Hal released the docking clamps. She jockeyed the shuttle away from its moorings on the Argo while Hal activated the descent sequence. The hiss of the maneuvering thrusters filled the cabin as the autopilot positioned the shuttle for atmospheric entry. The ready-light appeared on the console.

"Everything okay on your side?" asked Barbara.

"I'm good," said Hal. "How about you?"

"Ditto."

They began the descent. The outer reaches of the atmosphere were navigable, but it was not long before they found themselves in the opaque soup of the storm. Streams of burning dust scorched the shuttle with long, angry streaks. The craft shuddered under the strains of the erratic changes in pitch and yaw forced upon it by the storm. Barbara found herself fighting the joystick in her increasingly ineffectual attempts to maintain the shuttle's attitude. The engines were guzzling fuel.

"Hal! How's the imaging?" shouted Barbara over the din.

"Lousy. We're heading in the right direction. That's all I can tell you," he shouted in reply.

Just then, the joystick forced itself from Barbara's grip as if in the throes of a tantrum. The shuttle tumbled end over end.

"Shit!" said Barbara. "I flew us into a dust devil!"

Her first impulse was to punch her way through the wind funnel, but she thought the better of it. Yielding to the main force of the dust devil, Barbara nudged the shuttle's nose away from the wind and surfed the funnel.

"We have zero visibility," said Hal.

"Can you clean up the signal?" replied Barbara.

"I'm trying," said Hal, "but we're still blind." She gripped the joystick and throttled the engines full force.

The shuttle whined under the sudden acceleration. Barbara muscled the shuttle's nose to its port side. It shuddered briefly, and forced its way through the funnel.

Still wrestling with the joystick, Barbara called to Hal.

"Where are we?"

"I've got a fix. We're going the wrong way. Turn us about and head northeast."

Barbara changed course. A few minutes later, Hal noticed a warning light on his console.

"We've only got enough fuel for one ascent with a full cargo," he said.

"How far are we from the base camp?" asked Barbara.

"About 100 miles" replied Hal.

Barbara cut the main engine and let the shuttle glide.

"Am I on course?" she asked.

"You're OK," he said, "I'll let you know if you stray."

Barbara had to fight the winds to keep the shuttle aloft and on course. At the lower altitudes, they became vicious. Not content with streaming along the shuttle's unoffending fuselage, they resorted instead to buffeting kicks and punches that resounded through the crew compartment like so many thugs. The fact that they were still flying blind under the direction of muddled guidance from the navigational array did little to mitigate the threats raining on them from all quarters.

Barbara was straining to see through the storm when a melon-sized clod of dirt splattered itself across the windshield with the speed of a bullet. Thousands of smaller but similar impacts peppered the port side of the shuttle.

"Hard to starboard!" yelled Hal.

Barbara reacted faster than Hal could form the words. They had strayed to within 50 yards of the eastern face of the Pavonis Mons volcano. The storm's relentless pounding of the volcano's mountainous slopes had set up a landslide that would have engulfed them in a chaos from which there would have been no escape had they not reacted as quickly as they did. The incident did, at least, reveal that they were very close to the base camp, if there was a base camp.

"How close are we to the landing site?" asked Barbara.

"About 10 miles," said Hal.

"Good. Deploy the air bags on my mark," she said.

The navigational array was revealing the faint profiles of facilities that had been assembled by a series of unmanned robotic emissions to Mars. The winds on the surface were no less forgiving that they were higher up and there was no possibility of a controlled landing.

"Mark!"

Air bags crafted from bullet-proof fabric blistered the shuttle's surface under the force of explosive compressed-air charges. They landed nose first and rolled over the ground like a golf ball bouncing along a green. Barbara sensed the shuttle coming to rest upside-down. It was designed for such a contingency, but she was in no mood to jump ass-backward onto the ground. She tweaked the maneuvering thrusters one last time. The shuttle rolled onto its belly.

Hal and Barbara sat quietly for a while, listening, as the storm raged unabated around them. The entire ordeal had lasted all of 20 minutes, but it might as well have been a lifetime. What they had just accomplished set them apart from every other member of their race and, despite their nervous exhaustion, they both felt new. The planet had raised an angry fist at them and they had prevailed. They felt pristine. They were the first man, the first woman, to claim a restless Eden by dint of intelligence, heart, and will. It would have been a fabulous time to make love, she thought wistfully. Hal sensed her mood. She felt a shy touch on her right hand. Her skin tingled playfully in response, and then yielded to the spreading warmth of Hal's hand as he grasped hers. It was the first time she had let a man touch her since her imprisonment and she liked it.

"You did good, Barbara."

She beamed at him and chuckled.

"Hal, do you realize those were the first words to be spoken by a human on this planet?"

He thought about it, and nodded.

"It says everything that needs to be said," he replied.

"Thanks."

Barbara looked around her at the crew compartment.

"There's no point in going out," she said. "Let's do some housekeeping. Retract the balloons. I'll start a systems check.

Hal went aft. Barbara started with the navigation system. She repaired a number of software glitches identified by the diagnostics program and recalibrated the system to compensate the limitations imposed on it by the storm. Despite all that, the imaging data were still muddled. Barbara resigned herself to the necessary tedium of a deep-level noise analysis.

In the meantime, Hal had retracted the balloons and reset the explosive charges. He saw that Barbara was absorbed in repairing the software, so he began inspecting the mechanical systems. He started with the engines and attitude thrusters and worked his way forward. At each step, he was impressed by how few repairs and adjustments he had to make. There was a lot to be said for not awarding government contracts to the lowest bidder.

He was inspecting the joysticks when Barbara shushed him. "Listen! We have a homing beacon." She transmitted a few commands to the habitat computers. Their instant replies informed Hal and Barbara that the base camp's critical systems were intact, including the greenhouse. They also transmitted a list of hundreds of lesser problems that needed attention. Hal reviewed the list.

"This stuff can wait a day or two."

Barbara nodded in assent.

"It's getting dark anyway. We might as well spend the night here," she said. "Besides, I'm beat. How about you?"

"I could sleep through a war right now."

At that, they set about making themselves as comfortable as possible. Despite the amorous tension that was building between them, they dozed off and slept like the dead.

BASE CAMP

Hal and Barbara awoke ten hours later to the same winds that had lulled them to sleep. They reconstituted some rations and peered through the windows as they ate. Visibility at best was 20 feet.

"So what's the plan?" asked Hal.

"There's no use spending the day here," said Barbara. "You go out and check the hull integrity while I get the rovers up and running."

They suited up and moved toward the airlock. Then it struck them. This was it — the first step of the first human on an alien world. It was just a baby step. But it was the necessary first of many such that would, in time, lengthen to bounding leaps. Hal opened the airlock and stepped aside.

"Ladies first," he offered.

Barbara hesitated.

"Go on, you've earned it," he said.

She entered the airlock. Hal followed and sealed the inner lock. Barbara opened the outer lock. The sudden drop in atmospheric pressure nudged them forward, as if encouraging them to start the real mission. Barbara looked around but there was nothing to see except the wind-driven curtains of dust. She descended the landing ramp and stepped onto the ground. It responded with a crunch so like that of the farmland surrounding Milton that it amounted to a homecoming in reverse.

Hal trotted down the ramp and jumped into the air. He landed with the nimbleness of a child playing hopscotch, and set about inspecting the shuttle's hull. Barbara lowered one of the cargo ramps. She climbed into the hold and began readying the rovers for their trek to the base camp. The rovers were essentially high-tech all-terrain vehicles and, despite the storm, Barbara looked forward to riding them across the plain that lay between them and the base camp. She loaded the time capsule onto one of the rovers and eased it down the ramp. She let the engine idle while she retrieved the other rover. That being accomplished, she walked to the shuttle's rear, where Hal was tinkering with the thrusters.

"How's it going?" she asked.

"Fine, except for the nozzles. They're fouled with dust. I've cleaned the worst of it, but we should cover them before we leave." Barbara helped Hal with some final cleaning and installed the covers. Taking one last look at the shuttle, they mounted the rovers and started for the base camp.

With five miles separating the shuttle from the camp, Barbara and Hal were tempted to make time crossing the plain. The less exposure they had to the storm, the safer they would be. They had no safe choice but to navigate by the base camp's homing signal and had almost stopped squinting into the storm when something prompted Barbara to look up. She slammed the brakes and pitched over the rover's front end. She landed on her back and found herself staring up at a boulder the size of a bus. Hal leaped off his rover and ran up to her.

"You OK?"

"I'm fine. More embarrassed than anything else," said Barbara.

"Let's take it easy the rest of the way. I can barely see my rover from here," said Hal.

They resumed the crossing more cautiously. At times they had to plow through dunes that appeared and disappeared at the wind's caprice only to reappear in the most inconvenient places. It took them two hours to traverse the remaining three miles. They paused when the sandy silhouettes of the base camp's facilities finally appeared in the murk. The habitat module, greenhouse, tool shop, and hangar were still standing. Their telemetry had not changed in any important way.

Hal and Barbara rode into the camp.

"We shouldn't leave these things outside," said Barbara. "Let's stop at the hangar first."

They rode past of the habitat and stopped in front of the hangar. Hal dismounted his rover and opened the bay doors. Barbara rode into the hangar and parked her rover. Hal followed suit. He closed the doors and together they trotted back to the habitat. Opening its outer airlock, they stepped inside. The storm had not breached the entry. It was as immaculate as it was on the day it was built. Barbara scanned the habitat's interior while Hal sealed the outer airlock. All the major systems were within their normal operating limits. The habitat was pressurized and at room temperature.

"How are we doing?" asked Hal.

"Cozy," answered Barbara. We might even have fresh vegetables with dinner tonight."

Hal pressurized the airlock's interior. Barbara released the inner seals and entered the habitat. Except for an assortment of minor warning lights on various computer consoles, the habitat was waking itself up as planned.

"Hey Barbara, you're tracking dirt all over our clean floors!" said Hal, teasingly. "Your Grandpa would be appalled."

For the briefest instant, Barbara reacted like a chastised child. She walked over to Hal and swatted him on the shoulder. A puff of rust-colored dust filled the space around them. They both coughed a little.

"Before we do anything else, let's sonicate the suits," said Hal.

"And then let's eat something," said Barbara.

They helped each other out of their pressure suits, all the while longing to disburden themselves of more than that. Neither them spoke of it and the moment passed. Hal sniffed the air while Barbara set the cleaning cycle.

"Do you smell coffee?" he asked.

Barbara closed the sonic cleaner and stood up.

"Yeah, I do," she replied. "I hope nothing's wrong."

They found the galley-kitchen-conference room. A pot of fresh coffee sat on the stove, no doubt a welcoming gesture on the part of a nameless but kind engineer. They set the pot on a table in the middle of the room and, talking very little, drank it at their leisure. The room's only window might as well have never been installed, so opaque was the view afforded by the filthy, implacable winds.

"I hope this storm lifts pretty soon. We're up shit's creek if it doesn't," said Hal.

"With Linda...gone...we could stretch our resources another six months or so," said Barbara. She was about to say something else, but stopped, and stared into the warm mug cradled in her hands. "I hate myself for sending her out there to plug a couple of leaks. Sometimes I think I'll never stop hating myself."

Hal said nothing. He put his hands around Barbara's and waited until she looked up at him.

"Barbara...how does it help the mission...how does it honor Linda's memory if all you can do is hate yourself?"

She held his gaze a little longer and then looked down at the mug again.

"I know it's irrational, but it's just that we both dreamed of doing this when we were just kids. She was so sure we'd make it. It's as if she took it as given that we were going, and started working to make it happen. She'd be thrilled just to be stuck in this storm swilling coffee."

"She would," said Hal. "And she'd be right. Listen, I'm no philosopher. I don't have the mind for it. But I've never thought that death ends everything. You have your journey to make and she has hers. We just didn't think it would turn out this way."

"Hal, I didn't know you were so thoughtful," said Barbara.

"I'm not. That's all the philosophy I can take for one day," said Hal. After a discrete pause, he changed the subject. "I'm in the mood for bacon and eggs all of a sudden. How about you?"

"Sounds good," she said.

Hal rose from the table. Barbara stopped him.

"At ease, Captain," she said. "I'll make them. You just sit and enjoy the view."

Not sure which view she meant, Hal laid back in his chair and enjoyed them both. His reverie was disrupted by a second philosophical thought for the day. The United States and her allies had spent billions of dollars on the Mars program with the intention of sending people there. And what do the first humans on Mars do? They occupy themselves with something as prosaic as making bacon and eggs. He and Barbara were about to sit down to the most expensive meal in history. He laughed at the thought of it.

"What's so funny, dear?"

"No matter where we go in the universe, sweetheart, it all comes down to bacon and eggs. Best we learn to enjoy the simple things, because that's all there is."

#

Hal and Barbara used the next three days to effect the repairs flagged by the camp's diagnostic and maintenance computer. They worked quietly and seldom spoke. They ate when they were hungry, slept when they were tired, and worked methodically. Time scheduled itself as if responding to a rhythm beyond the purview of their thoughts and intentions. Even when they had to work together, they seldom felt the need to speak. They complemented one another's movements so well that the repairs

369

seemed choreographed. Each completed task was another brick laid into the foundation of their growing rapport.

Barbara came to love Hal's voice. When he did speak, it was a gentle, rolling thunder borne on distant storms on an otherwise imperturbable horizon. His personality was much like his voice, and Barbara could not help thinking he would be a wonderful father. Hal was also experiencing Barbara in new ways. Before they landed on Mars, he related to her as a superior officer to whom he was powerfully attracted and for whom he would die in combat. But it was an intrinsically unequal relationship and he had often wished that he were not so drawn to such forbidden fruit. Recently though, he was learning that Barbara did not make any personal investment in the trappings and privileges of rank. It was a facade that she put on and took off as casually as she would a hat. He now saw that she was unpretentious to the point of being shy while at the same time being friendly and open. And, judging by the amount of time she spent puttering around the greenhouse and making salads, she had a roosting instinct as well. It was an endearing ensemble of traits.

#

Barbara awoke on the morning of the fourth day feeling uneasy. Something was wrong; specifically, something was missing. She rose and ascended to the kitchen. Taking in the panoramic view afforded by the room's windows, it took her a moment to register the fact that she had been awakened by silence. So acclimated had she become to the shrieking winds that their disappearance left a void that she experienced as a kind of deafness.

And then she registered the view. To her left and a hundred miles distant, the Pavonis Mons volcano dominated the equatorial skyline. Arsia Mons and Ascraeus Mons, each 500 miles to the south and north, pimpled the horizon. Straight ahead and a thousand miles to the northwest, Olympus Mons brooded over the land as a monument to the impartial violence of planet building. No virtual simulation of the place could even remotely duplicate the immediacy of being there. It was at once intimidating and exhilarating. Barbara walked up to the window.

"This is so cool!"

"Actually, it should be pretty warm today. Maybe 70 degrees."

Barbara turned around.

"Oh...good morning Hal. I didn't know you were up."

Hal looked up from a live weather display and smiled.

"Been up for a while. I finally got a beam on the Argus," he said. "The storm's breaking up into smaller cyclones, mostly to the south. We have a clear shot at that blue thing."

"How's the Argo?" she asked.

"Still sittin' pretty," answered Hal. "I also sent a report home. The guys were antsy wondering where we splattered ourselves."

"This calls for a little party," said Barbara. "Pancakes and sausage?"

"Sounds good," said Hal. "You want me to make them?"

No, that's all right. I'll do it," said Barbara. "Coffee?"

"Black."

"Jigger of whiskey?"

"Do we have any?"

"If I know the boys back home, they'll have a stash or two here somewhere."

#

Barbara spent much of the day in a halting conversation with Mission Control. The one-hour delay between a given transmission and its response drained the interaction of all its spontaneity, making it more like a series of monologues. At issue was whether they should first make the thousand-mile trek to the object on Olympus Mons in the northwest, or travel 700 miles to the southeast and explore the Valles Marineris, a chasm much like the Grand Canyon except that it was deeper and spanned the distance between New York and Los Angeles. There were compelling arguments in favor of each target, not the least of which was that each would be a geologic treasure trove. Olympus Mons eventually won out. The bluish-green object had reappeared and was much larger than first suspected. It was a bonus that inclined the mission planners to place the volcano first.

The transmissions for the day were over when the concussions from three loud explosions rocked the habitat on its foundations. Barbara's first thought was of Hal. He had spent the day in the hangar readying equipment and vehicles for the mission, and she feared the worst. She scrambled to the nearest window and almost wept with relief when she saw him standing in front of the hangar, staring at three craters about 500 yards north of the camp. She scrambled into her pressure suit and within five minutes was standing next to Hal.

"I'd say we just about got our asses blown off," he said wryly. "Let's check it out."

They were nearing the closest of the craters when the ground beneath them trembled for an unnerving half minute. They surveyed the four long-dead volcanoes before them, dreading to see any signs of activity so close to the camp. There were none. The mountains continued their brooding vigil over the lava plains of the northern hemisphere. The ground was once again still. Hal and Barbara jogged to the nearest crater.

They came upon a steaming chunk of black rock the size of a grapefruit. The crater itself was still warm from the impact. Hal jumped into the crater and nudged the object with his boot.

"I can move this back to camp by myself," said Hal. "It's lighter than it looks."

"Good. Let's check out the other craters," said Barbara.

The second crater was much like the first. The crater beyond it was the size of a football field. In its middle sat a watermelon-sized rock similar to the first two fragments. Barbara looked at the crater' rim and gasped.

"Hal! Is that water?"

She pointed to a stratum of rock six feet beneath the surface. It was sweating a clear liquid. Considering the heat of the impact, it could not have been liquid carbon dioxide.

"The impact must have melted the stuff," said Hal.

Barbara stepped back from the rim and said, "I think our trip up north will have to wait a few days."

#

The week that followed changed the world, or at least Mankind's view of it. The liquid was indeed water. That confirmation of a long-held expectation alone unleashed torrents of ecstasy among exobiologists the world over, who now could offer plausible scenarios for terra forming Mars, provided of course that there was no indigenous life on the planet. The meteorites proved to be fragments of a rogue meteor that was saturated with a slurry of substances ranging from amino acids to large, complex proteins of a type whose synthesis in nature was associated only with living things. This revelation sent a second surge of joy through planetary scientists, who speculated that the comet was a chip from a life-bearing planet. Hal and Barbara could have packed up and gone home right then and justified the expense of the mission. But Olympus Mons and the increasingly mysterious object in its flanks beckoned them more insistently than ever.

Howard L. Enfiejian

A CASE OF NERVES

The meteor strikes at the base camp were only the first of a series. The sonic booms from two more meteoric impacts rocked the port side of the Geophysical Roving Utility Battery, or GRUB, as it began the thousand-mile trek northwest toward Olympus Mons. Everyone involved with the mission agreed that the planet was moving through a debris field previously undetectable from earth. The consensus was that the comet that had nearly annihilated the Argo was only part of a larger assemblage of objects. These impacts occurred when the GRUB was 100 miles northwest from the base camp. Hal and Barbara had stopped to drill core samples from the vast lava plains that separated the Tharsis volcanoes from Olympus Mons. It was to be the first of several such stops. At one point, shock waves from a nearby impact almost knocked the GRUB over on its side. Seismographs at the base camp and elsewhere on the planet located the impacts. There was no pattern to them. It was as if a blind god were hurling boulders at them.

But the bombardment was also a weird sort of boon. Each impact was a reason to return to Mars, to study its crustal geology, to sample flotsam from the nether rim of the solar system. The cosmos was showering mankind with favors and threats.

Given the imminence of chaos and sudden death under these conditions, the Argo, the base camp, the Argus orbiter, and the GRUB were set to monitor each other continuously. Barbara and Hal transmitted raw data streams directly to Ground Control that included everything down to live conversations about the scientific findings. Thus they made their way across the lava plains, all the while contending with celestial artillery strikes that were mostly out of harm's way but close enough to voice threats through their gruff thunder. Hal and Barbara pushed themselves to the limits of their suddenly reduced life expectancies, but there came a point where they had to yield to exhaustion. They were not working effectively; they were making too many mistakes; they were short tempered. Some days into the ordeal, Hal broke two drill bits in succession. Barbara flushed until her blue eyes turned red.

"Pack it up, Private!"

She sulked back to the GRUB, leaving Hal to deal with the heavy equipment. He did not even try, but instead

377

followed her up the ramp. The obligatory pause in the airlock did nothing to quell their anger. Once inside, Barbara wrenched off her helmet and threw it into a bulkhead. Hal did much the same thing.

"Listen, putz, you keep pullin' that shit and we won't have anything left to explore this rock with!"

Hal's nostrils flared. He lock his gaze onto Barbara's. Without realizing it, they started circling each other like two wrestler's looking for an opening in each other's defences.

"Well, Missy, if you weren't such a busybody..."

Hal never completed the insult. Barbara flew into a rage that he would never have thought possible in her.

"Don't you EVER call me Missy again!" she hissed. She was in another place, in another time, seething at someone else. She punched him in the face and snapped a kick into his diaphragm in a movement faster than sight. Hal crumpled over in a gasping fit.

Barbara stood over him, for the moment oblivious to what she had just done. She stared at the gasping man doubled over at her feet and fell onto her knees.

"Oh-my-God, Hal, what have I done?"

She cradled his head in her lap and waited for the fit to subside. There was nothing else to be done. After awhile, Hal's breathing subsided into its normal rhythm. He lay quietly in

Barbara's lap, recovering his composure. He rolled over so as to look her straight in the eyes and smiled.

"Hey Babe, was it good for you too?"

The outburst had been oddly thrilling, but neither of them spoke of it. Barbara helped Hal to his feet. They unsuited and collapsed into bed, oblivious for once to the threats that had been driving them to distraction.

#

Barbara slept dreamlessly while her body recuperated from the abuse it had sustained. Deeper and deeper she fell into a feathery nothing until she landed on a bed with the softness of a kiss. She regained an awareness of sorts and, leaving her fleshy self to its slumbers, arose in a subtle, ethereal body. She felt light. Energy flowed happily through her limbs. Looking down, she noticed that she was naked. Looking up, she saw a wooden door not ten paces from where she stood. She approached it and was greeted by the scent of sandalwood. She paused a moment to savor the fragrance of the wood. Opening the door, she stepped out onto the roof of the GRUB. The Martian air was warm, soothing, and breathable. She sat down and enjoyed the moment.

The lava plain across which they had been traveling so frantically had no equal on Earth. And that was because Martian volcanoes had no peers anywhere in the solar system. The three Tharsis volcanoes at her back had been active for two-and-a-half billion years. The ground beneath the GRUB was a boiling red sea at the same time that life was first exploding across Earth. Ahead of her, the lavas became younger and younger until they draped the flanks of Olympus Mons and moved on beyond the western horizon, a mere 200 to 20 million years old. Time and memory fused into rock worn smooth by the forever winds of Mars. Each grain of sand so liberated became a mote of history bounding endlessly among the craters, canyons, plains, plateaus, and valleys of this patient and forbearing world. This was what she had been missing, thought Barbara to herself: a knowledge of, an intimacy with this ancient world that science alone could never provide. She decided then to allow herself many more such moments, come what may.

She had almost forgotten that she was dreaming when the lava under the GRUB shuddered and snapped free of the encircling plain. It rose into the air until it cleared the surface. Lightning storms appeared on all horizons, knifing their way along the ground until they fused into a ring of blue fire. Crevasses opened under their electric lashes with a rumbling agony that shuddered across the land. And if this were not surreal enough, the whole plain, all 1000 miles of it, broke loose from the planet's crust and began folding in on itself like the layers of steel in a fine Samurai blade yielding to the will of a swordsmith. Stadium-sized boulders that had been entombed for entire geologic ages shot into space like so much artillery, becoming celestial nomads in their own right.

So relentless was the folding that it shrank the entire lava plain to the size of a dictionary. As Barbara watched, the innumerable rock strata thinned into the parchment pages of a book bound with the hide of an animal that had become extinct when Mars was still a young world teeming with life. The covers were affixed to the spine with hinges forged from the same bluish-green metal that had made Olympus Mons so tantalizing a target.

Barbara jumped off the GRUB. Landing next to the book, she bent over and picked it up. She opened it to the first page, but could go no further. Each time she turned a page, it snapped back onto its nearest companion. After some fumbling, Barbara found that she could riffle the pages. There were millions of them. Each page had a picture on it. Riffling the pages had the effect of producing a kind of animated cartoon. It started by showing an accretion disk swirling around a protostar. The disk was midwife to the birth of nine planets and an asteroid belt. The view narrowed to the fourth planet from the infant sun. It was warm and moist and cloaked with a rich nurturing atmosphere. The land turned green. Blue oceans thrashed with life. Strange animals, many of them airborne, flourished on the land. The planet was a garden. The pages flowed on beneath Barbara's fingers. Over the aeons, humanoid beings evolved from reptilian forebears and rapidly developed a high culture and technology.

Then came the asteroid bombardments. Five centuries of intermittent pounding reduced the planet to a volcanic wasteland long since abandoned by the creatures in a vast Noachian effort to colonize the nearby stars. Some stayed behind to study and colonize the newly fertile third planet.

The book closed of its own volition. Barbara placed it on the ground. Turning, she saw the sandalwood door open. She walked through it, and saw her still-resting body. She laid upon it and let her subtle body sink into her refreshed physical body. Another refreshing interval of dreamless sleep left her suspended in dark oblivion. After an indeterminate interval of time had past, the odor of coffee suffused her benighted mind. Barbara followed the odor. It led to a portal of light. She entered it and...

...awoke to the smells of breakfast.

"Jesus," she said to herself, stretching, "how long have I been out? Oh...good morning, Hal. Sorry."

"Fourteen hours," said Hal.

Barbara sat up and almost immediately doubled over.

"Whoa! I've got fourteen hours worth of pee in me! Hal, help me to the bathroom?"

Hal helped her to lurch toward certain relief and returned to the galley, thinking that their journey was providing any number of novel ways to get acquainted with each other. A few minutes later, Barbara emerged from the restroom. Judging by her stride, she was a new woman.

"I hate to admit it, but this is one of those times when I really suffer from penis envy."

Hal smiled rakishly and said nothing. Barbara walked up to him and said, "Sorry for being such a bitch. From now on, let's just damn the torpedoes and enjoy the ride."

"Works for me," replied Hal. "I haven't been much of a gentleman myself."

Barbara laid her head on Hal's shoulder. She felt his muscles soften in a subtle gesture of acceptance and desire. It was an exquisite interlude. She lifted her head and looked at the rations that Hal was trying to revive.

"What's that supposed to be?"

"I was hoping it would turn into an egg-and-sausage omelet, but I'm not optimistic," said Hal. "At least it won't kill us."

They sat by the windows and ate quietly. Barbara paused from time to time and studied Hal's face. To look at him, he could have been a model for the first generation of GI-Joe action figures — tall, taut, and steel-eyed. But not cold. And certainly not malicious. His lethal combat skills notwithstanding, Hal exuded a quiet and consistent warmth. He could kill when circumstances demanded it and lose little sleep over it, but otherwise he had no use for violence. Again, Barbara could not help thinking that Hal would be a wonderful father. He also had another quality.

"You're always in the moment, Hal, aren't you?"

"Where else would I be?"

I don't know...it's just that wherever you go, there you are. Your attention is never anywhere it's not supposed to be," said Barbara.

"Nothing else makes any sense, I suppose," said Hal. "Besides, it wastes energy, makes you old before your time."

"And that's why things broke down so badly over the last few days," said Barbara.

Hal paused and thought it over.

"You're right. I lost my center. We were running around dodging bullets. We never did that before."

"And we'll never do it again," said Barbara.

The coffee proved to be far more palatable than the omelette, so Barbara and Hal sipped it at their leisure. Under most circumstances, this would have been a mundane ritual too inconsequential to merit comment. But under the prevailing circumstances, under Nature's version of an atomic war, it was an eloquent protest, a fist raised in defiance of a meaningless and abortive end to the mission and their lives.

Barbara drained her mug, a speculative look in her eyes.

"I had the queerest little dream last night," she said.

Hal looked up at her, his eyes a pair of question marks.

"The lava plains around us shrank and turned into a book, a history book, I suppose. I picked it up and flipped through the pages. They showed me that Mars was once teeming with life until a slow asteroid bombardment killed everything."

"How far did you get in the book?" asked Hal.

"About a third of the way," said Barbara. "It closed by itself. After a while, I woke up."

Hal looked out the windows. Tiny dust devils tripped across the ground like sirens of memory, taunting him, teasing him with the bits of history lofted by their Lilliputian tempests.

"Maybe the book closed because it isn't finished yet. A lot can happen in a few billion years," he suggested.

"I guess so. I'd love to see this place come alive again," said Barbara.

"Maybe it will," said Hal, "especially if there are no indigenous critters still running around.

Someone's bound to terraform the place. In the meantime, it's pristine and we have it all to ourselves."

A couple of mushroom clouds had formed quietly on the far horizon while Hal talked. By tacit consent, neither of them spoke of it.

They were cleaning the galley when the message board signaled an incoming transmission from Mission Control. They were to cease all drilling operations and proceed directly to the target on Olympus Mons.

Something had changed.

THE GATE

"This <u>is</u> intriguing," said Hal as he and Barbara stood facing the GRUB's forward wind shield. Shocks from the meteor strikes had loosened rubble on the flanks of Olympus Mons, causing a number of landslides along its base. One of these had occurred over the greenish-blue artifact. It had exposed enough of the object to suggest that it was the entrance to a corridor leading into the volcano's base. The disturbance had also left a small mountain of debris at the base of the entrance. The GRUB was outfitted with a plow, but this was more of a job for an earth mover. They suited up and went outside.

They were too close to the volcano to appreciate its immensity, and the deteriorating weather afforded little long-range visibility. They did, however, have a decent view of the immediate area. The artifact was two hundred feet above the lava plains and topped a thirty-degree slope. A few well-placed explosives could send the debris the rest of the way down the volcano's flanks. Barbara and Hal parted, each examining half the debris field with the aim of disturbing it to best advantage. They were not long in forming a plan to clear the debris from the artifact with a minimum of high explosives. These were placed accordingly. Barbara moved the GRUB to a safe distance while Hal readied the detonator. With everything in place, Hal closed the circuit.

The explosion rocked the GRUB. One set of wheels bucked into the air and hit the ground with an ill-tempered thud. Barbara and Hal fell over each other. Debris cascaded past them like an angry river. Clods of dirt pummeled the GRUB. Dust rained on them from all sides. It settled as the last of the debris grumbled into place below them. All was once again quiet. Hal and Barbara disentangled themselves and stood up.

"I guess I should've parked us farther away," said Barbara with a measure of flustered understatement.

"That would've been nice," said Hal. "Next time, I'll drive."

They peered through the forward windshield. It was a clear shot to the artifact. Just then, Hal noticed something.

"Barbara, do those look like steps to you?"

"They sure as hell do!"

Snapping their helmets shut, Hal and Barbara exited the GRUB. The first object was thirty feet from the artifact. It was readily recognizable as a slab of dressed basalt -- one of the commoner substances on Mars. They walked beside the steps, scrutinizing each in turn, yet hesitant to touch them.

"Hal, are you transmitting this?"

"I have been since we left the GRUB. The folks back home are due to be shocked and amazed in about forty minutes."

"Good. Keep transmitting."

The steps opened onto a basalt plaza. There was nothing to be done but cross it if they wanted to explore the artifact any further. Still, they hesitated. There was no telling what span of time their first footfalls would bridge, but it was likely to be hundreds of millions of years. The moment passed with the need to know more, and they stepped mindfully onto the plaza, savoring each moment down to the minutest interval that their minds could discern. They were among the commonest of movements, barely worth noting on an ordinary day. But this was no ordinary day. Future generations would acknowledge those first steps across that plaza as the most understated gesture of all time.

Barbara turned to survey the plain beneath them. It's features were obscured by a mantle of dust that loitered over the land as a vestige of the recent storms, but the view sufficed for purposes of revery. Barbara tried to imagine what sort of creatures had first made their way across the plain but, in the absence of fossil remains, she was only wasting oxygen. Hal touched her shoulder from behind.

"Anything wrong?" he asked.

"Yes and no. I'm just frustrated by how much we don't know," answered Barbara.

"Well, we won't learn anything by just standing around," he said.

They approached the door, if indeed it was a door. Its greenish-blue surfaces were defiantly flawless and shone through the dirt of the landslide as if bearing their own light. Barbara spread the fingers of one hand and touched the object. It transfixed her with a flash of impressions that danced along her arm, filling her with bits of information, shards of memory, sounds, smells, tastes, none of which she could process. Finally, one thing settled and became clear.

"I know how to open this thing," she declared.

"How?" asked Hal.

"I don't know how, I just do," she said.

Barbara stepped back from the artifact, partly to admire its monolithic splendor, when she sensed something about its dimensions.

"Hal, get some measurements off this," she said.

He opened the geophysics kit and promptly produced the numbers.

"It's 2.3 feet deep, 9.2 feet wide, and 20.7 feet high," he said.

Barbara thought for a few moments and said, "What are its proportions."

"One, four, nine," said Hal.

"Hmmm...the squares of 1, 2, and 3. The first three prime numbers," said Barbara. "I wonder what it means."

"Maybe it's something philosophical," he suggested.

"I guess we'll know pretty soon," said Barbara.

She squatted in front of the artifact's lower right corner and pushed it to the left. It moved so easily that it might as well have been waiting for someone to open it. It stopped quietly after moving one foot to the left, revealing a sliver of what seemed to be a corridor. It was black -- an impenetrable black. The surrounding sunlight made no encroachments on it, as if black itself were an object that shunned light. Intrigued, Barbara cautiously touched the area...

...and screamed.

Hal leapt instantly to her side. Her hand had disappeared, having been pulled into the opening. She struggled to keep her arm from being sucked in as well. Hal placed himself between Barbara and the door. Straining to his limits, he pushed against Barbara's shoulder, and slowly extracted her arm from the opening. It was like pulling a tooth. When finally they were clear of the opening, Hal examined Barbara's arm. It had been snapped and warped into a shape impossible to describe, and it was trailing a ribbon of black or, more precisely, a ribbon of nothing. It did not occupy the space around them. It was a vacuous intruder from a bizarre elsewhere. Hal pulled Barbara farther from the opening. The nothing attenuated its grip on her arm until at last it snapped back into the opening. As it did, Barbara's arm assumed it's normal form.

The ordeal had lasted less than a minute, but the agony of it left them sprawled on the ground. Barbara cradled her arm and rolled onto her back, all the while cursing her impulsive stupidity. Hal got up and retrieved the med-pack.

"Let me scan your arm," he said.

Barbara complied as best she could. Hal ran the scanner over Barbara's arm several times, from shoulder to fingertips. He smiled and deactivated the scanner.

"This must be your lucky day," he said. "According to the scan, you're fine."

"Scan my brain while you're at it. See if something activated my stupid-center," said Barbara.

"You want to rest for a while?" he asked.

"Hell no. I'll open that thing with my tongue if I have to," she said.

"Can I watch?" he asked.

"Sure," she replied with a coquettish smile.

Hal helped Barbara to her feet. Facing the door again, she swung it through several very un-doorlike curves. Hal stood to one side and watched. Each movement of the door revealed different swatches of the now-dreaded nothing.

"Hey, Barbara! Stop and look at this!" exclaimed Hal.

Barbara guided the door to rest and joined him.

"Look at where the door meets the corridor. Your last move pushed the door against it, but the material yielded and reformed itself. It moved in a direction I couldn't follow. It didn't make any sense."

"Did you record it?" she asked.

"Sure, I haven't missed anything," Hal replied.

"Good." Barbara paused, as if remembering something. "There's more to the sequence. Let me finish. That should tell us something...maybe...hell, who knows," said Barbara uncertainly.

The next few swings of the door did nothing to clarify anything. The door, which until then had been in plain sight, rolled sideways and disappeared. Before they could react, it rolled back into view and settled onto the plaza, revealing an ordinary-looking passageway.

Neither Hal nor Barbara spoke. Hal picked up a pebble and tossed it into the passage. It bounced a few times and came to rest a few yards from the entrance. Barbara entered the passage and picked it up. She tossed it back outside. Nothing untoward happened. She exited the passage and joined Hal.

"I just had a thought," she said. "This isn't a door at all. It's a combination lock."

Hal saw where Barbara was headed.

"A hyperdimensional combination lock," he said, completing her thought. "We're just seeing slices of it as it moves through our space."

#

The following hour found Hal and Barbara trundling in tandem down the passage in two heavily equipped rovers. It was straight and unadorned and yielded no hints as to its purpose or destination. They took their time, being careful not to overlook anything. They were about a mile into the volcano when the rectangle of sunlight at the tunnel's entrance winked shut. There followed a mellow thunder whose vibrations dissipated into the deeps of the long-extinct volcano.

"I hope you know how to open that thing," said Hal.

"I'm hoping that a simple push will do it," said Barbara.

"But you don't know that for sure?" he asked.

"Nope," was her unequivocal response.

They continued for another two unremarkable miles. Shortly after that, the darkness ahead of them widened and opened onto a space whose invisible heights swallowed the rovers' engine noises and lights. Hal stopped and prepared to take some soundings. Barbara pulled up next to him and cut her engine. Dismounting, she stood by Hal and watched as the computer assembled the results.

"You could fit an asteroid in this place," said Hal.

"And somebody took the trouble to level the floor," said Barbara.

The final image glowed in the unforgiving darkness.

"We must be in a huge magma pocket," said Barbara. "But I can't imagine what it was used for. Are there any other openings?"

Hal increased the resolution of the soundings.

"Something's interfering with the signals, but I think there are," said Hal. "We'll need to go in farther to get cleaner data."

"Let's leave a beacon here," said Barbara, "to be on the safe side."

The chamber's avid darkness swallowed them as they left the security of the corridor. The world suddenly shrank to the blurry white sphere cast by the rovers' onboard lights. Navigating under the erratic guidance of the sensors, they had ridden ten miles into the cavern when several blips appeared on the periphery of the image. They stopped to study them.

"Can you clean that up?" asked Barbara.

"I'm trying," replied Hal, "but there's still too much interference."

They studied the telemetry for a few quiet moments. The quavering images seemed to be artificial.

"I'll wager that the two structures ahead of us are either small or in ruins," said Barbara. "The structure to our right seems more substantial. "Let's head for that one."

Hal tried to clean up the image further, but to no avail. The large blip did however, remain stable through the various scans. The other two did not.

"Let's give it a try," he said. "It's only twenty miles away."

Hal and Barbara made their way cautiously through the darkness. Although the scanners continued to show unobstructed surfaces ahead of them, their instincts balked at the prospect of traveling fast and blind through nothingness. Always in the back of their minds lurked the fear of stumbling into hidden dangers. There was nothing irrational in this. Given the planet's violent geological history, it was possible that the sensors' muddled readings hid crevasses, subsidences, or other instabilities that had formed since the cavern was abandoned.

Two hours of cautious movement had passed when a greenish-blue rectangle came within range of the lights. Barbara and Hal slowed the rovers and stopped a hundred feet from the object. Surmounting a broad flight of steps carved from the cavern's floor was an open portal made, evidently, of the same metal as the entrance on the surface.

"I'll bet this is the first light that that thing has seen in two- or three-hundred million years," said Hal. "The first light since the dinosaurs were in their prime..."

"Why Hal, my contemplative disposition must be rubbing off on you," said Barbara.

"Rub away, oh captain of mine," said Hal, just barely resisting the urge to swat Barbara on her behind.

They dismounted the rovers and approached the steps. Barbara had placed her foot on the first riser when Hal grabbed her arm.

"Barbara, point the light over there. To the left of the door," he said. She directed the beam onto an oblong panel that she had not noticed.

"Do you see any carving on that?" asked Hal.

"I see something," said Barbara. They walked up to the panel. It was intricately inscribed with elegant, oddly angular figures that did not seem to be primarily decorative. The impression was further validated by the presence of other panels that flanked the first and continued on the right side of the portal. Barbara and Hal spent the next few hours meticulously photographing the panels in infrared, ultraviolet, and visible-light media. Most of the panels bore characters similar to those on the first, but not all of them. Some of the panels bore diagrams, possibly maps; others appeared to carry mathematical formulae.

"As far as I can see," said Hal, "that wraps it up for now. How about a break?"

"Fine with me," said Barbara. "I gotta pee in the worst way."

Barbara returned to her rover and savored the infantile pleasure of being able to relieve herself directly into the pressure suit, knowing that its recycling system would capture every drop and turn it into potable water. That done, she selected two liquid-food supplements and sauntered back to Hal.

"Chicken soup or tomato," she said.

"Does it really matter?" replied Hal.

"I don't think so," said Barbara.

"Chicken, then," said Hal.

They snapped the supplements onto the receptacles in their pressure suits and sipped at the hot liquid, all the while browsing the panels.

"I can't imagine how anybody's going to translate this stuff without a cipher," said Hal.

"I can't either," said Barbara. "Whoever built this place probably didn't make allowances for primitive intruders."

"The day's young yet," said Hal. "Maybe we'll find something beyond the entry."

Hal paused and looked at Barbara.

"You don't seem all that eager to go in there, he said.

"Au contraire," said Barbara, I always save the best for last, and then I stretch it out as long as I can."

She winked coyly at Hal.

"I understand. And I agree," he said.

They returned to the stairs and sat down. Staring into the darkness ahead of them, they finished the soup slowly and quietly.

#

Shortly after the Argo left Earth orbit, the governments of Nepal and the United States dispatched teams of archeologists to the catacombs under Kathmandu. A month later, these individuals urgently requested the services of physical anthropologists representing a broad array of specialties. These persons were duly recruited and dispatched. By the time the Argo entered Mars orbit, and after much gnashing of scholarly teeth, these luminaries could only agree that they were at their wits' end. Their findings were at once fabulous and dismal. The artifacts and the inscriptions had no correlates with any known civilization at any time in history. The skeletal remains were almost but not quite human, had no known relatives in any branch of the human family tree, and were old enough to undermine every prevailing theory of human evolution. Most galling of all was their discovery of a stone tablet containing exactly one-half of what seemed to be a cipher for the inscriptions. The panel had been cut such that every line of text was disrupted as if it were part of a vast puzzle whose pieces had been scattered across the aeons.

#

Setting the food canisters aside, Barbara and Hal stood and contemplated the portal. Their excitement grew with each step they ascended until they stood before the open entrance.

"Hal, does it seem to you that the outside edges of this thing have the same 1:4:9 proportions as the outer entrance?"

"Yeah, it does," said Hal. "You want some measurements?"

"Sure," said Barbara.

A minute or so passed.

"It checks out exactly," said Hal, "and so do the inner edges."

"That's cool," said Barbara, "the proportions 1:4:9 defining the boundaries of an empty space. I think you're right, Hal, it might be some kind of metaphysical statement."

They entered the opening cautiously, playing the spotlights along the columns that supported the corridor. Each was covered with symbols and drawings that ascended and disappeared into the lofty darkness beyond the range of the lights. Hal stopped to examine one of the columns.

"What you make of all this?" he asked.

Barbara looked over Hal's shoulder, enjoying his closeness.

"The characters are different from the ones outside and there are a lot more pictures. They're almost glyphic -- maybe parts of geometric theorems."

"Almost as if the whole place is a mathematical treatise," said Hal. "Too bad the owners didn't expect any illiterate tourists to drop in."

They resumed their walk down the corridor, neither of them speaking, until Barbara stopped short as if regaining her balance after a sudden misstep. She stumbled, confused and disoriented, until she recognized Hal holding her up by one arm.

"What's wrong, Barbara?"

She leaned into him for support.

"This place is a shrine...mathematics was part of their religion...oh shit...I think I'm gonna be sick..."

Hal led Barbara to one of the walls and helped her to sit down. She slumped into a fetal position, breathing slowly and deeply, willing herself not to vomit. The spasm passed.

"Oh God, just shoot me...I wonder if anybody's ever puked in a pressurized helmet," said Barbara, still panting.

"I'm sure somebody has," said Hal, "but if it were me, I wouldn't broadcast it. What happened?"

Barbara sat up with Hal's help.

"Damned if I know. One minute I'm here, and next thing I know, something rips me out of my body and stuffs me into another one. It...I...whatever... was a priestess. Here, but a hell of a long time ago. Then I got thrown back to now. Oh, man, I gotta lie down quick!"

Hal rolled her back onto the floor. One dry heave followed another until Barbara was sore and exhausted by the effort. Hal sat beside her, laid her head in his lap, and placed his hand on her side, all the while hoping that he was one of those people who were blessed with a healing touch. It was a refreshingly primal experience — a caveman's instinct for protecting his woman.

Barbara relaxed enough to fall asleep. Hal sat still for a while, watching her breathing as it ebbed and flowed, ever quieter, ever deeper. Suddenly, she gasped and woke up, panic-stricken.

"Oh, God! It's happening again! Damn you, bitch! Get out of my head!"

Barbara staggered up onto her feet.

"Hal, hold me and start talking. Recite the phone book if you have to. Don't lose me!"

He embraced her and started talking. Random numbers. Science trivia. Dirty jokes. He felt Barbara tense up as if grappling with an enemy. Finally her entire body braced for a final rictus of effort. Hal babbled on, barely permitting himself time to breathe. He held onto her, willing his defiant strength to meld with hers. Barbara hunched over and then arched her back as if finally wrenching herself free from someone's grip. She relaxed into Hal's arms and then, incongruously, started laughing.

"Oh, Hal! You are IT! You be De Man!"

"What are you talking about?" asked Hal, more confused than he had been in a long time.

Barbara pushed herself a few inches away from him and slapped his chest.

"What do you mean what am I talking about? I felt you inside my head. You are freakin' awesome. Without you, I'd still be fighting that bitch!"

"Who are you talking about?" asked Hal.

"That priestess, she answered, "was a woman, some sort of grand Pooh-Bah. Everybody sucked up to her."

Hal nodded. Barbara's outré experiences on the mission were starting to form a pattern. It had something to do with space, time, and mind — or rather the untapped power of the mind.

"Barbara, why don't you rest for a while? I'll go back and get one of the rovers. We can ride the rest of the way," said Hal.

"Don't bother," she replied. "The next room is only 200 yards away. There's nothing else beyond that."

"Pick that up from the priestess, did you?" asked Hal.

"Uh-huh."

They walked on. As Barbara predicted, they soon espied a flight of steps in the distance surmounted by a portal identical to the first.

"Well Dorothy," said Hal, "I guess we finally get to see the Wizard."

"And what would a guy like you wish for," said Barbara.

"A brain," said Hal. "I've never been so clueless in my life."

"I have a feeling you'll be on a distinguished waiting list."

Hal found unexpected comfort in the thought.

"And what about you?" asked Hal.

Barbara thought about it and seemed surprised at the answer that came to her.

"I want to go home," she said, "but all of a sudden I don't know where home is. It's sad, sort of."

They reached the stairs and started to ascend them when Barbara gripped Hal's arm.

"Turn off the lights for a few minutes," she said," I think we're missing something."

Hal complied. Darkness fairly leaped out of them from the walls, swallowing them in a blackness so dense it could have been a new form of matter. Their eyes adapted quickly, suddenly starving for light. They became two pairs of ravenous pigs rooting about for photonic truffles.

"Look through the portal," said Barbara. "Do you see what I see?"

Hal stood still and let his gaze become diffuse. It was not long before he stiffened with attention.

"I see a glow, but it's a color I've never seen. Bioluminescence? Could something be alive in there?"

"Possibly, and I don't want to piss it off," said Barbara. "Let's take it slow."

They instinctively muffled their footfalls as they felt their way up the steps. Moving with the stealth of two mice approaching a sleepy cat, Barbara and Hal gradually reached the portal and looked inside. The glow was there, but it was not emanating from anything, not even from a point within itself. It both belonged and did not belong in the space it occupied.

Over Hal's protests, Barbara crossed the threshold first. Nothing happened. He entered just behind her and together they circled the light. It was featureless, borderless, static, seemingly immune to decay. They had returned to the portal when Barbara braced as if listening to something.

"Relax. This thing isn't alive and it's not a threat," she announced. "It's the focus of this place, a gate of some sort."

"How do you know?" asked Hal.

"Beats me, I just know," said Barbara.

She walked up to the glow and touched it. Nothing happened for a few moments. Then it grew. Blobs of light coalesced into a shape identical to the portals through which they had just passed. Three or four yards wide, it floated inches from the floor. The inscrutable color shifted to a wash of opalescent glitter that in turn settled into a lambent robin's egg blue. The surface was distinct yet impalpable, as if it were both there and not there.

"Hal, what does it look like through the camera?"

"It doesn't look like anything," he replied, "it's not there."

"Can you see me?" she asked.

"I see you just fine," he confirmed.

"OK, so the camera works," said Barbara. "That means we could be sharing a delusion, or..."

"Or the camera's right," added Hal, completing her thought. "There's nothing there, and our brains are registering a visual event that has nothing to do with light."

Barbara was about to say something when the thing started changing. It seemed to be folding in on itself, but without losing volume. Whatever disappeared into the fold was replenished by something emerging from the fold. The effect was that of an Escher print whose surreal, transdimensional perspective lines made doors, floors, and stairs conform to impossible shapes that yielded glimpses of other worlds in other realities. Hal stepped back and viewed the sphere again through the camera.

"Hey Barbara! Look at this."

She stepped behind Hal and looked into the viewfinder.

"See that? It's phasing in and out," he said.

They stood musing over the images when an oblong mass of black light emerged from the axis of the fold. Its image in the camera was stable against the throbbing background. The subsequent shock of seeing two hands emerge from it would have sent them screaming out of the shrine but for their indomitable curiosity.

Barbara approached the hands. They were long, delicate, seven-fingered, and composed in a gesture formed from equal parts of invitation and supplication. She knew that the being whose hands they were bore no ill will against her. And they were familiar somehow, although Barbara could not imagine how or where she could have seen them. But there they were, their mysteries notwithstanding, patient and imploring. Barbara saw nothing else to do but take hold of them and step into the gate.

Hal watched incredulously as Barbara entered the gate with the nonchalance of someone entering a phone booth. Once inside, she behaved as if she were looking for something far away. Whatever it was, she found it and calmly stepped into the fold. Her body curled around it and vanished.

Hal came as close to panic as he had ever been in his life.

#

The Shtatàam was mortified. If she had had feet at the moment, she would have kicked herself. Twice now, the female from the third planet had accidentally folded time back on itself, spanning entire geologic ages as she did so. The female had no way of knowing what she had done, and now saw the Shtatàam as a threat. She had underestimated the female's latent powers and was at risk of rupturing the rapport that they had formed in the female's spacecraft.

Circumspection was imperative if the Shtatàam wanted to salvage what was left of their bond. She condensed her body into its native form and entered the Jash Tatàam that the female and her male companion had just discovered. Moving forward along its timelines to the female's sense of the present moment, the Shtatàam marveled at the immensities that the creature had spanned without intending to.

Vowing to make no more mistakes, the Shtatàam took a moment to become comfortable in this rarely used aspect of her body. This time she would not fumble through the density of threespace. She extended her arms through the quasispace created by the revived Jash Tatàam and gently invited the female to take her hands and step into the shrine's quasispace. She complied. It was then that the Shtatàam felt the male's presence. It was vast and, astoundingly, insinuated itself into the shrine's quasispace as a fortress around the female. It was raw, unsullied, loyal, and bore the auric impress of a gentle warrior. The Shtatàam left it intact.

#

Barbara felt the hands draw her gently into the sphere, but could not figure out whose hands they were. The space into which she had just stepped made no sense. The movements and directions to which she was accustomed amounted to little more than jerks and spasms in this place. Barbara felt like a newborn child receiving its first inchoate impressions of the blinding new world into which it had been pulled, kicking and screaming, by strange hands.

The creature at whose behest Barbara had entered the sphere sensed this and guided her deeper into the quasispace of the shrine. Barbara eventually saw a tall, vertical rift that spun about itself in the quasispace, furling and unfurling dimensions that she sensed more with her mind than she saw through her eyes. Despite the weirdness in which she found herself, Barbara felt lucid and confident. She walked up to the rift and stepped into it. The last thing she saw before she disappeared was the shock on Hal's face.

Barbara had no idea where she was, or what she was, for that matter. She was in the eye of a storm around which raged her unraveling body. Her detachment from the seeming disasters swirling around her was odd but curiously rewarding. She was a nexus for the infinite possibilities created by the permutations of space and time among the many dimensions in which the Cosmos lived, moved, and had its being. She had lost her sense of time and duration, but it did not seem so very long before her body and mind came together again, as if they had followed very different paths for a tryst in a very strange place.

Feeling more or less normal again, Barbara looked down at her hands. They were still nestled within the hands of the being who had led her to this place. She looked up and recognized the priestess from whom she had earlier recoiled in horror. She pulled away and started to run, but was preempted by a thought that formed in her mind before she could move. It was not one of hers. It had been put there by the priestess and it was, of all things, an apology. It resounded within her to such depths that she could not deny its sincerity.

The priestess relaxed as Barbara lowered her defenses, at which point she recognized the priestess as the same being she had encountered on the Argo.

Barbara felt her memory being sifted for words. The priestess wanted to talk to her. The sifting was gentle, discrete, and soothing. It reminded Barbara of the days, long past, when Richard would brush her hair after a bath until it shimmered.

The sifting stopped. Barbara was again alone with her thoughts. She looked about, trying to make sense of where she was. A word, roughly hewn, formed in her mind as if spoken by a voice long unaccustomed to speech.

"Nah-me...nahme...name?" stammered the priestess.

"Barbara," said Barbara.

"Bahh-bah-rah?" the priestess queried.

"No," said Barbara. "Barbara."

"Barr-barr-rah...Barbar-ah... Barbara?" said the priestess tentatively.

"Correct," said Barbara.

The priestess smiled with the pleasure of a child mastering her first words.

"Your name?" ventured Barbara.

"C-call...me...Shtatàam," replied the priestess.

"Shtatàam," said Barbara.

"Correct," said the priestess.

"It's a pleasure to meet you, Shtatàam" said Barbara and she extended her right hand.

The priestess looked at Barbara's outstretched hand, uncertain as to what she was expected to do. She sifted through Barbara's mind for the appropriate response and nodded. She took Barbara's hand and shook it.

"The...pleasure is... all mine, Barbara," she said, and then added, "Hug?"

"Of course," said Barbara, pleasantly taken aback, "I love hugs."

They stepped forward and embraced each other. Barbara's animal warmth blended with the priestess's effervescent energy. After a suitable interval, the priestess relaxed her hold on Barbara and stepped away.

"I have things...to show you," said the priestess.

"I hoped you would, Shtatàam," said Barbara.

"You hope correctly, Barbara," said the priestess. "I will show you where you are."

Up until then, a fog had obscured Barbara's surroundings. A flash of thought from the priestess burned it away. It was also possible, thought Barbara, that the fog was in her mind and that the priestess was simply disabusing her of an illusion. It was the simpler of the two explanations and so more likely to be correct.

Her orientation restored, Barbara looked at her surroundings. They were standing on a flawless white floor that spread out before them in all directions. The space overhead was the same flawless white as the floor. There was no telling if the floor rose to meet the horizon or whether the horizon dipped to meet the floor. The lighting throughout was even and easy on the eye. It came from nowhere and everywhere. As her eyes adjusted to the conditions, Barbara saw that the floor was inscribed with ruby-red lines. They formed no obvious pattern, but she sensed that they expressed a high-order geometry. The surrounding space was also marked by the same red lines. These disappeared into the sky. More subtle was the movement of colored spheres along the lines. Some traveled alone, others in groups. They all moved with a deliberation, with an intentness, that suggested consciousness. And moreover...

...she knew the place. She knew it from her earliest visions. The only difference was that they were filled with people, not the balls of light now moving around her. Barbara nevertheless opened herself to them. They were in fact alive and aware and glad to share their light with her. Most were happy, some were reserved, some contemplative, and a few — Barbara among them — were simply overwhelmed by everything. But they all were explorers and travelers, flushed with their new understanding of being. Barbara wondered if she too appeared as a ball of light.

Still sharing herself with the others, Barbara turned her attention to the priestess.

"Shtatàam, I know this place!" she exclaimed. -"I came here when I was a baby!"

"Some highly evolved spirits are born into threespace with their connection to the hyperspaces still intact," said the priestess.

Barbara was almost unnerved by how fast the priestess was assimilating the language. Her inflection was still off, but that undoubtedly would change quickly.

"Is that who these beings are?"

"Yes, they are learning to fold space," replied the priestess. "Someday they will learn to fold time. It's all a matter of evolution."

"This is a happy place, isn't it," said Barbara.

"Yes, the Creator means for us to be happy," said the priestess.

The priestess was quiet for awhile, as if she were assimilating more data. Barbara continued communing with the travelers until she sensed that it was time for them to leave. The priestess turned her attention to Barbara.

"Barbara, it's time for me to show you some things."

RITES OF PASSAGE

Barbara suddenly had no body: no eyes to see with, no ears to hear with, no nose to smell with, no tongue to taste with. She was transparent. Experiences passed through her as if she were not there. She was as close to nothing as she could be without winking out of existence altogether. And yet despite this, or perhaps because of it — she was not sure what to think — she had never felt so receptive or so aware.

To what ends the Shtatàam had done this to her was one thing Barbara did not then know, but she no longer suspected the priestess of harboring any ill will against her. Barbara sensed her on the frontiers of her vastly enlarged awareness, hovering, alert, curious to see what her gifted pupil would accomplish.

The priestess began unfolding space. The vermiform dimensions so liberated wriggled into Barbara's mind. They wove themselves into a lattice within which her understanding affixed itself. She saw possibilities within the life of the universe that trivialized her wildest dreams. Then she started moving. Her quaintly outmoded sense of place told her that she was passing through chasms of time and space at speeds that outpaced the very idea of speed.

Eventually she slowed to a stop. Still formless, Barbara found herself hovering in front of an elderly, supermassive sun. Its surface seethed and boiled; it's corona incinerated the very atoms of which it was made; it disgorged solar flares that rent its atmosphere. It was an angry giant shaking its hot fist at death. It was hard for Barbara to sense the priestess within so much chaos. It got a lot harder when the space around her shuddered and snapped. The shattered dimensions rebounded, hurling Barbara into the sun like a doomed asteroid.

#

Hal decided that he had seen better days. His shock at seeing Barbara disappear into what seemed to be the crack of doom was exceeded only by his feeling that she had somehow drawn a piece of himself into the crack with her. He had a gut sense of being pulled and stretched in directions that made no sense. It was nauseating and draining. His mind became a swamp where his thoughts lost their footing and slid into quagmires of inertia.

Fighting the urge to sleep, Hal forced himself to think of simple solutions to their problem, if in fact it was a problem. Of even that he was not sure. He called out for Barbara, hoping that radio waves could pass into the sphere. He used every frequency that his headset could generate. His efforts met with nothing but static. Hal then tried to walk through the portal's fuzzy surface as Barbara had done. His right boot had no sooner touched it when the surface condensed into adamantine crystal.

Next, he scanned the sphere through every medium available to him. The equipment reacted as if nothing was there to scan. Finally, feeling witless and clueless, he retrieved a geologist's hammer from his rover. Bracing for the effort, Hal struck the sphere with all of his considerable strength. The hammer rebounded with a force that would have ripped his arm off had he not released his grip on the handle. The hammer shot into the darkness beyond the pale of the spotlights and struck an invisible wall. It was his final effort. Hal's last thought was that he had been willing to die for Barbara from the moment he met her. Evidently it was time to make good on his promise. The thought soothed him as he slid into the void of his drained body.

#

Barbara was well beneath the sun's surface when she realized what had happened. The priestess had either abandoned her or moved beyond the range of her mind. Incredibly, she could still sense Hal. His presence had somehow followed her through the crack. Even now, Barbara felt him all around her, protecting her with the tenacity of a dragon guarding his treasure.

Then she started to sink. The weight of the star bore down on her. The dragon spent his remaining strength in trying to be the immovable object that would defy this irresistible force. He also understood the inherent contradictions in this that voided all hope of success. He yielded. The death rattle that escaped the dragon's crushed body reverberated throughout the enfeebled vastness of the ancient star as it squandered its final scraps of fuel and imploded.

The last of her protection gone, Barbara understood just how deep pain can go. All around her, gravity's hammer had pounded the sun's native hydrogen into helium, carbon, oxygen, iron, and other heavy atoms by successive fusions, each more violent then the last, until the exhausted star had no recourse but to collapse under its own dead weight.

The implosion slammed Barbara deep within the sun's core. It was Satan's own crucible. Even at that, it barely contained an inferno that threatened to incinerate the very atoms cowering within it. It was a place where molten lava amounted to nothing more than a tepid bath. The extreme gravity prevailing within the core twisted space into macabre forms that gripped Barbara with a coffin-like claustrophobia. It suffused her mind such that her most elusive thoughts were soon pinned down like so many butterflies in a display case. The last thoughts to be so captured was her knowledge that millions of years had to have passed for her to have seen the star's death throes so quickly. Everything and everyone she had ever loved was nothing more than dust in the wind. This thought was soon pinned down among the others. All that was left was pain, pressure, heat, and their kindred malefactors.

But there came a time when even the atoms within the core could no longer tolerate gravity's despotism. Countervailing forces rose within the core that soon overwhelmed the strictures formed by the implosion.

The star went supernova, and so did Barbara. Shards of thought, language, perceptions, feelings, ideas, and cherished illusions fled the cataclysm among shards of exotic matter from the dismembered star. Their flight was futile. A shock wave soon overcame everything in the star's vicinity and annihilated everything in its way.

The cataclysm ignited a catharsis. It left Barbara so empty that even her form was formless. She became a field of unsullied awareness, perfect in its composure, perfect in its emptiness. After an irrelevant span of time had passed, another presence moved into

Barbara's awareness. It set up vibrations from which her mind emerged. It was a rebirth of sorts, and Barbara was glad that the first object in her mind's eye was the priestess. It was she who had acted as midwife to her emergence from nothing.

"Hello, Shtatàam," said Barbara. "I thought you had left me."

"No, Barbara," answered the priestess, "I never left you, but I did have to leave your awareness. It is the only way in which a novice can complete the Awakening, which you did, incidentally. I am pleased."

The priestess paused to let Barbara assimilate her ordeal.

"It is time for a well earned rest, Barbara," said the priestess.

"You're right, Shtatàam," replied Barbara, "but how can I be tired when I'm not in my body?"

"There will be time for thought later," said the priestess, "but now you must sleep."

"I think I will, Shtatàam. But I'm concerned about my companion. I lost him during the initiation. He's... important to me."

"Be still, Barbara," said the priestess.

"If you say so, Shtatàam, goodnight, I think," said Barbara

"Goodnight," said the priestess.

#

Thorhaaken lived on a planet whose skies were dominated by two suns and three moons. True night was thus rare, and life on the planet had evolved accordingly. The times when the suns and moons fell into alignment on one side of the planet were those in which darkness enshrouded the planet's far side. The Dark Hours had long been special to Thorhaaken's race. They were times for retreat and reflection. Entire religions were devoted to them. During the Dark Hours, a few venturesome souls, Thorhaaken among them, withdrew into the Torrid Wastes. There, they slept with two eyes closed and one eye open. This eye stared into the heavens, unperturbed by the distractions of sunlight. The Order of the Third Eye encouraged this meditation. The wisdom so gained had guided Thorhaken's people for millennia.

But the Order had of late come under attack. Secular political factions wanted to quash the order and ban its teachings. Some of the factions pressed the point by seizing priests and publicly cutting out their third eyes. These were roasted on the spot and eaten by prominent party leaders "for all eyes to see", as they never tired of saying.

These atrocities sickened Thorhaaken, and he had devoted his life to creating an underground counterrevolutionary movement. He was under increasing pressure to unleash his forces. Thorhaaken was not by nature violent and he had entered the Torrid Wastes that night hoping desperately for a sign from the heavens. It came when he was in the deepest of the Dark Hours.

A feeble star suddenly brightened. It soon banished the night with its cold blue light. Thorhaaken's two sleeping eyes boggled open with recognition. One word formed in his mind.

"Supernova."

These violent stars were not unknown to his race, but they were rare, fabulously rare, and were the stuff of myth and legend. Never had a supernova appeared during the Dark Hours. This fact was not lost on Thorhaaken. His was a highly evolved soul, and it was flooded with impressions, with intimations of the powers yet to evolve among his people. A alien thought surfaced in the fertile chaos of his mind that he would one day meet a female whose rebirth into a higher order of being had been heralded by the supernova. A surge of power such as Thorhaaken had never known lent order and purpose to his mind.

He left the Torrid Wastes and loosed a holy war upon the shocked and dazzled tyrants of his world.

#

Barbara awoke on her back. "My back!" she thought. I have a back!" It was a homecoming and she was glad of it. Despite the marvels the priestess had shown her, Barbara enjoyed being human again. It offered too many animal comforts and simple pleasures to be despised and abandoned. She stretched languidly, saw what she was wearing, and sat up, confused. She was wearing her formal dress uniform. At her side lay, not the traditional saber, but the Samurai sword that Richard had given her. Barbara stood carefully, anxious not to chip the lacquered sheath, and looked around. She was in front of a large lean-to against which a ladder had been propped.

"OK, I'm asleep or something and this is a dream," muttered Barbara to herself, "might as well play along."

Other than the lean-to, she saw nothing but rocks, mountains, and more rocks. The sky was a pale blue nothing. It was virginal, as if it had never seen a cloud. The terrain was black. She looked inside the lean-to. Nothing. Somebody evidently wanted her to climb atop the structure. She steadied the ladder and cooperated. The added height revealed nothing new, except for what seemed to be a crater, a basin, or maybe a pit. It was too far off for Barbara to be sure. There seemed to be nothing else to do but get close enough to find out. Taking her bearings, she descended the ladder and started walking.

It was not long before Barbara noticed something odd about the terrain, something subtle but pervasive. As she hiked toward the pit, she got the feeling that everything around her was both new and old, pristine yet primeval. She knelt and ran her fingers across the ground. It was like fresh sandpaper, all grit and not a mote of dust. She stood and gazed around her. Everything from the rocks to the mountains had the same character. And then, the answer came to her. She was back home, on Earth, but not the Earth that any human being had ever walked or would ever walk. It was the Earth of four and a half billion years ago, when its crust had cooled enough to be stable. She was most likely standing on a protocontinent that was itself floating on an ocean of molten lava.

Barbara then understood her impression of newness. The planet was utterly sterile. Nothing, not so much as an amino acid, existed in this place. The land was barren, protean, and silent. It's only activity was to continue birthing itself.

Barbara's awareness of this became a nexus of contrary perceptions: old and new, fertile and barren, hot and cold, stiff and malleable. She held them, not as contradictions, but as paradoxes that would inspire her to deepen her understanding of the nature of things. It anchored her in the midst of this surreal but preternaturally lucid dream, if in fact it was a dream.

She eventually reached her target. It was a cylindrical pit roughly hewn into the ground. Picking up a rock, Barbara knelt beside the rim and tossed it in. She listened carefully, waiting for the sound of impact. It never came. She was about to stand when she did hear something — something as incongruous as her own presence in this place.

A torrent of whispers rose from the pit's invisible deeps and gushed onto the ground. They were fractured and muddled to the point of being unintelligible. Barbara remained by the rim, trying to make sense of the whooshing sounds. Most of it was noise, but a few words and phrases emerged from it.

"...come...us...show...with...Self... with us...show you...we...us...your... let us...come...show...true..."

Barbara assessed her situation. There was no point in staying on the surface. She had done what the dream's governing spirits required of her. She detected no duplicity in the voices flowing past her. If anything, she felt like Alice chasing the White Rabbit down his hole. She unsheathed her sword and, smiling grimly, jumped into the pit.

Barbara's cry of "banzai!" echoed along its sheer rock walls as she fell into the darkness.

#

When next she was aware of anything, Barbara thought she was a bug trapped in a spider's web. She was surrounded on all sides by white filaments that glistened with their own light. She was shackled to the filaments in a way that hobbled her every move. After a while, she gave up the struggle and went limp. Her mind relaxed in kind. She then realized that she could fuse all of her faculties and make of her body one sense. Barbara used herself thus to search for anyone who might be in her predicament. She found none, but it was not long before something found her.

Barbara's first reaction was fear -- fear that the spider had found her and was on its way to suck her dry. The fear grew as the thing approached. Her memories of being bound and tortured in the catacombs under Kathmandu flooded her every sensibility until she contracted into a nutshell of anguish. The thing set upon her, insinuating itself into her mind. She was too terrified to scream.

"Relax, Barbara, it's only me."

It was the priestess.

"Oh-my-God! You just scared the livin' shit out of me, Shtatàam!"

The priestess smiled.

"Strictly speaking, Barbara, you scared the shit out of yourself. Fear makes us stupid."

The filaments around Barbara stopped quaking as she relaxed.

"So where am I and why am I so stuck?"

"Think of the web as your life, or lives to be more precise, with all of their possibilities, explored and unexplored."

"Ok, but why am I stuck?"

"You're bound by the circumstances of your life, as are we all. There's nothing wrong with that. It's all part of The Game," said the priestess.

She tweaked the space around them. Barbara floated free of her bonds -- bonds that she herself had most likely forged. The priestess folded space again, only this time more severely. She and Barbara left threespace, where the web spread in all directions, and jumped into fourspace. The web flattened and became a glistening map depicting the vast and intricate topography of Barbara's lives.

"So that's my life," mused Barbara out loud, "can I look at it up close up?"

"Of course," said the priestess, "it's your life."

"But can I do it without getting trapped?" Barbara asked.

"From here you can," said the priestess. "Just think, or feel, your way into any place that interests you. When you're finished, think your way back to me. I'll be here."

Barbara looked at the matrix. Her life was an embarrassment of riches. Everything beckoned her. Picking a point remote from the mission, she thought her way toward it. Time and space as she knew them condensed from the higher dimensions, wrapping themselves around her as she assumed the body germane to the life she had chosen.

The next thing she knew, she was flopping around in an intertidal pool left by the receding waters of an ancient sea. She partook of both fish-mind and hyperdimensional magus-mind.

427

Her fish-mind was driven by its instinct to be wet. Her magus-mind knew the creature as a primitive lung fish from ancient Earth, torn between its watery instincts and its equally compelling drive to struggle onto dry land. Its lidless eyes stared into the sky, comprehending nothing. Barbara pulled away from the fish and concentrated on another life strand.

She found herself next in a weird kind of darkness. It was warm and wet and threatening. She forced her way deeper into it. When she could go no farther, Barbara pulled back into the light. Her face was awash in blood. Her every move was a study in rage. She was possessed by the raw fury of a mother defending her baby against an otherwise certain death. She readied herself for another lunge. Her baby wailed with fear. A renewed surge of fury drove Barbara deeper into the wet darkness than she had been able to go just moments before. She pulled back when a roar resounded through her body. Barbara was once again in the light. Before her lay a Tyrannosaurus Rex, eviscerated and choking on its own blood. Calm once again, Barbara felt the weight of a carapace and three horns on her face. She was a young female Triceratops awash in the blood of her first kill in defense of her baby. The infant waddled up alongside her and warily approached the dead predator. Sensing no more danger, it played at charging and goring the carcass. The infant's best efforts did little more than dimple the hide. Barbara looked at her baby with the saurian version of motherly pride and jumped off the time line.

She did not land. This time, she took to the air, gliding along the thermals rising from a lush valley hundreds of feet below. Two wing tips appeared on the edges of her field of view. She was a Pterodactyl watching the world go by at a safe height. Up here, she was unassailable and at peace. The afternoon sun eventually sank behind the mountains that flanked the valley. Seized by a longing to fly even higher, Barbara's bird-like brain lofted her into the open sky. From there, she flew out of the one life and into another.

She hit the ground running. It was dark. She was among a throng of women fleeing into the recesses of a long, tortuous cave. Shouts, cries, screams, and the din of battle hounded their every step. Some of the women ran with torches to light the way. The bouncing light tricked them into seeing phantom enemies at every turn. This was just as well. Fear made their feet fly.

Barbara looked down. She was carrying a baby. Her baby. A human baby. The realization gave her the fleetness of a gazelle. She bounded ahead of the others and was the first to enter a secret chamber. She found an obscure recess in the cave's wall and climbed in, all the while shielding the baby with her body. The other women soon filled the chamber. Among them was a short woman with wavy blond hair -- a rarity in this dark haired tribe. For a long moment, they looked at each other with a thrill of deep but inarticulate affection.

The chaos of the battle eventually subsided into a frightening stillness. The women fell into an agony of unknowing, anxious to keep their young quiet. After too long a time, the women heard shouts of victory. Several among them heard the gravelly voices of their mates. Fear left the chamber like an exorcized demon. The men's jubilant cries grew louder as they approached. They bounded into the chamber, each searching for his mate, mother, or child. Among them was a muscular giant with kind eyes, clearly the tribe's leader. He sought out Barbara and ran to her. She reveled in his embrace, the dirt, sweat, and blood of battle notwithstanding.

Again, she folded time and warped space. In a tap-dance of jumps, she was a Celtic priestess, a gladiatrix, a peasant, a queen, and so on until she approached her incarnation as Barbara Llandry. There, she stopped, unwilling to vitiate that life with too much foreknowing. All the while, Barbara as magus hovered in hyperspace, contemplating the drama of her incarnations into the denseness of threespace. The Shtatàam approached.

"Well done, Barbara," said the priestess, "any thoughts?"

Barbara noticed that the priestess's English was more colloquial with their every conversation. Her's was an enviable learning curve.

"I do, now that you mention it. Time is part of us. We can fold space and time with our minds. We can project our minds anywhere we want. But there's a spiritual, or maybe a moral, imperative that limits what we can do. It's as if there's a story that must be told, down there, in threespace," said Barbara.

"You're right, Barbara," said the priestess, that's where all the tales are told. We have infinitely many facets to our being and infinitely many ways of knowing them. Threespace is a theater and we are all members of the company."

The priestess paused, a playful energy fluttering the space around her.

"Would you like to see how big the story is?" she asked.

"Sure," said Barbara.

With the priestess's help, they flew over the living tapestry of her lives. Every time Barbara thought they had reached the end of her days, the priestess showed her more, and more, and yet again more, until Barbara learned that the only limits to her sense of being were those imposed by her limited vision. From far away and long ago came the words of a cryptic sermon. "The time-being has the quality of flowing. So-called today flows into tomorrow, today flows into yesterday, yesterday flows into today. And today flows into today, tomorrow flows into tomorrow."

The priestess smiled and led Barbara far beyond her lives until they coalesced into a perfect faceted ruby poised in the deeps of hyperspace. Her's was not the only jewel to be so bedazzling.

"Look around you, Barbara."

They were surrounded by other points of light, all spun into a web of interbeing that addled her awareness.

"Isn't it wonderful to be so small in the midst of all this?" said the priestess. "No end to life and no end to our joy in it."

She paused for effect, and continued.

"You've done well, Barbara, very well. We must part now. Return to your people and become a teacher. Oh...and that man who has devoted entire lifetimes to you? Go back and hold on to him like grim death. You are a resplendent pair. Besides, he needs you at the moment."

Barbara was torn between her impulse to find Hal and desire to prolong this parting.

"Shtatàam, will we ever meet again?"

"Oh yes, we'll cross paths again. Remember, life is big. Really big."

At that, the priestess folded hyperspace and left. Barbara did likewise. But instead of heading back

to Hal, Barbara felt the priestess nudge
her toward a bizarre anomaly in
fourspace. It changed shape as various
timelines engaged and disengaged it at
random intervals. One such timeline
formed in front of her. She followed it
into the flux. Once inside, a schizoid
profusion of dimensions and
quasidimensions, of times and
pseudotimes swirled and tumbled around
her. The region dead ahead of her
cleared, revealing a black disc. The
ambient dimensions wove themselves into
a bewitching arabesque around the disc.
They reminded her of the endless
patterns woven around the center of a
fabulous red carpet on the floor of a
library situated on the second floor of
a stately white house.

Barbara passed through the dark
center and fell asleep. As the darkness
blanketed her, she did not even wonder
how long she would be out. She was in
Wonderland. Time was irrelevant.

#

Barbara hovered between sleep and
wakefulness, only indolently aware of
her surroundings. The sun warmed her
comfortable linen clothes, while the
lush grass on which she lay cooled her
back. She wanted to sleep on but she
sensed someone standing over her. Two
taps on her side from the person's foot
woke her up.

"Hey, Pookie, planning to sleep the
day away, are you?"

Barbara leapt to her feet in one clumsy movement.

"Grandpa?"

She looked around. The house, the lawn, the garden, the porch -- all were as they should be, or should have been. To look at it, it was just an ordinary day, another preciously ordinary day, in Milton. For the first and only time in her life, Barbara Llandry fainted. Richard caught her and laid her on the grass. He knelt beside her, gently tapping her cheeks until she came to. She propped herself up on her elbows and stared at the hale old man beside her.

"Are you, is all this, real?"

"Yes and no, in that order, more or less," said Richard, "except that I'm dead. A friend of yours, a fascinating woman, conjured the scenery from our memories."

Barbara sent thoughts of gratitude into hyperspace, hoping that the priestess would sense them.

"But why did she do all this?" asked Barbara.

"So we could have breakfast," said Richard as if it should have been obvious. "It's what you wished for a few months ago, isn't it?"

"Uh, yea, I suppose so," said Barbara, "I wrote it in my private mission log, but I had no idea that...that..."

"Wishes come true?"

"You might put it that way," said Barbara, "but it was just a rhetorical yearning."

"Well, continued Richard, "it worked regardless of what you thought you were doing."

Just then, the sounds and smells of breakfast swirled around them like an enchantment.

"I hope you're hungry," said Richard as he started toward the kitchen. Barbara followed, the bounce of a child in her steps again. The smells in the kitchen almost made her weep as they entered through the back door. Crackling on the stove were fried eggs and bacon, cooked exactly as she liked them. A pot of tea sat steeping on the antique, wide-planked table. Steam rose and curled in the air like smoke from a fairy's chimney. Richard motioned for her to sit.

"Sorry about the timing, Pookie," said Richard, "this is more of an early dinner."

The grandfather clock sounded 4:00 p.m. as he sat down across the table from Barbara. He settled into the chair with the bittersweet longing of the newly departed for the simple pleasures of ordinary living.

"I assume you still like to have your breakfast cooked like this," he said.

"It couldn't be more perfect," said Barbara, "it's a dream come true."

Richard poured the tea. They ate in silence for a while. Every morsel that passed Barbara's lips was a reliquary of memory. She savored them as much as she did the food, thus satisfying two appetites with the sweep of one fork. When they did speak, it was of simple things rendered exotic by the otherworldly setting in which they were uttered.

The afternoon was waning when Barbara rose to collect the dishes.

"Don't bother," said Richard, "they'll fade away soon enough."

"But I'd like to, Grandpa, one last time," said Barbara.

"I understand, sweetie," said Richard as he rose and moved toward the porch swing.

Barbara kept the back door open so that she could see the sun set behind the corn. Their appetites had wiped the plate clean, but Barbara went through the motions anyway. A part of her enjoyed being domestic. It was something she seldom indulged but, considering her experiences of late, it was a calming sort of return to the pleasures of the hearth.

A mellow squeak disrupted her reverie with a polite insistence that brooked no refusal. Barbara finished the dishes with that briskness of which only women are capable and joined Richard on the porch. Cricketsong filled the air. Fireflies rose to soften the coming night with their fey lanterns. It was a perfect moment, complete within itself, lacking nothing and alive with possibilities. Frank's root-beer stand became an oasis of light. People came and went, enjoying their drinks under his light and then fading to black. Whether they were phantoms or souls resting for a moment amidst their sojourns Barbara could not say. She decided it was none of her business and turned her attention to Richard.

He was ageless, robust in a way that defied his body's fleeting weaknesses. Barbara knew that his was an evolved soul, always at the ready among those whose nature it is to lead by example and encouragement. He had spent his life just passed helping people to see through deception to discern the real. What he would do next she could not imagine. Richard was evidently thinking the same of her.

"You've evolved, Barbara. You're no longer quite human. I can see it in your eyes. I used to think of them as two warm, flawless sapphires. Now I see two dark stars. I see worlds within you, sweetheart. When you get back home, share those worlds with anybody who will listen. A lot of us, I suspect, are ready to take the same leap that you did if you'll show them how."

Richard paused to acknowledge someone in the distance with a discrete nod. Barbara followed his gaze and saw a woman sitting under the blue glare of the root-beer stand. She was stunning. No, thought Barbara, she was a goddess — — a goddess eating french fries with a casual elegance that flouted convention. The woman looked at her and smiled.

"Grandpa, who is that woman?"

"Natasha."

Barbara sat up with a jolt that almost toppled Richard.

"Can I meet her?"

"Sorry, Pookie, it's not in your cards, at least not this time around. She just wants to see her heart's savior."

"And that would be me?"

"That would indeed be you," said Richard.

Barbara waved to Natasha. She waved back and smiled again.

"Well, sweetie, that's my cue to leave; can't keep the little woman waiting. We're..."

Barbara cut him short.

"You're soul mates. Honest-to-God soul mates."

"You bet. We're joined at the hip."

Richard rose to leave. Barbara stood facing him, devouring him with her eyes.

"Understand something, Barbara. No matter where we go, no matter what happens to us, I'll always love you. Never forget that. Now go save your own soul mate."

Barbara embraced her grandfather with the frantic intensity of someone who will never really be ready to let go. But she had to. Clinging served no one's interest. Richard jumped over the porch rail and hit the grass with an agility far beyond his apparent age.

Natasha rose and met him half-way, in the middle of Main Street. They joined hands and walked away, two blithe spirits finally free to revel in each other. Night had by then fallen in earnest. Barbara entered the house and turned on the lights. She wandered the first floor, letting her feet lead the way. Tears pooled in her eyes as she walked, crowning everything she saw with spectral haloes. Why she should be mourning all of this puzzled her at first. When she returned to earth, she would find the house essentially unchanged. So why did she feel like she was bringing up the rear of a funeral?

The answer came in its own time. Everything around her was the stuff of dreams and memory, her's and Richard's. It was a house of spirits and shades that would soon take its place among the dusty ghosts of Jake's Mule Barn. That time was at hand. She turned off the lights and went upstairs. Everything on the second floor was reminiscent of a certain endearingly incorrigible sidekick with long blond curls. Barbara wondered where she was, what she was doing, whether a new body had formed around her. Of one thing only was she certain. Linda was very far away. It would be a long time before they met again.

Barbara went into her bedroom. Everything remained as she had left it. She sat on her huge pencil-post bed and stroked the blankets. She arose and opened the window next to the bed. Cricketsong filled the air. Barbara kicked off her shoes and got under the covers. She made a point of lying off to one side so as to leave room for the memory of her friend. She took a deep breath and settled in for her last night among the shadows, memories, and dreams of her youth. The crickets serenaded her to sleep.

The house held its shape for a while. Finally, when it had served its purpose, it dissolved, leaving no trace.

#

By the time she found Hal, Barbara had become fairly proficient at folding time and space without the Shtatàam's help. She sought him out with her mind and heart until she heard him calling her name from one of the timelines. Barbara focused on the Jash Tataam, knowing that it would compensate any temporal disturbances created by her body as it condensed back into threespace. She materialized within the sphere. Hal was lying next to it, barely conscious. Barbara leapt from the sphere and landed next to him. The simple fact of her presence revived him.

"Hey, soldier, no sleeping on guard duty!" said Barbara.

She helped him to his feet. He was still weak and fell into Barbara's arms.

"Oh, man, if we weren't on Mars, I'd swear I'd been hit by a goddam train."

"You were, sort of," said Barbara, "I'll explain later. For now we need to get some food into you. You look like hell."

"I yield to your tender mercies, Commander," said Hal as his legs went out from under him. Barbara eased him to the floor and dashed off. She returned with a hot cannister and snapped it into Hal's pressure suit.

"Chicken soup," she announced, "good for what ails you."

When she was sure that Hal could feed himself, Barbara picked up a spotlight and explored the room. Like the cavern outside, it too bore inscribed panels on its walls. She strolled along them until one in particular caught her eye.

"Hey, Hal," she said, "this is weird. I think I found exactly one-half of a cipher.

Hal rose cautiously and walked over to Barbara's side. She was in front of a panel that had been cut in half. Only one of the pieces had been mounted. The inscriptions seemed to make more sense than anything they had yet seen.

"Looks like a mathematical cipher," said Hal. "But why would anyone provide just half a cipher?"

"Beats me," said Barbara. "Let's take some pictures and get out of here."

An hour later, the rovers were packed and ready to go. Hal stopped short, as if suddenly remembering something.

"By the way, Barbara," he said, "did you see anything inside that contraption?"

441

SEGUE

It was a relief to sit down and eat a proper meal in the light of day, especially given the psychedelic revelations that the cavern had unleashed after aeons of patient stewardship. The ambience fostered by the sounds and smells of simple cookery afforded time for reflection.

Upon returning to the GRUB, Barbara and Hal set up the next raw-data transmission. The digitized images that streamed toward Earth were received with a speechless shock that mounted as each image was unscrambled, cleaned up, and displayed across the monitors of receiving stations the world over. The critical mass exploded when someone noticed that the image of the bisected tablet was a perfect mate to the similarly bisected tablet found in the catacombs under Kathmandu. Reactions to the discovery would not have been more intense had Moses descended Mt. Sinai at the same time bearing the Tablets of the Law. Meanwhile, the two greatest explorers in history sat down to a pot of reconstituted Irish stew.

Barbara ate quietly, trying to form an answer to Hal's disarmingly simple question, a question she had evaded during the trip back to the GRUB. How could she describe an evolutionary leap to people who were almost but not quite ready for it? She looked up at Hal. He was engrossed by some shards of rock that he had found in an odd corner of the shrine. He stared at them fixedly, forgetting at times to eat. She was grateful for the distraction.

Finally, he looked up.

"Check this out, Barbara."

Hal pushed the rocks across the table toward her.

"Take a few minutes and look at these. Tell me what you see."

Barbara set the stew aside. The rocks were jagged like flint. Colorful crystalline spicules flowed across the shards' glassy surfaces like minuscule porpoises in a choppy sea. She looked closer. The movement was no illusion. The spicules were moving toward the middle of their respective surfaces and disappearing into them. Fresh spicules appeared along the margins and joined the flow. She looked up at Hal.

"The shards are fluid," said Barbara, "but I can't imagine how it's done."

Hal pressed the point.

"Neither can I, but does the effect remind you of anything?"

The answer was obvious.

"It's just like the fissure that formed in the gate. It's also like what happened to the wreckage on the Argo. I'm guessing that this stuff may be pieces of a larger device."

Barbara sighed, pocketed a small piece of the device, and resigned herself to the necessity of transmitting the weirdest mission report of her life. She rose and went over to the communications console.

"Hal, be a dear and heat the rest of the stew. I may be here awhile."

#

The next morning found the GRUB making its way up the northeastern face of Olympus Mons toward the summit. A direct ascent was the clearest path to it, but it was also fairly steep. Speed had to be tempered by caution so as to avoid potentially disastrous rollovers. The weather began to pose threats of its own. As the day wore on, increasingly violent winds threatened to envelope the GRUB in yet another dust storm. For minutes at a time, Hal and Barbara had to pick their way through opaque gusts of wind that blinded the Argus's otherwise all-seeing eyes. It took them twelve hours to traverse the one-hundred miles between the shrine and the summit. Nightfall found them parked on level ground surrounded by blinding winds. Mission Control had yet to respond to Barbara's surreal report, so there was nothing to do but go to sleep.

Deep into the night, Hal was awakened by a discrete alarm from the communications console. It was an encrypted message for his eyes only. A few seconds later, a terse message floated across the monitor:

"Have reviewed last mission report. Concerns raised about Commander Llandry's stability given recent pressures. Do you see signs of psychosis or delusional behavior?"

Hal looked at Barbara. Never had he seen her sleep so imperturbably. She lay on her side, mouth open, breathing deeply. He sat still for some time, watching the tidal ebbs and flows of her ribs. He had no doubt that her brain was busy making sense of what she had experienced inside the shrine. He looked back on the mission, to their shared combat experiences, to Barbara's capture and subsequent torture, to everything that he knew or had heard about her. He knew then, with his heart and with his head, that Barbara was one of the few people on Earth stable enough to have coped with such a patently bizarre mission.

Hal turned back to the console and entered an equally terse reply."

"NO."

He deleted the message from the console and went back to bed, falling asleep easily amidst the insanely wailing winds.

Sunrise brought with it a welcome calm. Barbara and Hal awoke to clear skies and boundless visibility. They had no sooner risen from bed when the view afforded by the departed storm transfixed them with the tenacity of spikes hammered through their feet. The virtual-reality training simulations had done nothing to prepare them for the immediacy of the vastness surrounding them. Not a mile away, was a caldera that could have swallowed Rhode Island. The mellow descent of the volcano's slopes, covering as they did an area the size of Texas, spoke volumes about lava flows that had persisted for hundreds of millions of years, burning their way into the planet's crust and memory. If ever a mountain could be said to brood over the secrets of the gods, this was it.

Hal moved first.

"Coffee?"

Barbara looked at him as if he had wrenched her from a vision.

"Uh, yeah, ...sure, whatever."

She drifted distractedly in the general direction of the lavatory while Hal started breakfast. He was showing a flair for turning space rations into palatable meals and she was happy to let him indulge it. She was brushing her teeth when a familiar yet elusive bouquet of odors filled the cabin. Drying her lips, she poked her head out of the lavatory door.

"What's cooking?"

"Come out and see."

Barbara dressed and brushed her raven hair. A minute later, she sat down to an intriguing meal. Hal sat down opposite her.

"And this is?" she queried.

"Ground beef, rehydrated and mixed with miso paste, formed into lewdly suggestive patties, and seared to perfection for Mademoiselle's delectation," said Hal. "For the rest, we have honey-sweetened grapefruit juice, and dried apricots, boiled and dusted with sugar and cinnamon."

The food was fun and fanciful and sat well in Barbara's stomach. As they ate, she reflected on how Hal Major was the best thing to have come into her life in years. He was her ground, her stepping-off place, a haven that she could count on. He had proved that he was willing to take a bullet for her. He had stepped into her heart and taken his rightful place next to Richard. She did not like to imagine life without him. She hoped that he felt the same.

Hal looked up and saw Barbara looking down at her plate, distractedly picking at her food.

"Everything OK?" he asked.

She answered with a smile. "It's more than OK. You're...it's...all a girl could want."

Hal looked at her with that blank, deer-in-the-headlight expression peculiar to men the world over when confronted with the vagaries of a woman's mind.   Barbara laughed and rose from the table.

"I'll clean the dishes," she said. "Go freshen up and don't worry your pretty little head over anything."

An hour later, Hal and Barbara were in their pressure suits, exiting the GRUB's airlock.   Their first jolt at seeing Olympus Mons within the safety of the GRUB's habitat module was trivial compared to the vertiginous shock of venturing forth to stand, naked, at the crater's brink.   It's farthest rim was vague, insubstantial, grainy as a dream, a world away.   It misted into the horizon, taunting the puny explorers with its remoteness.   The chasm in between was a sucking void.   The ground beneath them threatened to betray their feet by subsiding into dust.   Everything around them resurrected the maxim of superstitious sailors in bygone days about the edge of their flat Earth: "Here there be dragons!"   Pulling back from the rim did little to mollify their bodies' primitive, but well-founded, vertiginous fears.   Their pilot's composure prevailed, however, to the point where they could function in the context of this hugely enlarged place.

"Let's take a walk," suggested Barbara.

Having acclimated herself to the incongruities of their surroundings, Barbara approached the rim and steadied herself at its brink.   She abandoned herself to the volcano's mocking girth.

Without realizing it, she raised her arms as if to embrace the gods who had created and tenanted the place. Her interior sense of Self grew in proportion so that she no longer felt humiliated by the mountain. She was, instead, filled with humility in the best sense of the word.

And that was when the tears came.

This surprised her. She reflexively raised her hand to wipe them from her cheeks, but was stymied by her glassteel visor. The upwelling tears became a river that brought with it memories of a small girl, warming herself before a pot-bellied stove in a ramshackle bar in a town on a planet millions of miles, and ages, away -- a small girl marveling at the mineral deposits inside a hot enamel basin full of water. The neglected basin was as firmly rooted to the stove as this volcano was to the planet. Both had established a millennial presence in their respective homes. Both were archives of stratified memory. Both were open to the sky and anything it had to give them.

The river flowed its course and dried up. Only one duty remained. Barbara stepped back from the rim, looking for Hal. He was a hundred yards away, prospecting for drilling sites.

"Hal? I need your help with something."

He nodded and trotted along the rim to her side.

"What's up?"

"I want to leave the time capsule here."

His nuts-and-bolts attention to the drilling site fell away into a compassionate softness.

"Sure, Barbara. Anything you say."

A half-hour later, Hal was riding shotgun atop the capsule that he and Barbara had muscled onto one of the rovers. She was heading for a gentle decline within the rim that she had espied from the GRUB. She brought the rover to a slow stop. Hal stepped back so as to leave Barbara alone with her thoughts. It was a thoughtful but unnecessary gesture. Any lingering concerns she may have had were hushed by the solace of having come so far to keep her promise to Richard, Natasha, and all those who had been blasted to dust by the dawn of Man's nuclear age.

She bent over, placed her hands on the capsule, and pushed. The canister slid easily into the crater, rolling over the sands with a whoosh rendered soft and distant by the thin atmosphere. It speeded up briefly and then came to a slow stop. The sands disturbed by the capsule's passage followed in its wake, burying it as they settled into a new resting place within the crater.

Barbara stood up, disburdened of a weight she had carried so long that it seemed to be a part of her. She felt light, free to move on. She approached Hal, timidly, with one request.

"Hold me."

She walked into an embrace that had
bided its time, waiting for this moment.
Barbara felt Hal's aura enfold her with
a deeper embrace that brought with it a
lambent warmth that soothed even as it
aroused. Their sense of time and place
fell away. They forgot where and when
they were, and they did not care. Their
Jiddashin's meld was sufficient unto
itself. Barbara understood why so many
Martian lovers were content to linger
indefinitely before the Jash Tataam.

Hal relaxed his hold on Barbara and
lifted her face to meet his own.

"You've changed," said Hal.   "No,
that's not quite it. You've come into
your own. When I look into your eyes, I
see..."

Hal paused and looked up at the sky
as if searching the stars for the right
words. He decided they did not exist
and pushed on.

"...entire worlds inside of you.   I
feel them when we're close like this."

At that moment, Hal wanted to rip
their visors off and die with the warmth
of Barbara's face against his own. She
sensed his thoughts and pulled him
closer, drawing and releasing a deep
breath in one seamless movement.

"We have to leave. Soon," she
muttered.

"What do you mean?" asked Hal.

"I don't know. We just have to get
out here," said Barbara.

Hal looked at her bemusedly but said
nothing. Then, a dark orange smudge in

the northwestern sky caught his eye. Within minutes, the smudge became a flaming white ball that shed vindictive pieces of itself as it passed overhead and disappeared behind the southeastern horizon. Seconds later, the mountain shuddered. Pieces of rock, disturbed by the tremor, leaped into the crater's maw. A crescent of fire formed on the horizon. It did not subside with the chaos of impact.

Barbara and Hal raced back to the GRUB. The rover popped a wheely as it bounded up the cargo ramp at speeds for which neither was designed. It stopped, inches from the habitat module. They scrambled through the airlock. Without so much as removing their helmets, they established an uplink with the Argus. Barbara summed up the situation in two words.

"Oh, SHIT!"

.

HEGIRA

The GRUB bounded down the east face of Olympus Mons as if fleeing hordes of infidels. It left countless unexamined geological curiosities in its dusty wake, moving with a relentless intensity that bespoke the crew's disquietude over what the Argus had revealed.

Mars had betrayed them. To all appearances, it was a tepid ember bearing the scars of its violent youth, a place whose ravaged surface had few new tales to tell, a place of storms whose winds shrieked with the malice of senile Harpies. It was a world peopled with memories that sulked within its vast and glorious ruins. ·New life would have to be imposed on it from without.

But Mars harbored one last pustulent secret. The planet's encounter with the debris field had been a mixed blessing that had harried the Argo's doughty crew. It was also a scalpel that had just lanced a very old boil.

The meteor that passed over Olympus Mons pulverized the northwest face of Pavonis Mons, not two-hundred miles from the base camp. Sheets of long-repressed lava lapped the volcano's base, threatening the crew's access to the mission habitat. Thermals rising from the lava agitated the overlying atmosphere, threatening to become the malicious eye of a cyclopean storm.

Hal set the shortest possible course to the eruption. Barbara ran a battery of diagnostics. Mission Control provided delayed opinions on various logistical issues. Two hours later, the GRUB leapt onto the flatlands like a cheetah intent on pursuing its prey to the death. Hal barely blinked as he negotiated hazards at speeds that made no allowances for mistakes. At first, his sense of urgency pushed his harried awareness ahead of the GRUB and out of the present moment. A few near collisions quickly disabused him of that particular folly. He focused only on the exigencies of the moment. He knew he could not alter the flow of time by worrying about it, so he gave it up. His world condensed into a tunnel strewn with dangers. As the hours passed, Hal's mind retreated into solitude. His eyes bypassed his brain and assumed control of his body.

It was getting dark when a tap on his shoulder widened Hal's awareness. He brought the GRUB to a stop.

"You've been at it for ten hours," said Barbara. "Time to stop and rest."

"But I'm not tired," protested Hal. "I'm good for three more hours at least."

"Indulge me, love," countered Barbara. "I've eaten and slept. I suggest you do the same."

Hal was loathe to move.

"That's an order, soldier."

"Yes, ma'am," said Hal in a tone of mock submission.

He vacated the darkened cockpit and set about following orders.

Barbara checked the GRUB's integrity and made some minor corrections. The cockpit was still warm with Hal's presence. She settled into his seat and resumed their dash across the plains. Her experiences within the Jash Tataam endowed her with a limited prescience. She compensated for obstacles before she saw them. She pushed the GRUB to its limits. As the hours and miles passed, Barbara's prescient awareness of Pavonis Mons became increasingly worrisome. The lava was flowing hotter and faster, as if responding to mounting pressure. She sensed pent-up forces massing beneath the surface, becoming increasingly unstable. They were racing toward hell.

Barbara stopped the GRUB when she had traversed three-quarters of the plain. A firestorm dominated the horizon ahead of them. She exited the cockpit and came upon Hal. He was awake, refreshed, and staring out of the windows. She joined him. He knew what was coming.

"We have to get off this planet," she said.

"I know," he concurred, "we could initiate the launch protocols from here."

"And bypass the base camp," Barbara added. "I have a feeling it won't be there anyway."

They studied the telemetry that the Argus had been transmitting continually over the last few days. The northwest face of Pavonis Mons was gone. In its place, a cauldron of molten lava spilled onto the northern, western, and southern plains. It would not be long before their escape routes vanished under a blistering sea of lava.

"Our best bet is to skirt the north face," said Hal. "It'll save us a hundred miles or so compared to the southern route."

"I agree," said Barbara. "But we have to leave now. I'll bet the farm that we haven't seen anything yet. You take the wheel. I'll set up the remote-launch protocols."

The hours that followed were the grimmest of the mission. The base camp had sustained heavy damage. The greenhouse was gone; the hangar roof had collapsed. The habitat module's environmental systems were down. The entire facility had taken on the forlorn mantle of a ghost town. In this light, Barbara's rough landing of the shuttle so far from the camp was providential. The cumbersome gap between the base camp and landing site placed the vehicle out of harm's way for the moment.

Barbara had the craft ready for lift-off when an urgent message from Mission Control lit up the communications console. It warned of increasing solar flare activity and the possibility of an ion storm. Up until then, Barbara had regarded the dangers of the mission as a rite of passage, a gauntlet thrown upon the ground to test Mankind's mettle. But this latest danger tainted everything with malice. They were under siege. It was as if they had insulted the gods by daring to leave home for new worlds. Barbara walked over to Hal and put her hand on his shoulder.

"Step on it. We're in for an ion storm," she said.

The ground beneath the GRUB shuddered as additional magma pockets coalesced and discharged their burdens into the main torrents of the eruption. The effect was already visible to the Argus. Barbara sensed that the worst was yet to come. She set about preparing the Argo to receive the shuttle. To that end, she configured the navigation systems to calculate, revise, and recalculate launch trajectories as ground conditions changed.

The work did not go well. Barbara could not focus. Her thinking was muddled. She was easily distracted. Finally, she leaned back on her seat and closed her eyes. A few quiet breaths led her to the reason for her unease.

Fear had constricted her normally supple awareness. She had closed herself off, become deaf to the inner cues that had served her so well for years. At that moment, her larger self was simply prodding her to put on her pressure suit and make sure that Hal did the same. Hence the unease. She rose and entered the airlock to suit up. That done, she removed Hal's pressure suit from its hook and brought it forward into the cockpit.

"Here, Hal, put this on. We're headed for a world of trouble."

Barbara relieved him until he was suited up. Her mind finally clear, she returned to work. It went well and she was soon free to look at the solar-flare report. It was a wildcard that could render their meticulous calculations useless, and for once Barbara was glad that Mars had no magnetic poles. Any ionic shock waves that did hit the planet would at least not be focused on the surface. There was some comfort in that. She was, however, feeling restless, so she went into the cargo bay and readied the rovers for instant deployment should the GRUB be crippled. That done, she returned to the telemetry monitors. The renewed lava streams were broadening under the pressure of additional magma volume. Any more delays on their part could cut off their escape route. Already, red sheets of lava were visible through the GRUB's forward and starboard windows. Ascraeus

Mons brooded darkly on their port side. Barbara knew then what Odysseus must have felt when he braved the waters between Scylla and Charybdis on his way home after the Trojan War. The experience was not conducive to clarity, so she put it out of her mind and joined Hal in the cockpit.

"Need a break, love?"

"Thanks, but I'm fine."

Hal did not take his eyes off the horizon.

"We're in deep shit, aren't we?" he asked flatly.

"The Devil's very own doo-doo," replied Barbara as flatly.

"Let me guess," said Hal, "the only way for us to make time is to stay within spitting distance of the lava."

"You guessed it, Bucko," replied Barbara.

"I feel toasty already," said Hal as he grimly altered course.

Neither of them spoke for a long time. Staying safely abreast of the lava flows was an ordeal in itself. The terrain before them had been shattered by the meteor's impact and dangers abounded. The hours droned on. The sun reached its zenith and began its afternoon descent. They were still making good time and it was likely that they would reach the shuttle late in the afternoon.

The colors created by the afternoon light cast the volcanoes into surreal relief. Barbara felt as if they were traveling through a painting. To their left, Ascraeus Mons glowered as it had for hundreds of millions of years, a sullen study in terra cotta pastels. To their right, Pavonis Mons seethed with the malice of the proverbial evil twin. It mocked the falling sun with its own defiant fires. It stood out, belligerent, refusing to cower under the coming night.

That was when the tremors began.

They rolled across the plain like prophets of doom, each louder than the last. The GRUB shuddered as each wave passed under it. Subsequent waves lofted it ever higher into the air, whence it dropped onto the tortured ground beneath. Barbara and Hal sealed their helmets and pressurized their suits. Barbara got up and went aft to the cargo ramp to check that the rovers were still ready to move the instant circumstances demanded it. She was returning to the cockpit when an explosion hurled her into the air. She hit the GRUB'S ceiling and fell face down to the deck. Stars danced before her eyes against a black background. Willing herself not to faint, she crawled the rest of the way to the cockpit. She stumbled into her seat and strapped herself in.

Hal had to fight the GRUB's increasingly erratic controls, but the calm set of his face assured Barbara that he was far from yielding the fight. He reminded her of a doughty helmsman from bygone days lashed to the wheel of his ship during a hurricane. She transferred the telemetry to the cockpit monitors and assessed their situation. The volcano's entire northwestern flank was gone. It its place, sheets of molten lava threatened to overwhelm the entire region. She zoomed in on the base camp in time to see it overwhelmed by a torrent of lava. The habitat building withstood the heat for a few seconds before it slouched into oblivion. The hangar and its cache of equipment melted outright. The fuel reserves exploded into mushroom clouds visible through the starboard windows. Through it all, the shuttle stood at the ready, thirty miles distant, imploring them to sacrifice everything to speed.

Barbara shut down the environmental systems and all non-essential lighting. She glanced at Hal, wondering in passing how long it had been since they had last spoken. She dismissed the thought and routed all power to the engines and computers. Secondary explosions from the volcano pelted the GRUB with no end of rocks and man-sized clods of white-hot soil. The glassteel enclosure buckled slightly. The plain ahead of them was littered with enough fresh debris to seriously impede the progress of a vehicle the size of the GRUB.

Hal squeezed it through fifteen more miles of maze-like obstacles, but not fast enough. The expanding sea of lava was gaining on them. Barbara touched Hal's arm.

"Run her into the ground, Hal. We'll use the rovers the rest of the way."

Hal nodded and throttled the engines. The GRUB bounded through a maze of hot house-sized boulders. Pieces of the vehicle snapped off with its every side-swiping collision. Barbara monitored the remaining telemetry. An incoming message from Mission Control warned of the imminent arrival of the ion storm. She was about to say something to Hal when the GRUB reared into the air like a wild stallion and landed to the sound of snapping metal and shredding wheels. Hal had misjudged the path through yet another debris field. The GRUB lay on it's side, in the grip of a death rattle. Unfazed, Hal unbuckled his restraints and left the cockpit just as Barbara regained her footing.

"We have to lower the cargo ramp manually," he said.

"And fast. Look at that," replied Barbara, pointing through the shattered glassteel dome at the eruption. The lava flows were gaining on them again.

A surge of strength that bordered on the superhuman sent them into the aft cargo bay. Releasing the airlock manually, they muscled the rovers down the twisted ramp and onto the burning ground. They felt the heat through the soles of their boots as they turned the rovers about and pitted them against an environment for which they were not designed. But they made better time. The smaller vehicles could negotiate a more direct route to the shuttle than could the GRUB.

Even with their improved progress, Hal and Barbara barely kept pace with the implacable lava. Matters deteriorated even more when the first waves of the ion storm blinded the Argus and confused all of the remaining computers. When finally they cleared the debris field, the shuttle was still not visible, and the rover's telemetry had become erratic. Their chances of finding the fastest route suddenly plunged to something between nil and zero.

And then Barbara checked herself. By focusing on the eruption, she had again blinded herself to alternate possibilities. She looked behind her. The lava was gaining on them and there was nothing they could do about it. She estimated five minutes before the lava engulfed them. Hal cut in.

"I can see the shuttle. Maybe ten miles."

Barbara sighted down Hal's outstretched arm. The shuttle glittered in the distance, confused by the storm but otherwise ready to fly. But that wouldn't matter, she said to herself, if they were minutes away from being fried. She ignored the eruption and assessed the possibilities. These narrowed to two. They could persist in trying to outrun the lava, which was pointless, or she could...and she backed away at the thought. She could bend threespace and divert the lava flow but she would have to do it without the shrine or the Shtataam. In principle, she knew how, but only from the perspective of hyperspace. It provided a map. Folding threespace while immersed in it amounted to flying blind through a hurricane.

Contemplating the demands ahead, Barbara saw that she could not operate the rover and bend space at the same time. She would have to ride shotgun with Hal and that would slow them down even more. The ground ahead of them glowed red in the light of the advancing nightmare. Fear threatened to freeze her thoughts when she heard a whisper at the edge of her mind.

"The story must be told!"

It was the priestess. No sooner had she voiced the thought than she left. Barbara was alone with its maddening ambiguity.

She pulled up beside Hal.

"At this rate, we're fried," she said. "There's something I can try, but I have to ride shotgun behind you."

"But that'll slow us down to nothing," he said.

They felt the heat at their backs rise with the ticking of their few remaining seconds.

"Hal, if you love me then you'll trust me on this!"

He slowed the rover. Barbara gauged their relative speeds and positions and jumped. Hal sensed her coming. He extended his right arm and guided her to a safe spot behind him. The rover slowed under the added burden. The lava was less than thirty feet behind them. The heat seared her back.

She screamed.

The lava overtook them. Sheets of sizzling hell besieged the hobbling rover. Hal felt Barbara's agony but rode on, vowing to die honorably. The shuttle's running lights were considerably closer, but Hal figured they might as well have been a thousand miles away, for all the good they could do. The first rivulets of lava made their way to within inches of the rover's wheels.

And stopped.

Hal was beyond questioning anything and rode on through sheets of lava that parted as he defied his way through them. Something tugged at his mind, but he banished it, determined to stay focused in the midst of this inexplicable parting of a hateful Red Sea. Three, four, five times it persisted. Three, four, and five times he pushed the thought away. It returned for a sixth assault, intent on prevailing. It broke his concentration. The shock of the assault stunned him. The rover limped to a halt. The lava remained cowed. He turned around to face what he thought was the scorched husk of his great love.

He was wrong.

Barbara was indeed burning, but with flames such as Hal had never seen. Whips of energy flogged the air around them, creating odd spatial distortions. He peered into the flames. Barbara was at their source, in a trance. Her thoughts were inarticulate in and of themselves. Words from Hal's mind formed around them in urgent scraps: "not sure how long I can do this...move...lava getting ahead of me...love...

Hal moved.

The lava continued to part before the rover. The shuttle was clearly visible and in imminent danger of being annihilated. Hal felt Barbara's strength tickling his back. Then it withdrew, but only briefly. The spatial distortions protecting the rover came together and carved a path through the lava to the shuttle. He did not understand the spatial manipulations that held the path open, but he did feel Barbara groaning under the effort of sustaining them.

He steered the rover into the path. As they approached the shuttle, Hal heard Barbara's gasping thoughts. They seemed to be coming at him from far away, from a place where time dilated: "c-o-n-s-e-r-v-e f-u-e-l...j-e-t-t-i-s-o-n c-a-r-g-o...A-r-g-o i-n t-r-o-u-b-l-e...I'-l-l l-e-a-d..."

Hal skidded to a stop beside the shuttle. It hummed with expectancy, alert to the smallest command. Seconds later the lava arrived, forming a malicious circle around the launch site, smugly biding its time until Barbara perished under the burden of effort. Hal picked her up and ran into the shuttle. He felt her mind. It was exhausted but lucid. Stopping for nothing, Hal went to the cockpit and placed Barbara in the co-pilot's seat. Dropping into the pilot's seat, he surpassed his personal best in completing the launch sequence. That done, he overrode the autopilot, trusting that Barbara would compensate.

The shuttle rose vertically, just as Barbara's tired mind lost its grip on the lava. The circle closed, but the lava had to content itself with swallowing the cargo module that Hal ejected before taking off for the relative haven of the sky. Barbara relaxed. She slipped into a well-deserved indolence. They had tons of fuel to spare, so Hal set a course for the volcano and circled it lazily at a safe distance. The Argus was still blinded by the storm and the Argo's computers were babbling. The situation was volatile, but there was nothing to be done until Barbara was up to it.

With the most pressing threats beneath them, Hal relaxed and contemplated the eruption. Its was a cruel yet awesome beauty, indifferent to any living thing whose misfortune it was to stand in its way. Much of the universe was like that, thought Hal. It did not play fair by any human standards and never rescued us from our own stupidity and arrogance. That was our problem. Despite all that, or maybe because of it, the beauty beneath them was undeniable, and it was sad that their hobbled computers left him as the only one to have such a privileged view of it. Luckily, the mission planners had foreseen such a scenario and provided the crew with a few mechanical cameras and a cache of shielded film. Hal loaded one and started shooting. He was into a third roll when Barbara woke up.

"Look out a window," he replied between shots, "any window."

She rose and went to Hal's side.

"Oh my God!" was all she could say before lapsing into a humble silence. Hal finished shooting the third roll and turned to face Barbara.

"Feeling up to getting us out of here?"

"Sure, let's do it."

They seated themselves as before. Hal prepared the shuttle for its last flight. Barbara centered herself into a single-point meditation. The reduced stress of their current situation made it easy for her to create an optimum path to the troubled Argo. Curious, she looked at the navigation readouts and chuckled.

"Ignore the computer, Hal, it wants to slam our asses onto Phobos."

Hal smiled and switched off the monitor.

"Better?" he asked.

Barbara reached out and squeezed his hand affectionately.

"I'll take that as a yes," said Hal.

"OK, love, this is what we'll do," said Barbara. "The path to the Argo is shifting. She's in trouble. I can't talk fast enough to feed you the course variations, so I'll meld with you. You'll see what I see. If you get confused, I'll compensate." She looked at him appraisingly.

"By the way, Hal, did you know you were psychic?"

He returned Barbara's gaze.

"To be honest, sweetheart, I started wondering about that in flight school," confessed Hal. "Every so often I could see several seconds ahead of the action. Sometimes things were fuzzy; other times they were clear. After a while, I figured out that clear sight meant few or no alternative paths ahead. Blurry sight meant nothing was cast in stone. It saved my butt more than once."

"And all this time I thought you got by on reflexes and good looks," said Barbara.

Hal smirked at her.

"That's part of it too," he admitted.

"Jesus, Hal, at this rate our kids are going to be..." Barbara cut herself short, appalled at her indiscretion.

Hal countered with a feigned nonchalance.

"Don't stop on my account."

"Oh, it was nothing; it's just that if two people like us had children, hypothetical children, I mean, then we -- I mean they -- couldn't hide anything from them. From the hypothetical children, that is. But being hypothetical, they're not really real. Neither are the parents. The parents are hypothetical too; they're not..."

Hal looked on in amazement. He had never before heard Barbara babble, would never have suspected her to be susceptible to it. He did the gentlemanly thing and pulled her foot out of her mouth.

"This is all very interesting, Commander, but we still have to dock with our flaky mother ship."

Barbara was grateful for the diversion. She consolidated her hold on threespace. That done, she reached out for Hal's mind but stopped at its threshold. It would be arrogant and immoral, she realized, to create the link before Hal made it clear that he was ready for it. She did not have to wait very long. He spoke directly to her mind.

"Let's rock-and-roll, sweetheart."

Free of the restraints imposed on their minds by their three-dimensional bodies, Barbara and Hal communicated at the speed of thought.

Barbara tied him into her mind's eye. He gasped at the sight.

"First time in a spacefold?" she said, feeling playfully cocky.

"I've never eaten any funny mushrooms, if that's what you mean," he said.

"Relax. You'll get used to it," she assured him.

Hal found himself surrounded by fractured dimensions. He could only imagine them as pieces of colored glass whose edges skewed along lines that were not really lines. They were "of the other." The other what, he wondered, but he aborted the thought. Barbara was in charge. She would take care of everything.

In time, Hal saw a kaleidoscopic pattern in the fractured dimensions -- a kind of funnel. He was hovering just inside it's mouth. He ventured inside and looked through its neck. It was a tunnel that burrowed through an interdimensional house of mirrors. At its far end, he saw the Argo but was not sure how to get there.

"You're in," said Barbara.

"In what?" asked Hal.

"Don't think too much. It'll distract you," she said. "Just set your sights on the Argo. I'll lead you to it. Your body will fly the shuttle."

"Couldn't we just think our way to the Argo?"

"I could expand our minds to include the Argo," she said, "but...it's hard to explain. Let's just say that a wise woman told me that threespace is where the story must be told. No exceptions."

"OK," said Hal.

Barbara started the ascent slowly. Hal needed to be at least somewhat acclimated to the spacefold if he were to keep the shuttle on a smooth trajectory. He adapted quickly. Barbara surmised that his incipient prescience was working to his advantage.

Hal was fascinated by the experience. His awareness bifurcated the instant Barbara sent him into the corridor. Half of him heard her thoughts. The other half flew the shuttle. His sense of being was poised between the two, balanced and relaxed.

"Faster. We've cleared the volcano," said Barbara.

They circled high above Pavonis Mons.

"Take us into orbit," she continued.

The shuttle ascended steeply. The lustrous facets of the corridor blurred into grey as the shuttle accelerated toward its rendezvous with the Argo. Barbara made minute corrections to the shuttle's speed and trajectory. Their linked minds worked faster than any computer. Seconds later, they shot out of the spacefold and back into threespace. The Argo was less than a mile away, listing into a decaying orbit. Hal nudged the shuttle close to the disoriented ship. Its maneuvering thrusters were firing erratically. Every so often, the ship changed attitude quickly and unpredictably. It was a pilot's nightmare. Hal opened his prescient eye. Everything was blurry. Every possible path to the Argo's docking module was a crap shoot.

He moved the shuttle to within a hundred feet of the ship. It was not as fuzzy as it had been. Hal took advantage of the opportunity and brought the shuttle to within three feet of the docking airlock. The Argo shifted. He compensated. It shifted again. He compensated again. The situation showed signs of blurring back into chaos. In one virtuoso movement, he fired the shuttle's maneuvering thrusters. It hit the Argo hard, but accurately enough for Hal to close the docking mechanism.

An observer on the ground would have seen nothing untoward. If anything, she would have admired the shuttle's unerring ascent into the sky, where it turned into a shooting star that sought out and embraced its heavenly mate.

"Fanciest flying I've seen in a long time," said Barbara.

"Thanks. Let's get out of here before anything else goes wrong," he said.

They secured the shuttle, entered the Argo, and headed to the command module. What they found would have been merely pitiful had it not portended so many disasters. The quantum chaos wrought by the ion storm had reduced the computers to gibbering fools. Nonsense streamed across monitor after monitor. Barbara cursed and began a multilevel shutdown, starting with the most complex -- and most vulnerable -- systems and working her way down to the cruder but stabler ones. These she left alone. A modicum of ship wide sanity eventually prevailed.

"Damn!" said Hal.

"What's up?"

"The maneuvering thrusters have been guzzling fuel," said Hal. "We're flying on fumes. By my calculations, we're not nearly maneuverable enough to go home."

Barbara crossed the room and checked his calculations.

"And we may not even be able to correct our decaying orbit," she added.

"We're not really equipped for it, but I could rig up something to siphon fuel from the shuttle," Hal suggested.

"Do it," said Barbara. "I'm just wondering if we'll have to dump the cargo module to reduce our momentum. That way we save fuel. I'll go crunch a few numbers and get on the horn with Mission Control."

For the next hour, they set about their separate tasks. No matter how she worked the numbers, they were on an unforgivingly tight fuel budget. Something would have to go. Hal fared much better. Fuel was flowing back into the Argo, and he had gone on to reconfigure the deranged fuel pumps.

Barbara was fifteen minutes into the earthbound transmission when a low-level navigation system exceeded its resources and crashed. Several thrusters misfired, twirling the Argo like a corkscrew. The seals between the shuttle and the Argo snapped, as did Hal's improvised siphon. Fuel shot into space, freezing instantly. The shuttle tumbled end over end, falling toward the planet, leaving gushers of frozen fuel in its wake. Hal muscled his way back to the controls and closed the fuel line. Barbara made frantic efforts to reboot the system.

The shuttle glowed red as it plunged into the atmosphere. Seconds later, it exploded, precipitating an incendiary chain reaction. Like beads on a pyrotechnic necklace, the frozen blobs of fuel exploded sequentially back to the Argo. Shock waves from the fireballs broadsided the ship, pummeling it out of orbit and into space. At a shouted order from Barbara, Hal released the cargo module. It leapt off the Argo under its own centripetal force and fell toward Mars.

Barbara finally rebooted the computer. Together with Hal, she fought to regain control of the ship. When finally it yielded the contest, the Argo was in a high, elliptical orbit around the planet. Barbara dreaded the inevitable question but voiced it anyway.

"How much fuel did we save?"

"We couldn't maneuver our way out of a phone booth," Hal said. "Not unless we lighten our load big time."

"At least we're in a stable orbit, and that gives us time," said Barbara. She paused, as if coming to a difficult decision. "As of now, the Argo is no longer a research vessel," she said. "That means she's grossly overloaded and over equipped. How about it? You in the mood for a spacewalk?"

"You have to feed me first," said Hal.

"Done," said Barbara.

Their adrenaline rush subsided while they ate and devised a plan. Barbara would run simulations on the effects of severing nonessential components. Hal would hack away under her guidance.

They worked slowly and sadly. Each severed component was a piece of themselves cut away and abandoned. They had made the outbound crossing bristling with the tools of discovery. The Argo and her crew had dazzled earthbound scientists with every mile they put behind them. She was a great, if untested, ship. She would go down in history next to her namesake, the stuff of legend in her own right.

But now, she was a skeleton. Like many heroes, she had died young. The Argo's severed pieces persisted in following her around the planet, as if afraid of facing the void alone. Her dismemberment complete, the Argo's disburdened engines ignited, bellowing a white-hot requiem that the gods could not with impunity ignore.

The violence of the Argo's departure scattered her anguished parts on their own lonely voyages into forever. Each of them submitted to the Goddess of Necessity, making peace with their destinies as the mute bards of tales yet untold.

Had our surface-bound observer persisted in watching the sky, she would have seen the newborn star shed glittering pieces of itself before shooting toward a distant blue star that had just risen above the planet's darkening horizon. She might have fancied that they were lovers racing toward a long-awaited tryst. Were she a loving soul, she would have blown a kiss into the sky and wished them well.

#

Jets of water splashed and gamboled down his back, each a tiny masseuse loosening the tensions of the mission from his tired shoulders. Hal turned to face the shower head. The water pounded away at his scalp, forehead, eyes, and cheeks. Worry drained from his face like so much soap scum. He had turned around again when Barbara entered the module. She was barefooted and dressed in a sheer white robe. The steam blurred her body into a figure seem dimly at the edges of a dream. She approached the shower haltingly, like a school girl on her first date.

"Hal? Mind if I join you?"

Her words washed away his last and oldest cause for unease.

"Sure, if you don't mind a tight squeeze."

"I don't mind at all."

She slipped the robe off her shoulders. It fell to the floor forming, in its erotic disarray, a cascade of silken sand dunes. She opened the shower door and stepped inside. A blind man could have seen that Barbara was beautiful, but this, this was more than a pair of mortal eyes could take. Hal welcomed her with a warm, wet embrace that she savored through every pore in her body and returned with all the force of her pent-up ardor. She wrapped her mind around his. He returned the gesture as best he could. Memories of their past lives together, of their shared agonies and ecstasies, rose and raced around them. In the calm center of the storm, Hal and Barbara resumed that journey of unharried and intimate knowing granted to perennial lovers at the soul level through body after body, life after life, world after world, age after age. They were Eros and Aphrodite to each other, forever coupled and never tiring of it. Within the bounded infinity of a few breaths, Barbara and Hal surrendered to passions that are understood the world over and need no explanation.

In the months that followed, as the Argo fell toward home in a graceful curve, a child was conceived. In itself, this was unremarkable and hardly worth mentioning were it not for the fact that it was the first of its kind to be conceived off-world.

LEAVETAKING: late summer 2093

The decades passed. Radical innovations in propulsion extended mankind's grasp of the cosmos to Pluto and made possible the contemplation of interstellar ventures. Hal and Barbara had a daughter, Gwendolyn, who followed in Richard's footsteps and then leapt beyond them to become a preeminent paleoarcheologist.

Through it all, the big white house in the Iowa prairie beckoned to all those who knew and loved it. Barbara and Hal retired there. Gwendolyn spent as much time there as her off-planet career permitted. If anything, the place enchanted her more than it did her mother. The abysses of extraterrestrial history that Gwendolyn explored on her hands and knees with picks and shovels gave her ancestral home the alluring comfort of a well-worn enchanted blanket. Seven years into their retirement, Hal was hoeing beans in the garden when an oddly persistent breeze buffeted his face. He stood and glance up at Barbara's study. During all their years together, Hal had never known Barbara to sleep in chairs. She was constitutionally incapable of it. That morning, however, she was slumped over her desk, very still, hands flaccid.

Hal dropped his hoe and ran inside.

\#

Barbara's study was itself a study in comfort. Visitors who ventured inside came upon bright oriel windows that afforded a view of gnarled maple trees whose branches swept the sills on windy days. On either side of the windows, antique Persian rugs were flanked by bookcases housing everything from rare books to proposals for prototype interstellar probes. Overstuffed chairs were scattered among several old library tables. A Russian chandelier hung from the ceiling near the windows, underneath which was Barbara's desk.

On that morning, Barbara was busy composing the metaphysical poetry that had become her passion of late. She was savoring the afterglow of a creative rush when a sudden burst of pain detonated in her chest and tore into her left arm. She collapsed, slumping onto her desk. As she did so, the paper on which she was writing slid to the floor.

During those final seconds, Barbara called upon the last of her soldierly strength to rally and rise from her desk. All she succeeded in doing was to knock open a malachite box, which contained her most precious possession — the dark blue shard of stone that Hal had given to her on Mars. It bounced onto the floor and came to rest on the paper.

For some time, nothing happened. The study assumed an unwonted stillness that went unchallenged until a diaphanous, crystalline shroud condensed from the air and encircled the desk. The crystals formed and reformed in a fractal waltz that reflected light in impossible ways, in impossible directions. Within this organized chaos, a shapeless but intelligently directed form sweated its way out of Barbara's body. Drop by drop it coalesced into a fluid, humanoid form that shot out the windows and hovered above the garden, invisible against the cloudless sky. The shroud dissolved into scintillae of light that vanished, leaving the study unchanged.

Except for the stone. It burned with a fierce midnight blue light and started folding in on itself faster than it had ever done before. It would be several hours before it returned to normal.

#

Barbara had made her funeral plans known only to Hal. She shuddered at the thought of being embalmed and wanted to be buried in a pine casket, so that her dust would mingle quickly with the Earth from which she was so often separated. He did so. She wanted to be buried in her admiral's uniform. He did so. She wanted her grave to be marked by a plain blue stone monolith cut in the proportion 1:4:9. He did so. With one addition. He inscribed Barbara's last words on the monolith — those that he had found written on the paper that had fallen to the floor beside the desk. Hal cherished them as the bearers of her last raw passion.

The funeral was an open-casket affair limited to family and friends. It took place in Milton's only graveyard. After everyone had paid their last respects and gone, Hal performed one last service for his wife. Whenever they wore their dress uniforms, Hal always noticed that Barbara's Medal of Honor hung around her neck like a millstone. She never stood straight. She pursed her lips. She was prone to the thousand-yard stare of combat veterans laboring under the weight of a secret and unrequited grief. It was a burden that was not following her into the grave.

Hal bent over Barbara's body and gave her one last lingering kiss. As he did so, he removed the medal from her neck, intending to pass it on to Gwendolyn. He folded Barbara's hands over her heart and nestled within her fingers the stone that had fallen so innocuously on top of her last poem.

Thus was it over. Hal was alone as he had never been alone before. The cemetery was empty except for the sun, the birds, the sky, and the husk of his beloved. He stared at her coffin for a long time. Grief bypassed his brain and settled into his bones. He wanted only to fall into the grave face down with the part of his heart called Barbara Llandry.

After a while, Hal lifted his tired eyes and read the inscription on the stone.

Indra's Net

There are things reflected
in the petals
of every blossoming flower
that bespeak the freewheeling
of newborn galaxies
in the stellar afterbirth of
a time
long since dispersed into
dust
now blown lightly
from the pages
of a seldom read book
sitting on a desk
in a room
with a view
of a budding tree...

A warm breeze cooled Hal's salty cheeks and went on its way. He paid it little heed. It returned and lingered in a most un-breeze like way. Something, a ghostly hand perhaps, caressed his face. He felt the warm, wet presence of a pair of lips upon his own. A voice formed inside his head, whispering "Soon, my love, very soon..."

The grief in Hal's bones lessened a little. He bent over and picked up a handful of rich, black soil. Sifting it carefully through his fingers, he sprinkled it over Barbara's body and blew a kiss into the wind.

It was time to leave. Hal made his way among the inscribed stones toward the old iron gate. He closed it carefully, making sure that the lock snapped into place. He walked up Main Street towards the middle of town. He paused to look at the grand white house on his right before continuing toward a ramshackle bar and a few drinks next to an old pot-bellied stove.

ABOUT THE AUTHOR

Howard L. Enfiejian holds a doctoral degree in neurobiology from Rutgers University and Robert Wood Johnson Medical School. He has been a science writer since 1982. His ghost-written projects have appeared in a number of peer-reviewed academic journals and independent publications, as have projects written under his own name.

Dark Star is Howard Enfiejian's first novel. An early version of *Dark Star* was among the finalists in the 1998 James Jones First Novel competition.

Printed in the United States
830400001B

9 781403 389770